MULTICULTURAL EDU

MW00637449

James A. Banks, Series Editor

(continued)

Race, Empire, and English Language Teaching
SUHANTHIE MOTHA

Black Male(d)
TYRONE C. HOWARD

LGBTQ Youth and Education: Policies and Practices
CRIS MAYO

Race Frameworks
ZEUS LEONARDO

Class Rules
PETER W. COOKSON JR.

Teachers Without Borders? The Hidden
Consequences of International Teachers in U.S.
Schools
ALYSSA HADLEY DUNN

Streetsmart Schoolsmart
GILBERTO Q. CONCHAS & JAMES DIEGO VIGIL

Americans by Heart
WILLIAM PÉREZ

Achieving Equity for Latino Students
FRANCES CONTRERAS

Literacy Achievement and Diversity
KATHRYN H. AU

Understanding English Language Variation
in U.S. Schools
ANNE H. CHARITY HUDLEY & CHRISTINE MALLINSON

Latino Children Learning English
GUADALUPE VALDÉS ET AL.

Asians in the Ivory Tower
ROBERT T. TERANISHI

Our Worlds in Our Words
MARY DILG

Diversity and Equity in Science Education
OKHEE LEE & CORY A. BUXTON

Forbidden Language
PATRICIA GÁNDARA & MEGAN HOPKINS, EDS.

The Light in Their Eyes, 10th Anniversary Ed.
SONIA NIETO

The Flat World and Education
LINDA DARLING-HAMMOND

Diversity and the New Teacher
CATHERINE CORNBLETH

Frogs into Princes: Writings on School Reform
LARRY CUBAN

Educating Citizens in a Multicultural Society, 2nd Ed.
JAMES A. BANKS

Culture, Literacy, and Learning
CAROL D. LEE

Facing Accountability in Education
CHRISTINE E. SLEETER, ED.

Talkin Black Talk
H. SAMY ALIM & JOHN BAUGH, EDS.

Improving Access to Mathematics
NA'ILAH SUAD NASIR & PAUL COBB, EDS.

"To Remain an Indian"
K. TSIANINA LOMAWAIMA & TERESA L. MCCARTY

Education Research in the Public Interest
GLORIA LADSON-BILLINGS & WILLIAM F. TATE, EDS.

Multicultural Strategies for Education and Social
Change
ARNETHA F. BALL

Beyond the Big House
GLORIA LADSON-BILLINGS

Teaching and Learning in Two Languages
EUGENE E. GARCÍA

Improving Multicultural Education
CHERRY A. MCGEE BANKS

Education Programs for Improving Intergroup
Relations
WALTER G. STEPHAN & W. PAUL VOGT, EDS.

Thriving in the Multicultural Classroom
MARY DILG

Educating Teachers for Diversity
JACQUELINE JORDAN IRVINE

Teaching Democracy
WALTER C. PARKER

The Making—and Remaking—of a Multiculturalist
CARLOS E. CORTÉS

Transforming the Multicultural Education
of Teachers
MICHAEL VAVRUS

Learning to Teach for Social Justice
LINDA DARLING-HAMMOND ET AL., EDS.

Culture, Difference, and Power, Revised Ed.
CHRISTINE E. SLEETER

Learning and Not Learning English
GUADALUPE VALDÉS

The Children Are Watching
CARLOS E. CORTÉS

Multicultural Education, Transformative Knowledge,
and Action
JAMES A. BANKS, ED.

RACIAL MICROAGGRESSIONS

USING CRITICAL RACE THEORY TO RESPOND TO EVERYDAY RACISM

Daniel G. Solórzano
Lindsay Pérez Huber

TEACHERS COLLEGE PRESS
TEACHERS COLLEGE | COLUMBIA UNIVERSITY
NEW YORK AND LONDON

Published by Teachers College Press,® 1234 Amsterdam Avenue, New York, NY 10027

Copyright © 2020 by Teachers College, Columbia University

Front cover painting, *Social Consciousness Through Intergenerational Knowledge: Sustaining a Cycle of Justice*, by Luis-Genaro Garcia. www.LuisGenaroGarcia.com. Copyright © 2020. Reprinted with permission of the artist.

An excerpt from ["Certain moments send adrenaline to the heart,..."] from *Citizen: An American Lyric* by Claudia Rankine is reprinted with the permission of The Permissions Company, LLC, on behalf of Graywolf Press, graywolfpress.org, and Penguin Random House UK. Copyright © 2014 by Claudia Rankine.

The photographs "Untitled, Harlem, New York, 1947" and "Department Store, Mobile, Alabama, 1956" are reproduced courtesy of and copyright © The Gordon Parks Foundation.

Chapters 2 and 3 contain text from "Racial Microaggressions as a Tool for Critical Race Research," by L. Pérez Huber & D. G. Solórzano, 2015, *Race, Ethnicity, and Education, 18*(3), 297–320. Reprinted with permission of Taylor & Francis Ltd, http://www.tandfonline.com.

Chapter 5 contains text from "Theorizing Racial Microaffirmations as a Response to Racial Microaggressions: Counterstories Across Three Generations of Critical Race Scholars," by D. Solórzano, L. Peréz Huber, & L. Huber-Verjan, 2020, *Seattle Journal for Social Justice, 18*(2), 185–215. Reprinted with permission.

All rights reserved. No part of this publication may be reproduced or transmitted in any form or by any means, electronic or mechanical, including photocopy, or any information storage and retrieval system, without permission from the publisher. For reprint permission and other subsidiary rights requests, please contact Teachers College Press, Rights Dept.: tcpressrights@tc.columbia.edu

Library of Congress Cataloging-in-Publication Data is available at loc.gov

ISBN 978-0-8077-6438-1 (paper)
ISBN 978-0-8077-6439-8 (hardcover)
ISBN 978-0-8077-7909-5 (ebook)

Printed on acid-free paper
Manufactured in the United States of America

Contents

Series Foreword

This illuminating and informative book about racial microaggression is being published at a propitious time because the devastating effects of the COVID-19 pandemic have poignantly revealed the deep racial and social-class divisions and disparities within the United States (Villarosa, 2020). During the pandemic, many middle- and upper-class professionals work virtually while sheltering in their homes while most low-income and low-status essential workers have to take buses, subways, and other forms of public transportation to get to their work sites or face the possibility of being fired from their jobs. One of the consequences of this difference is that African Americans, Latinxs, and immigrants—who are heavily concentrated in low-status jobs—have been infected with the coronavirus virus and died at much higher rates than middle-class and upper-income workers, who are disproportionately White (Mays & Newman, 2020).

Another startling example of the racial and social-class divide in U.S. society was the images of lines of cars at food banks in different cities, some several miles long, that were shown on national television news every evening after the U.S. economy was brought to a standstill by the pandemic in late April and early May 2020. Unemployment has reached its highest level since the Great Depression that began in 1929 and lasted through the 1930s (Cohen, 2020; Schwartz, Casselman, & Koeze, 2020). Food insecurity, while affecting a large number of Americans, including many Whites, has been highest among people of color. Racial and social class divisions during the pandemic were also manifested in the digital divide that was revealed when most school districts shuttered schools and instruction became virtual. In some city school districts, such as Chicago, Detroit, Los Angeles, and Philadelphia, whose populations consist primarily of students of color, a large proportion of the students have not received consistent instruction because they lack tablets, computers, or reliable Internet connectivity (Goldstein, 2020). Nine out of ten students in the Detroit Public Schools did not have access to tablets, computers, or the Internet until the school district was given a $23 million grant by local foundations (Williams, 2020).

The COVID-19 epidemic and its painful consequences have seriously challenged the idea of "American exceptionalism" (Grandin, 2019). In May 2020, the United States had the highest number of deaths from the pandemic of the major nations. The U.S. health care system, because of its lack of preparation for the pandemic and infrastructure problems (Case & Deaton, 2020; Rosenthal, 2020), was in disarray during the early phases of the pandemic (Egan, 2020; Villarosa, 2020). The COVID-19 pandemic not only revealed the deep racial and social class divisions within American society (Blow, 2020), it also stimulated the rise of anti-Asian racism and microaggressions (Stevens, 2020). President Donald Trump called COVID-19 "the Chinese virus" and the "Kung Flu virus." Some Asian Americans have been victims of racial hostility and attacks. The anti-Asian events and expressions evoked, for many Asian Americans, painful and repressed memories of the Chinese Exclusion Act of 1882 and the internment of Japanese Americans during the 1940s (Stevens, 2020).

Solórzano and Pérez Huber have adapted the definition of *racial microaggression* developed by Chester Pierce, the noted Harvard University psychiatrist:

> The subtle, stunning, repetitive event that many whites initiate and control in their dealing with blacks can be termed a racial microaggression. Any single microaggression from an offender to a defender (or victimizer to victim) in itself is minor and inconsequential. However, the relentless omnipresence of these noxious stimuli is the fabric of black-white relations in America. (Pierce, 1980, cited in this volume, p. 31)

Solórzano and Pérez Huber expanded the definition constructed by Pierce to encompass all people and communities of color. In his American Educational Research Association (AERA) Distinguished Lecture in 2019, Solórzano defined racial microaggressions as "a form of systemic everyday verbal or non-verbal assaults directed toward People of Color. They are also layered assaults, based on a Person of Color's marginalized identities. . . . [T]hey are [also] cumulative assaults that take a physiological, psychological, and academic toll on People of Color" (cited in Harmon, 2019). Solórzano and Pérez Huber detail many graphic and authentic examples of racial microaggressions throughout this book that will enable readers to comprehend and recognize indicators of microaggressions when they experience or witness them.

The vivid examples and descriptions of racial microaggressions in this book enabled me to recall and to categorize incidents that I have experienced personally or witnessed during my life's journey. When I was an undergraduate student enrolled in an anthropology class at Chicago Teachers College (now Chicago State University) that consisted of very few African American students, the White professor, while discussing a topic related to race, looked directly at me and asked, "Mr. Banks [class discourse in college classes was formal in the early 1960s], what do Blacks think about this?" I was traumatized and embarrassed by his question and was speechless. An African American woman in the class, who was older than me and who had probably had past experiences with professors like this one, was offended by his question and made a harsh comment to him. His anger at her comment was palpable. He retaliated against her, and she received a low grade in the class.

The University of Washington has a large number of Asian American students, many of whom come from families that have lived in the United States for generations. These students are sometimes asked, "Where are you from?" When they answer "Los Angeles" or "San Francisco," the next question is, "Where are you *really* from?" This racial microaggression assumes that these students were not born in the United States and are Asians, not Asian Americans. When Michelle Obama was a student at Whitney Young School, a magnet high school in Chicago, she said that she wanted to attend Princeton University. A college counselor told her that she wasn't "Princeton material" (Obama, 2018). Obama had a successful academic experience at Princeton and later graduated from Harvard Law School. Obama did not internalize the college counselor's view of her but was determined to defy and resist it. The engaging and realistic examples of racial microaggressions in this book, which inspired me to recall the ones detailed above, will enable readers to comprehend the concept, identify examples, and to understand the adverse effects that racial microaggressions have on their victims.

This book not only contains myriad examples of racial microaggressions, it also describes the heavy psychological and physiological consequences that the victims of racial microaggressions experience, including discomfort, anxiety, confusion, stress, and hypertension. Solórzano and Pérez Huber also describe actions that perpetuators of racial microaggression can take to lessen the negative consequences for victims, including acknowledging the harm and apologizing to victims. The authors embed their conception of racial microaggressions within a critical race theory framework. They describe how racial microaggressions are a manifestation of structural and institutional racism within U.S. society and argue that "perpetrators of racial microaggressions should own the responsibility of dismantling everyday racism, whether it be the racism that they carry out themselves or the racism perpetuated by institutions" (p. 50).

The major purpose of the Multicultural Education Series is to provide preservice educators, practicing educators, graduate students, scholars, and policymakers with an interrelated and comprehensive set of books that summarizes and analyzes important research, theory, and practice related to the education of ethnic, racial, cultural, and linguistic groups in the United States and the education of mainstream students about diversity. The dimensions of multicultural education, developed by Banks (2004) and described in the *Handbook of Research on Multicultural Education, The Routledge Companion to Multicultural Education* (Banks, 2009), and the *Encyclopedia of Diversity in Education* (Banks, 2012), provide the conceptual framework for the development of the publications in the Series. The dimensions are content integration, the knowledge construction process, prejudice reduction, equity pedagogy, and an empowering institutional culture and social structure. The books in the Multicultural Education Series provide research, theoretical, and practical knowledge about the behaviors and learning characteristics of students of color (Conchas & Vigil, 2012; Lee, 2007), language minority students (Gándara & Hopkins 2010; Valdés, 2001; Valdés, Capitelli, & Alvarez, 2011), low-income students (Cookson, 2013; Gorski, 2018), and other minoritized population groups, such as students who speak different varieties of English (Charity Hudley & Mallinson, 2011) and LGBTQ youth (Mayo, 2014).

This book describes ways to identify and mitigate racial microaggressions in colleges and universities. A number of other books in the Multicultural Education Series analyze and discuss problems related to diversity in higher education and ways in which higher education institutions can be reformed to address those problems. These books include *Engaging the "Race Question": Accountability and Equity in U. S. Higher Education* by Alicia C. Dowd and Estela Mara Bensimon (2015); *Race, Empire, and English Language Teaching: Creating Responsible and Ethical Anti-Racist Practice* by Suhanthie Motha (2014); *Achieving Equity for Latino Students: Expanding the Pathway to Higher Education Through Public Policy* by Frances Contreras (2011); *Americans by Heart: Undocumented Latino Students and the Promise of Higher Education* by William Pérez (2011); *Asians in the Ivory Tower: Dilemmas of Racial Inequality in American Higher Education* by Robert T. Teranishi (2010); *Immigrant-Origin Students in Community College: Navigating Risk and Reward in Higher Education,* edited by Carola Suárez-Orozco and Olivia Osei-Twumasi (2019); and *Campus Uprising: How Student Activists and Collegiate Leaders Resist Racism and Create Hope*, edited by Ty-Ron M. O. Douglas, Kmt G. Shockley, and Ivory Toldson (2020).

Solórzano and Pérez Huber not only describe how people of color are victimized by racial microaggressions, they also detail how they exemplify resiliency and efficacy by responding to racial microaggressions in creative and innovative ways, as Michelle Obama did when she rejected the advice of her high school college counselor and exemplified efficacy and strong determination by pursuing her education goals.

One of the most edifying and inspiring parts of this book consists of the definition, examples, and descriptions of what the authors call "racial microaffirmations," which are the powerful and transformative ways in which people and communities of color respond to racial microaggressions. The authors describe a telling example of racial microaffirmations in which Henry Louis Gates, Jr., the eminent African American Harvard University scholar, explains in a letter to his daughters why he "still nod[s] or speak[s] to black people on the streets and why it felt so good to be acknowledged [with a nod] by the Afro-Italians who passed [his] table at the café in Milan"

(Gates, 1994, cited in this volume, p. 84). Gates said that he "enjoy(s) the unselfconscious moments of a shared cultural intimacy, whatever form they take, when no else is watching, when no white people are around. . . . And I hope you'll understand why I continue to speak to colored people I pass on the streets" (pp. 84–85).

The African American teachers in my segregated schools in the Arkansas Delta in the 1950s and 1960s were keenly aware of the racial microaggressions that we experienced daily in Marianna, Arkansas, including when we went to the movie theater and had to use the colored entrance and watch the movie upstairs in the small room where the movie projector was located, which made it difficult to hear the movie because of the clinking sound of the projector (Banks, 2020). Our teachers responded to these microaggressions by constructing racial microaffirmations that included learning about African Americans such as Booker T. Washington, George Washington Carver, and Mary McLeod Bethune in our social studies lessons and singing each day in morning exercise both the "The Star Spangled Banner" and the Negro National Anthem, "Lift Every Voice and Sing." Our teachers wanted us to develop a national identity but also an identity with our cultural community that would provide us with resiliency, affirmation, and hope.

The concept of racial microaffirmations, which the authors define and illustrate with rich examples, is important to illuminate so that students and faculty of color will not be perceived as mere victims of racial hostility and institutional racism. Examples of the resistance of racial and ethnic groups to institutional racism in the United States, such as journalist Ida B. Wells's campaign against lynching in the 1890s (Giddings, 2008) and the civil rights movement of the 1960s and 1970s (Garrow, 1986), have been a consistent and integral part of the American saga. Okihiro (1994) argues that it was groups on the margins of society, such as African Americans, American Indians, and Asian Americans, that kept the United States committed to the ideals stated in its founding documents, such as the Constitution and the Bill of Rights. These groups challenged the nation to live up to ideals such as justice and equality when it seriously violated them with practices and institutions such as the takeover of Indian lands, slavery, lynching, and the internment of Japanese Americans during World War II.

This timely and significant book will help faculty and administrators in colleges and universities to identify racial microaggressions that take a heavy toll on students and faculty of color, to take actions to mediate the effects of racial microaggressions, and to better understand the ways in which structural and institutional racism give rise to racial microaggressions, and thus must be the target of reform.

I hope this needed, illuminating, and visionary book will receive the wide and warm reception that it deserves.

—James A. Banks

REFERENCES

Banks, J. A. (2004). Multicultural education: Historical development, dimensions, and practice. In J. A. Banks & C. A. M. Banks (Eds.). *Handbook of research on multicultural education* (2nd ed., pp. 3–29). San Francisco, CA: Jossey-Bass.

Banks, J. A. (Ed.). (2009). *The Routledge international companion to multicultural education.* New York, NY & London, England: Routledge.

Banks, J. A. (2012). Multicultural education: Dimensions of. In J. A. Banks (Ed). *Encyclopedia of diversity in education* (vol. 3, pp. 1538–1547). Thousand Oaks, CA: Sage Publications.

Banks, J. A. (2020). *Diversity, transformative knowledge, and civic education: Selected essays.* New York, NY & London, England: Routledge.

Blow, C. (2020, May 3). Covid-19's race and class warfare. *The New York Times.* Retrieved from https://www.nytimes.com/2020/05/03/opinion/coronavirus-race-class.html

Case, A., & Deaton, A. (2020). *Deaths of despair and the future of capitalism.* Princeton, NJ: Princeton University Press.

Charity Hudley, A. H., & Mallinson, C. (2011). *Understanding language variation in U.S. schools.* New York, NY: Teachers College Press.

Cohen, P. (2020, April 17). Straggling in a good economy, and now struggling in a crisis. *The New York Times.* Retrieved from https://www.nytimes.com/2020/04/16/business/economy/coronavirus-economy.html

Conchas, G. Q., & Vigil, J. D. (2012). *Streetsmart schoolsmart: Urban poverty and the education of adolescent boys.* New York, NY: Teachers College Press.

Contreras, F. (2011). *Achieving equity for Latino students: Expanding the pathway to higher education through public policy.* New York, NY: Teachers College Press.

Cookson, P. W., Jr. (2013). *Class rules: Exposing inequality in American high schools.* New York, NY: Teachers College Press.

Douglas, T.-R., Shockley, K. G., & Toldson, I. (2020). *Campus uprisings: How student activists and collegiate leaders resist racism and create hope.* New York, NY: Teachers College Press.

Dowd, A. C., & Bensimon, E. M. (2015). *Engaging the "race question": Accountability and equity in U.S. higher education.* New York, NY: Teachers College Press.

Egan, T. (2020, May 8). The world is taking pity on us: Will American prestige ever recover? *The New York Times.* Retrieved from https://www.nytimes.com/2020/05/08/opinion/coronavirus-trump.html

Gándara, P., & Hopkins, M. (Eds.). (2010). *Forbidden language: English language learners and restrictive language policies.* New York, NY: Teachers College Press.

Garrow, D. J. (1986). *Bearing the cross: Martin Luther King, Jr., and the Southern Christian Leadership Conference.* New York, NY: HarperCollins.

Giddings, P. J. (2008). *Ida: A sword among lions: Ida B. Wells and the campaign against lynching.* New York, NY: HarperCollins.

Goldstein, D. (2020, May 9). The class divide: Remote learning at 2 schools, private and public. *The New York Times.* Retrieved from https://www.nytimes.com/2020/05/09/us/coronavirus-public-private-school.html

Gorski, P. C. (2018). *Reaching and teaching students in poverty: Strategies for erasing the opportunity* gap (2nd ed.). New York, NY: Teachers College Press.

Grandin, G. (2019). *The end of the myth: From the frontier to the border wall in the mind of America*. New York, NY: Henry Holt & Company.

Harmon, J. (2019, May 7). Daniel Solórzano delivers AERA Distinguished Lecture. *UCLA Ed & IS*. Retrieved from https://ampersand.gseis.ucla.edu/daniel-Solórzano-delivers-aera-distinguished-lecture/

Lee, C. D. (2007). *Culture, literacy, and learning: Taking bloom in the midst of the whirlwind*. New York, NY: Teachers College Press.

Mayo, C. (2014). *LGBTQ youth and education: Policies and practices*. New York, NY: Teachers College Press.

Mays, J. C., & Newman, A. (2020, April 8). Virus is twice as deadly for Black and Latino people than Whites in N.Y.C. *The New York Times*. Retrieved from https://www.nytimes.com/2020/04/08/nyregion/coronavirus-race-deaths.html

Motha, S. (2014). *Race, empire, and English language teaching: Creating responsible and ethical anti-racist practice*. New York, NY: Teachers College Press.

Obama, M. (2018). *Becoming*. New York, NY: Crown Publishing Group.

Okihiro, G. Y. (1994). *Margins and mainstreams: Asians in American history and culture*. Seattle, WA: University of Washington Press.

Pérez, W. (2011). *Americans by heart: Undocumented Latino students and the promise of higher education*. New York, NY: Teachers College Press.

Rosenthal, E. (2020, May 6). We knew the coronavirus was coming, yet we failed. *The New York Times*. Retrieved from https://www.nytimes.com/2020/05/06/opinion/coronavirus-health-care-market.html

Schwartz, N. D., Casselman, B., & Koeze, E. (2020, May 8). How bad is unemployment? 'Literally off the charts.' *The New York Times*. Retrieved from https://www.nytimes.com/interactive/2020/05/08/business/economy/april-jobs-report.html

Stevens, M. (2020, March 29). How Asian-American leaders are grappling with xenophobia amid coronavirus. *The New York Times*. Retrieved from https://www.nytimes.com/2020/03/29/us/politics/coronavirus-asian-americans.html

Suárez-Orozco, C., & Osei-Twumasi, O. (2019). *Immigrant-origin students in community college: Navigating risk and reward in higher education*. New York, NY: Teachers College Press.

Teranishi, R. T. (2010). *Asians in the ivory tower: Dilemmas of racial inequality in American higher education*. New York, NY: Teachers College Press.

Valdés, G. (2001). *Learning and not learning English: Latino Students in American schools*. New York, NY: Teachers College Press.

Valdés, G., Capitelli, S., & Alvarez, L. (2011). *Latino children learning English: Steps in the journey*. New York, NY: Teachers College Press.

Villarosa, L. (2020, May 3). Who lives? Who dies? How Covid-19 has revealed the deadly realities of a racially polarized America. *The New York Times Magazine*, pp. 34–39, ff. 50–51.

Williams, C. (2020, April 23). $23M to get Detroit students tablets, internet amid pandemic. *Associated Press*. Retrieved from https://apnews.com/cb984f50631e4a35c17418182c63f94e

Acknowledgments

This book project would not have been possible without the support, insight, critical dialogue, and critiques from our friends, family, and colleagues. We can never recognize everyone by name, and we hope that those that we do not list will forgive us. We acknowledge collectively, those who have contributed to our thinking and theorizing of racial microaggressions, including those who served as coauthors with us in the past. We also acknowledge important places and organizations that have supported us and our scholarship. We end with personal acknowledgements to our mentors, friends, and families who have made our careers and scholarship possible and have fulfilled our lives.

This work would not be possible if not for Dr. Chester Pierce, who set the foundation for all research on racial microaggressions. We thank you, Dr. Pierce, for your many contributions and for giving academia a name for everyday racism. A special thanks to Professor Peggy Davis for introducing us to Dr. Pierce's work. Many colleagues have offered their support over the years and contributed toward our development of racial microaggressions and racial microaffirmations. Many of these scholars have coauthored (with one or both of us), and others have offered important insights and feedback on our ideas about racial microaggressions presented in this book. Thank you to Walter Allen, Grace Carroll, Miguel Ceja, Bert Cueva, Dolores Delgado Bernal, Valerie Gomez, Layla Huber-Verjan, Rita Kohli, Maria Ledesma, María Malagón, Laurence Parker, Derald Wing Sue, Verónica Vélez, Octavio Villalpando, Kenjus Watson, and Tara Yosso. We are forever grateful for your collaboration. We would also like to thank Dr. James A. Banks for his support of this work to be included among a significant list of highly influential books on social justice and education. We are honored to be included in this series. Thanks also to Brian Ellerbeck and John Bylander, our editors. We would also like to thank Luis-Genaro Garcia for providing the artwork for our book cover.

There are many other scholars whose work has been critical and influential to our work in Critical Race Theory (CRT) in the law and education. We wish to thank legal scholars Derrick Bell, Kimberlé Williams Crenshaw, Richard Degaldo, Charles R. Lawrence III, Mari J. Matsuda, Margaret Montoya, and Jean Stefancic, whose work has played a significant role in theorizing racial microaggressions from a CRT perspective. There have been many other scholars within and outside the field of education that have contributed to our use of CRT. We wish to thank Rudy Acuña, Gloria Anzaldúa, Patricia Hill Collins, Dave Gillborn, Tyrone Howard, Gloria Ladson-Billings, Don Nakanishi, Gordon Parks, William Smith, Dave Stovall, and William Tate for their work that has informed our theorizing.

There are also many important students across the years we wish to acknowledge. We thank German Aguilar-Tinajero for his editing assistance with this book project. Many others have played an important role in the development of CRT and racial microaggressions. I (Lindsay) would like to thank Tamara Gonzalez and Gabriela Robles, my graduate students in the Social and Cultural Analysis of Education (SCAE) program at California State University, Long Beach (CSULB), who have worked with me to collect data on racial microaffirmations (some of which we present in this book). I would also like to thank SCAE alum Lorena Camargo Gonzalez, Dolores Lopez, and Brianna Ramirez for each of their contributions to racial microaggressions. Finally, I am grateful to my community of SCAE graduate students, and colleague Nina Flores at CSULB, for pushing my thinking and teaching work. I (Danny) would like to thank my former students at East Los Angeles College, California State University, Northridge; California State University, Bakersfield; and the University of California, Los Angeles (UCLA), who have worked with me on research and teaching. I would like to thank the hundreds of past and current students from the UCLA Research Apprenticeship Course (RAC), some already mentioned here. RAC began in the Graduate School of Education & Information Studies at UCLA in 1995 and continues to this day. Well over 500 students have come through the RAC, and it has been an incubator for the development of Critical Race Theory in Education. It is a space where ideas are shared, challenged, and pushed forward. Countless contributions to the field of CRT have come from current and former members of the RAC—I see myself in you.

There are several organizations that have supported us and our work over the years that we would like to acknowledge here. The Latina/o Critical Legal Theory (LatCrit), Inc., community of scholars has included and supported our work as education scholars for over two decades. This has been a critical site of knowledge production for CRT, and we have appreciated the opportunity to engage with LatCrit. We would like to thank Nancy Parachini and the UCLA Principal Leadership Institute, as well as the UCLA Teacher Education Program for their support to integrate racial microaggressions research into their teacher and administrator training. The UCLA Center for Critical Race Studies in Education serves as another important venue for dissemination of CRT scholarship in education, and we thank those whose vision began it: Alma Itze Flores, Tanya Gaxiola Serrano, and Ryan Santos. We appreciate the support of the Ford Foundation Fellowship Program, where we both have received dissertation (Lindsay) and postdoctoral (Danny) fellowships to pursue our research ideas. For decades, this fellowship program has and continues to diversify U.S. faculty ranks by supporting PhDs of Color from all fields. We would also like to thank Chon Noriega, Carlos Haro, and the UCLA Chicano Studies Research Center for their support of our work over the years and for their commitment to improving the Latina/o education pipeline. Finally, we thank the Critical Race Studies in Education Association where we have presented our work since its first annual meeting in 2007 in Chicago, Illinois. This organization provides an important space for CRT scholars in education and beyond to come together to move the field forward.

I (Danny) want to express my gratitude to the people who helped me through this book project. Though not here, I begin by thanking my parents Elizabeth and Manuel Sr. for their unwavering love and support through this and other chapters of my life. To my brothers Ronny and Manuel Jr.: I give special thanks to you for your love and support throughout my life. To my best friend, wife, and life partner, Laura Telles: Your strength, support, and love has contributed so much to this and all the work I do. I also want to thank my nieces, nephews, and godchildren for your support—you inspire me. Thanks to my coauthor, Lindsay, whose wisdom, intellect, and commitment have guided us on this and other research and writing projects. Over the years I have been blessed with many mentors but three stand out—thanks to Leobardo Estrada, David Drew, and Arturo Madrid for continuing to guide me and serving as a model on this long journey. I want to acknowledge my teachers from grammar school to graduate school. Special thanks goes to the Catholic nuns, priests, brothers, and lay teachers who instilled in me the importance of struggling for "social justice." They accomplished this, in part, by teaching social justice through the works of Jesus Christ and Catholic Social Teaching.

When I (Lindsay) was in elementary school my family (my parents, two younger sisters, and myself) lived in a small studio apartment in Los Angeles County. We shared one open room with a trundle bed that my younger sister and I would sleep on, while my parents and little sister slept on a couch or on the floor. I remember asking my parents one day, "Why do you let us sleep on the beds?" My father replied, "You both have to go to school, so you get the beds." This was an important message I was taught early on. Education is a big deal. My first conversations about the importance of education began in my home with them, and I thank them for this—for always believing in me and for always supporting me.

I would like to thank the mentors I have had over the years that have made my pursuit of an academic career possible. My coauthor, Danny, is a true role model for exceptional mentorship, and I will be forever grateful for the many years of his support, patience, care, and encouragement. It is an honor to write this book with him. I was lucky to have mentors early on that encouraged me to pursue graduate school. Thank you to Lisa García

Bedolla, Jeanett Castellanos, and Ramon Muñoz. Each of these mentors are like family, an academic family that have always been there and always believed in me. My academic family also includes my colleagues and dear friends Maria Malagón and Verónica N. Vélez, who have supported me personally and intellectually and have been there every step of the way during my academic trajectory. Finally, and most importantly, I thank my partner, Guillermo Verjan. We have shared 20 years of our lives together, and I will always be grateful for his unconditional love and support. I thank my daughters, Layla and Luna, who have played an active role in this book. They have both been note-takers, time-keepers, illustrators, collaborators, and copresenters during meetings and conferences. Layla has also been my coauthor on earlier work, also included in this book. I am so grateful to be their mom. They are the loves of my life, my joy, the two most important reasons I do this work.

Artist's Statement

Social Consciousness Through Intergenerational Knowledge: Sustaining a Cycle of Justice

ABOUT THE COVER ART

In his book *Pedagogy of the Oppressed* (1970), Paulo Freire calls on educators to unveil the reality of oppression that exists in marginalized communities and commit to social transformation through the process of praxis. He adds that critical pedagogy should include a critical and liberating dialogue to challenge oppression and needs to be cofacilitated between students and educators to achieve social transformation.

Based on conversations that developed between the authors of this book and myself regarding the interdisciplinary knowledge of art, critical education, and Critical Race Theory, the work on the cover of this book is a representation of Freire's idea of a critical pedagogy. The image is inspired by the continued activism of Erika Huggins, human rights activist, poet, educator, Black Panther Party leader, and former political prisoner. The image reflects a moment of transformation for a group of students who are developing their own social consciousness through the teaching that is taking place in the real-life settings and circumstances of their communities. It presents the ways in which an activist (that takes on the role of an educator) draws on her lived experiences to explain how past forms of racism targeting People of Color have sustained modern forms of racism in the media (i.e., "China Virus," "Kung Flu") systemically and have caused intergenerational trauma. The historical and contemporary signage references the history of racism in the United States. However, the image also represents the response and resistance to racism, anchored by Victor Hugo Green's The Negro Motorist Green Book. This guidebook was published annually from 1936 to 1966, and was created for African American travelers to find lodging, businesses, and gas stations that would serve them during the Jim Crow era. It also provided information on places to avoid along travel routes that could be dangerous for African Americans to pass through (i.e., "sundown" towns). The guidebook was recognized as a form of shared knowledge among Black communities and was quite literally a navigational tool. The Green Book represents the resistance of Black communities to the racism and violence perpetrated by whites during the time.

Response and resistance to racism is also represented through the development of students' own social consciousness—a new generation of youth activists (illustrated towards the bottom of the image) that understand how the historical circumstances of the past have shaped current activist movements like Black Lives Matter, the American Indian Movement, Immigrant Rights, and the LGBTQ Movement. These movements have led to new generations of activists like the young Girls of Color in Radical Monarchs (radicalmonarchs.org), uniting in solidarity and a shared struggle to become radical leaders of change in their communities. And the cycle of justice continues.

Teaching Art for 14 years in the high school I attended enabled me to understand my students and their communities. It allowed us to understand our community's past and present struggles and we found ways to change those circumstances both inside and out of the classroom.

—Luis-Genaro Garcia

Luis-Genaro Garcia, PhD (education), is a Los Angeles artist and former high school art teacher of 14 years from South Central Los Angeles. His approach to art education uses art and ethnic studies as tools of resistance by drawing on the theoretical frameworks of the funds of knowledge, critical pedagogy, and Critical Race Theory. His critical arts-based research focuses on using critical education frameworks along with the ethnic, personal, and historical experiences of working-class Students of Color in order to challenge, navigate, and transform the institutional circumstances that exist for Communities of Color. He is currently an assistant professor of art education at California State University, Sacramento. Learn more about his work at luisgenarogarcia.com.

Origin Stories

How We Came to Study Racial Microaggressions

You've given me a name for my pain.

—Detroit High School Student, Spring 2001

In the spring of 2001, after I (Danny)[1] presented our team's research on racial microaggressions at the University of Michigan, the audience lined up for questions and answers. A young African American high school student came to the microphone. She stood there crying. When she finally spoke, she said, "Thank you. You've given me a name for my pain." This comment remains with us because this young woman expressed the raw and real feelings that many People of Color have since expressed from many different age groups, communities, and walks of life. This high school student showed us that these two words, *racial microaggressions*, are a powerful way to acknowledge and name the everyday pain and suffering that People of Color experience. This book builds on that acknowledgment and on earlier research on racial microaggressions we began in 1995.

DANNY'S STORY

I (Danny) came to my work in racial microaggressions long before my first publication in 1998 (Solórzano, 1998a). I have spent most of my academic life searching for, collecting, and analyzing books, journal articles, newspapers, magazines, and other written and visual materials on the everyday racialized experiences of Communities of Color (see Solórzano, 2013). Indeed, I have spent many hours, days, months, and years in libraries and archives of all sizes practicing my craft of knowledge exploration, recovery, and recreation. I have searched in bookstores, video stores, secondhand stores, antique stores, estate sales, yard sales, and photo archives looking for materials to help me better understand the cultural wealth that exists in Communities of Color (Yosso, 2005; Yosso & Solórzano, 2005). The following story is about how I used the tools of Critical Race Theory (CRT)

1

to identify and analyze the concepts of marginality and racial microaggressions. I begin by telling my story of how I came to CRT and how that led me on a journey to discover and utilize the concepts of marginality and racial microaggressions in my research, writing, and teaching. I end by reflecting on the journey and where I see the challenges and opportunities facing the field of racial microaggressions.

My Journey to CRT

I was first introduced to CRT in July of 1993 at the library of East Los Angeles College, a community college in Southern California.[2] I came across an article in the *Chronicle of Higher Education*[3] by Peter Monaghan (1993) titled "'Critical Race Theory' Questions Role of Legal Doctrine in Racial Inequality." Although I didn't know it at the time, this was my first "critical race moment."[4] The article introduced me to an emerging field that was challenging the orthodoxy of race, racism, and the law. It also mentioned and led me to CRT's founding legal scholars, such as Derrick Bell, Kimberle Crenshaw, Richard Delgado, Cheryl Harris, Linda Greene, Lani Guinier, Charles Lawrence, Mari Matsuda, Margaret Montoya, and Patricia Williams.[5] Critical Race Theory in the law seemed to be a framework that began to answer some of the questions that had been troubling me—especially questions on how we center race and racism in our academic research and teaching. Yet, two reactions also went through my mind as I read the article: My first reaction: This framework is a new and powerful way of looking at race and racism in the law and by extension the social sciences, humanities, and education.[6] My second reaction: I've seen this before. In the days that followed I realized the language of CRT in the law resonated with my previous training in race and ethnic studies and Freirean critical theory. At that point, I returned to some of the early foundational writings in these fields and tried to connect and put them in conversation with CRT.[7] In order to secure time for this academic journey, I asked for and received a sabbatical to immerse myself in the CRT legal literature, incorporate it with my background and training in race and ethnic studies and Freirean pedagogy, and apply them to social science and educational research. Figure I.1 represents a model of my intellectual journey to CRT.

My Journey to Marginality

My experience with the concept of marginality predates my introduction to CRT. In 1987, I received a Ford Foundation postdoctoral fellowship in sociology to study the career paths of Chicana and Chicano PhD scholars. This multimethod study surveyed an initial sample of Chicana and Chicano Ford predoctoral, dissertation and postdoctoral fellows on issues related to their experiences with race and racism in academia (see Solórzano, 1993). At

Figure I.1. My Journey to Critical Race Theory

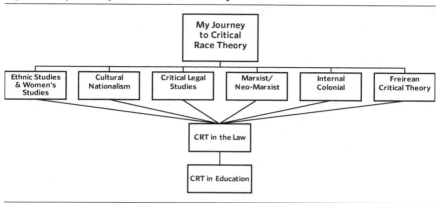

the same time, I was creating another data set of life history interviews with Chicana and Chicano PhD scholars in mathematics, science, and engineering (MSE).[8] I began by using the tool of marginality to frame their journey to, within, and beyond the academy (see Collins, 1986). I was looking at how these scholars experienced racial/ethnic, gender, and class marginality. I differentiated the related concepts of the margin and marginality. I defined the margin as a complex and contentious space or place where People of Color[9] experience race, gender, and class subordination. In those complex and contentious spaces or places, People of Color are forced out of the center and into the margins of society and their academic fields (hooks, 1990).[10] I then defined marginality as that complex and contentious status of subordination experienced by People of Color. The construct of marginality was a useful analytical tool for me in understanding the problem of the underrepresentation and subordination of People of Color—especially within the academy. I also recognized that W. E. B. Du Bois theorized about racial marginality in the late 19th century. As early as 1897, Du Bois introduced the concepts of the veil, second-sight, double-consciousness, and two-ness. He wrote:

> After the Egyptian and Indian, the Greek and Roman, the Teuton and Mongolian, the Negro is a sort of seventh son, born with a *veil*, and gifted with *second-sight* in this American world,—a world which yields him no true self-consciousness, but only lets him see himself through the revelation of the other world. It is a peculiar sensation, this *double-consciousness*, this sense of always looking at one's self through the eyes of others, of measuring one's soul by the tape of a world that looks on in amused contempt and pity. One ever feels his *twoness*,—an American, a Negro; two souls, two thoughts, two unreconciled strivings; two warring ideals in one dark body, whose dogged strength alone keeps it from being torn asunder. (p. 194, emphasis mine)

Although Du Bois never referred to these concepts as marginality, his insight was clearly the precursor to the concept of marginality that Robert Park (1928) introduced to the field of sociology in 1928—31 years later. According to Aldon Morris (2015), Park never acknowledged what his thinking owed to insights from Du Bois.[11]

Using CRT as a basic framework, I analyzed the life history interview data looking for experiences with and responses to racism, sexism, and classism. Specifically, after all the interviews were conducted and analyzed, some thematic patterns around marginality emerged (Glaser & Strauss, 1967; Strauss & Corbin, 1990). Specifically, I began to: (1) identify all the examples of and reactions to racial, gender, and class marginality, (2) determine whether patterns could be found in the types, contexts, effects, and response to race, gender, and class marginality, and (3) find examples of text or "autobiographical moments" that illustrated the different forms of and reactions to marginality (see Culp, 1996). In this analytical process, I found examples and began to compare these raced, classed, and gendered experiences across the scholars in my study.

My Journey to Racial Microaggressions

In 1994, I was analyzing the interviews and writing an initial manuscript on marginality titled "A Critical Race Analysis of Marginality: Examining the Career Paths of Chicana and Chicano Doctoral Scientists."[12] I came across an article in the *Yale Law Journal* by Peggy Davis (1989) titled "Law as Microaggression." This was the first time I saw the word *microaggression* in either a title or a narrative. To examine the concept of microaggression, Davis takes readers on a brief elevator ride and describes the following incident:

> The scene is a courthouse in Bronx, New York. A white assistant city attorney "takes the court elevator up to the ninth floor. At the fifth floor, the doors open. A black woman asks: 'Going down?' 'Up,' says [the city attorney]. And then, as the doors close: 'You see? They can't even tell up from down. I'm sorry, but it's true'" (pp. 1560–1561).

Davis (1989) describes the many explanations for the Black woman's question "going down?," from the possibility that she was just being congenial, to a broken elevator display. However, the white city attorney jumped to an assumption that the Black woman was unintelligent. His comment was based on a stereotype, and as Davis (1989) interprets, was a microform of racism—that is, not just a personal slight, but an instance of racialized harm. Davis (1989) goes on to define microaggressions as "stunning, automatic acts of disregard that stem from unconscious attitudes of white superiority and constitute a verification of black inferiority" (p. 1576). Davis

(1989) cites the origins of this concept in the work of Chester Pierce. At footnote number five in the article, Davis's first Pierce citation is a two-page unpublished manuscript in 1986 titled "Homoracial Behavior in the U.S.A." (Pierce & Profit, 1991. The Davis article had a total of five Chester Pierce citations and led me to Chester Pierce and his colleagues' (1978) definition of microaggressions as

> subtle, stunning, often automatic, and non-verbal exchanges which are "put downs" of blacks by offenders. The offensive mechanisms used against blacks often are innocuous. The cumulative weight of their never-ending burden is the major ingredient in black-white interactions. (p. 66)

The Davis article, the Pierce citations, and this definition started me on a journey to find, understand, and utilize the concept of racial microaggressions in my research and teaching. I went on to read (and re-read) all the works of Chester Pierce.[13] Indeed, I wanted to know how and why he came to work on microaggressions.

Bringing Racial Microaggressions to My Work on Marginality

In 1994–1995, I went back to my study of Ford Fellows and reanalyzed the data using the analytical tool of racial microaggressions. I also reanalyzed the life history interviews from my sample of Chicana and Chicano PhDs in MSE. I continued to use CRT as a framework to examine how racial and gender microaggressions affect the career paths of these Chicana and Chicano scholars. I had three objectives for these studies: (1) to extend and apply Critical Race Theory to research in education, (2) to recognize, document, and analyze racial and gender microaggressions against Chicana and Chicano scholars, and (3) to hear the voices of survivors of discrimination by examining the effect of race and gender microaggressions on the lives of these Chicana and Chicano scholars. As I analyzed the data, three patterns of racial and gender microaggressions were found: (1) scholars felt out of place in the academy because of their race and/or gender, (2) scholars felt their teachers/professors had lower expectations for them, and (3) the scholars reported subtle and not so subtle experiences with race and gender discrimination.

As I used the tool of racial microaggressions to reanalyze the Ford and MSE scholar data, I began to see the power, complexity, and utility of the concept. For instance, in the interview passages below, I began to re-code for racial and gender microaggressions. A Chicana biochemist recounts the following:

> Sometimes you don't know it's gender discrimination when you're in the midst of it because it's *so subtle*, but when you mature and you

look back, you realize that, yes, there were distinctions by which young males were really encouraged to participate in math courses, in math clubs, and the intense extra-curricular activities whereas the young women were encouraged to be more auxiliary. (personal communication, June 14, 1988)

Another Chicana biologist shares:

I can't tell you how many times I've been told *"you're not like the rest of them," "you're different,"* or more specifically, *"you're different from other Mexicans."* Ever since my college days, I have been told this time and time again. (personal communication, June 16, 1988)

A Chicano mathematician mentioned a feeling that some of the other scholars expressed about the experiences of many minority professors in the field:

It wasn't the time period when I got my PhD that causes problems for me. It is the *subtle racism* in my department that no matter how much I produce, I am and will forever be a *"target of opportunity,"* or an *"affirmative action professor"* and that means that I will never be seen by my colleagues as their equal. (personal communication, June 27, 1988)

Throughout these interviews, a majority of the participants expressed a sense that each individual racist and sexist act could be overcome. For instance, the day-to-day slights, the remarks, the attitudes, the behaviors of others were negative experiences they learned to live with. However, the cumulative effect of these individual acts over time is what affected these scholars. A Chicano biologist reinforces the illustration:

There are overt and blatant forms of racism but there are also the *constant and subtle negative experiences* that can wear down one's spirit. The *racism just below the surface.* It is the *accumulation* of these racist events that wear you down . . . What bothers me is the constant retort from non-Hispanics that, "I was being too sensitive about racial issues." (personal communication, June 16, 1988)

As I worked my way through this analytical process of moving from marginality to racial microaggression, I came to define racial microaggressions as one form of systemic everyday racism used to keep those at the racial margins in their place. Racial microaggressions can be

- verbal and nonverbal assaults directed toward People of Color, often carried out in subtle, automatic, or unconscious forms;
- layered assaults that are based on a Person of Color's race, gender, class, sexuality, language, immigration status, phenotype, accent, or surname; and
- cumulative assaults that take a physiological, psychological, and academic toll on People of Color.

In 1998, I published an article based on the Ford scholars in the *International Journal of Qualitative Studies in Education* titled "Critical Race Theory, Racial and Gender Microaggressions, and the Experiences of Chicana and Chicano Scholars" (Solórzano, 1998a). As far as I can tell, other than the 13 works of Pierce and his colleagues, this was the first empirical research article to examine racial microaggressions (see Wong, Derthick, David, Saw, & Okazaki, 2014).

My Continuing Journey:
University of Michigan Law School Case (2000–2003)

In the fall of 1999, University of California, Los Angeles (UCLA), professor Walter Allen contacted me and asked if I would be part of a team of researchers who would conduct campus climate studies and serve as expert witnesses for the *Grutter v. Bollinger* affirmative action case (*Grutter v. Bollinger*, 2003). *Grutter* was a federal case making its way through the lower courts and was challenging the use of race in admissions at the University of Michigan Law School. Professor Allen mentioned that the 6th Circuit Federal Appeals Court agreed to let student interveners enter the trial. As a result, the federal district judge stopped the proceedings and set a July 31, 2000, date for submission of all reports, briefs, and other supporting materials on behalf of the student interveners.

In January 2000, Professor Allen convened his team to design a campus climate study of the University of Michigan Law School and its four main feeders—University of Michigan Undergraduate, Michigan State University, Harvard University, and the University of California, Berkeley.[14] Our multimethod design incorporated surveys, focus groups, interviews, document analysis, and other public records. We went into the field to gather data at each of the universities in March of 2000. We submitted the final report to the court on July 31, 2000. The federal trial in the Eastern District of Michigan resumed in January 2001.

The final report to the federal court was published in the *UC Berkeley La Raza Law Journal* and titled "Affirmative Action, Educational Equity and Campus Racial Climate: A Case Study of the University of Michigan Law School" (Allen & Solórzano, 2001). Data from our *Grutter* study was turned into two additional articles. Our first article focused on the experiences of African American students and was published in the *Journal of Negro Education* and titled "Critical Race Theory, Racial Microaggressions and Campus Racial Climate: The Experiences of African American College Students" (Solórzano, Ceja, & Yosso, 2000).[15] Later we published an article on Latina/o[16] students in the *Harvard Educational Review* titled "Critical Race Theory, Racial Microaggressions, and Campus Racial Climate For Latina/o Undergraduates" (Yosso, Smith, Ceja, & Solórzano, 2009).

My Continuing Journey to Racial Microaggressions

Since those first articles on racial microaggressions, I have continued to work with colleagues on research and conceptual manuscripts. For instance, our work on racial microaggressions included publications on a second affirmative action federal court case in California (Solórzano & Allen, 2000; Solórzano, Allen, & Carroll, 2002), on racial battle fatigue (Smith, Yosso, & Solórzano, 2006, 2007), on teachers (Kohli & Solórzano, 2012; Ledesma & Solórzano, 2013), on visual microaggressions (Pérez Huber & Solórzano, 2015a), on microaggressions as research tools (Pérez Huber & Solórzano, 2015b), on microaggressions and social work pedagogy (Pérez Huber & Solórzano, 2018), and encyclopedia entries and policy briefs (Pérez Huber & Solórzano, 2015c; Solórzano & Pérez Huber, 2012). Much of my recent work has been conducted in collaboration with my coauthor, Lindsay. She will further explain how we came together to do this research, but first she will tell her story of coming to the work of racial microaggressions.

LINDSAY'S STORY

If I (Lindsay) think about where and when my interests in studying race and education began, I would have to go back to my undergraduate years at UC Irvine. There I began a major in political science as a college student interested in the law and politics. However, as I began taking courses, I felt a disconnect. That disconnect was between my own experiences and those that I studied in my classes, between the conflicting demands of college expectations and my first-generation college student status, between my world and the world of higher education. Then I found ethnic studies. My college counselor, Ramon Muñoz, encouraged me to take courses in the new Chicana/o studies major. I still remember my first course on race and citizenship, taught by political scientist Dr. Lisa García Bedolla. I was hooked. I remember searching through the university course catalogue for any class with "race" in the title in my department. When I took all of those, Ramon encouraged me to add another major in Chicana/o studies, because many of these classes already fulfilled the requirements. By the end of my undergraduate career, and because of the mentorship I received at UC Irvine, I knew that I wanted to pursue a PhD program that joined my interests in race, ethnic studies, and education.[17] At the time there were few programs in the country that had this explicit focus. My top choice became the PhD program in Social Science and Comparative Education (SSCE) with a specialization in race and ethnic studies at UCLA. I was accepted first as a master's student, then as a PhD student, and this was where I first learned about Critical Race Theory (CRT) and racial microaggressions.

My Early Training in CRT and Racial Microaggressions

My research in racial microaggressions began with the training I received while a graduate student in education at UCLA. I was first introduced to the concept of racial microaggressions in 2004, during my first year of study at UCLA. I remember two graduate seminars I took in that year that assigned readings on racial microaggressions, one taught by my coauthor, Dr. Daniel Solórzano (Danny), professor of education, and the other by Dr. Walter Allen, professor of higher education. I did not learn until later that Danny and Walter had worked together as expert witnesses on racial microaggressions in the *Grutter v. Bollinger* affirmative action case. Nor did I know that what I had read that year was some of the first empirical research to be published about racial microaggressions and the experiences of Students of Color. What I did learn that year was this: There was a name and a framework for the experiences I had lived.

I was initially drawn to these frameworks because they allowed me, as a Woman of Color, to recognize how racism, patriarchy, capitalism, and other systems of oppression are embedded in social institutions, and how those systems shape our everyday experiences. I remember specific moments in my life—for example, when my high school counselor encouraged me to pursue a vocational program rather than college, or, when I became an expectant mother and was told that pursuing a doctoral degree would not be possible—I felt the pain of microaggressions, but did not have a name or an explanation for it. I believe this is exactly why I was so drawn to the concept when I encountered it in graduate school. I began my training in CRT in education working on research with Danny.

The UCLA Chicano Studies Research Center (CSRC)

Shortly after my first year in the program, I began working with Dr. Carlos Haro (then assistant director) at the UCLA Chicano Studies Research Center on a conference to feature Latina/o education. This conference would become the UCLA CSRC Latina/o Education Summit, and we would have our inaugural meeting in March 2006 at the UCLA campus. The summits were designed to examine the critical transitions in the educational pipeline for Latina/o students, from K–12 to higher education, with an emphasis on recommendations for improving the educational outcomes for our students.

On our first panel at this summit was the superintendent of Montebello Unified School District, a small urban district in the eastern Los Angeles area. During his presentation, he announced that he had to leave to address an "urgent issue" in his district. At the time, we did not know what this issue was. However, as the day progressed, conference participants and audience members began getting the news by text and social media that students across Los Angeles were walking out of their schools in protests of H.R. 4437, the Border Protection, Antiterrorism and Illegal Immigration Control Act of 2005. H.R. 4437 was a bill introduced in Congress and passed by the House of Representatives in December 2005.[18] H.R. 4437 was a bill that further criminalized the undocumented by imposing stricter penalties and punishments, expanded the border wall, and threatened anyone providing shelter for the undocumented with felony charges (see Pantoja, Menjívar, & Magaña, 2008).

At the end of the day, conference participants engaged in a collective discussion to devise next steps in improving the Latina/o educational pipeline. A young woman graduate student raised her hand during this discussion and stood up. She said, "This entire day we have been discussing how to make education better for Latina and Latino students. However, I am undocumented. My experience has not been represented here today, and I don't feel that my experience has been included in these discussions," and she sat down. In 2006 there was very little research on the experiences of undocumented students, particularly those in higher education. In the report I coauthored and disseminated for the conference (Pérez Huber, Huidor, Malagón, Sánchez, & Solórzano, 2006), there was a brief mention of the only study I had found at the time, authored by a sociology graduate student at UCLA, Leisy Abrego (now Dr. Leisy Abrego, UCLA professor of Chicana and Chicano studies).[19] The undocumented Latina student had called our attention to the irony of holding an all-day conference focused on improving the Latina/o educational pipeline without the representation of undocumented student experiences, while at the same moment, students were demonstrating against anti-immigrant sentiment for undocumented communities.

By the end of the conference that day, we had learned that students were walking out not only in Los Angeles but across the state and across the nation. By that evening, Spanish-language radio in Los Angeles was announcing another protest planned for the following day in downtown Los Angeles and asking everyone to wear white shirts to show peace and solidarity. On March 26, 2006, I participated in this protest with my young daughter, and with other graduate student friends from UCLA, all of us wearing white. As we arrived in the downtown area, we expected to join perhaps a few thousand people near City Hall. However, when we got there everywhere we looked we saw people wearing white. Looking north toward the direction of City Hall we saw a sea of people, tens of thousands moving forward, intermittently breaking into chants: "¡El pueblo, unido, jamás será vencido!"[20] The feeling of community among so many people was almost overwhelming. Perhaps for the first time in Los Angeles history, downtown was effectively shut down by the masses of people protesting for immigrant rights. Indeed, by day's end history had been made. It was reported that more than half a million people participated in what became the largest immigrant rights demonstration in the history of the United States.

I remember vividly walking past a street corner and seeing a little girl, Latina, maybe 7 years old, holding a protest sign that read "Racism Must Die for Humanity to Live." Her words were like a bright spotlight, demanding recognition of the racism that pervades immigration discourse and dehumanizes undocumented immigrant Latina/o communities. Because of my training in Chicana/o studies as an undergraduate, I knew that anti-Latina/o racism had targeted our communities, both immigrant and U.S.-born, for more than a century in the United States.[21] Indeed, what was happening was a cumulative response to decades-long anti-immigrant policies that have targeted undocumented Latina/o immigrants in California and across the nation. In 2006, it had been only 10 years since Proposition 187 was passed by California voters, a ballot initiative that sought to ban undocumented (mostly) Latina/o immigrants from health care, social services, and public education (García Bedolla, 2005). A ban on Spanish language instruction in schools was passed just a few years later in California with Proposition 227 (Pérez Huber, 2011). Shortly after this historic event, I began working on several studies to more carefully examine the links between racism, immigration, and education, using CRT.

My Journey to Racist Nativism

The first project I undertook was in response to the woman graduate student who voiced her concern at the 2006 Latina/o education summit. I began working with another graduate student and friend, Maria Malagón, on a study that examined the experiences of undocumented Latina/o college students attending public higher education in California (Pérez Huber & Malagón, 2007). To my knowledge, this was the first study in education to utilize CRT, and specifically LatCrit (Latina/o critical theory) to examine the experiences of undocumented Latina/o students. We found that in everyday experiences on college campuses, there were indicators of "institutional neglect," the ways that racist beliefs and ideologies about undocumented Latinas/os surface on college campuses through institutionalized and informal policies and practices that marginalized undocumented students.

During this time, I also began working on another study with Danny and with my peers Veronica Vélez, Corina Benavides Lopez, and Ariana de la Luz researching the media portrayals of the students who participated in the walkouts, protests, and other forms of activism against H.R. 4437 in 2006. In this study, we found that there was a range of contradicting portrayals of Latina/o youth from across the nation who participated in the activism for immigrant rights (Vélez, Pérez Huber, Benavides Lopez, de la Luz, & Solórzano, 2008). Most concerning to us was that the discourse used to frame these youth reflected the racist and nativist perspectives that have historically pervaded Latina/o immigration. The findings in this study led our research group to further theorize what historian George Sánchez (1997) called "racial nativism." Sánchez (1997) used the concept to describe the historical and persistent link between race and immigration that prescribes nativist responses (formally and informally) toward immigrants and that shapes constructions of an "American" identity (Sánchez, 1997). This, we believed, was precisely what we saw happening in 2006 to undocumented Latina/o communities. As my thinking around these issues developed, I worked with my graduate school peers Véronica Vélez, Corina Benavides Lopez, María Malagón, and Danny to further theorize. We met several times over the summer and fall of 2006 at East Los Angeles County Library to discuss our ideas. Ultimately, we utilized CRT and, specifically, Latina/o critical theory (LatCrit) to build from Sánchez's (1997) concept of *racial nativism* to develop the concept of *racist nativism*. We theorized the concept of racist nativism as

> the assigning of values to real or imagined differences, in order to justify the superiority of the native, who is to be perceived white, over that of the non-native, who is perceived to be People and Immigrants of Color, and thereby defend the right of whites, or the natives, to dominance. (Pérez Huber, Lopez, Malagon, Velez, & Solórzano, 2008, p. 43)

What was distinct about our theorizing of racist nativism was the desire to locate the discussion of racist nativism as a "symptom" of an often-unspoken ideology of white supremacy that justifies and (re)produces all forms of racism. Here, Robert Carter's (1988) metaphor of racism as a "symptom" of the "disease" of white supremacy was critical, and will be further explained in Chapter 3.[22] In my research that followed, I focused on how discourses of racist nativism emerged in the educational trajectories of undocumented and U.S.-born Chicana/Latina college students. I found racist nativism emerged through everyday practices of subordination in their schools and universities that were often supported by institutional policies. These practices assigned values to these women as "not belonging" and made clear distinctions of their perceived "non-nativeness" within educational institutions, while reinforcing belonging and nativeness to white students. Subjugation of the Spanish language, marginalization from college preparatory courses, and exclusion from financial aid programs (for the undocumented students), were only a few of the practices and policies in place that hindered educational access for these students, from K–12 to higher education (Pérez Huber, 2009a; Pérez Huber, 2010; Pérez Huber, 2011). Through this work, I found that many of the practices that subordinated students throughout their educational trajectories were forms of racial microaggressions, the everyday subtle (and sometimes not so subtle) reminders that they were not as capable as their white peers, and even worse, that opportunities for educational access and social mobility should be reserved for those peers. These studies provided empirical evidence of how microaggressions in everyday schooling experiences were shaped by structural inequities and institutional racism.

Bringing Together CRT and Chicana Feminisms

As my research progressed in this area, I began to delve deeper into the area of Chicana feminist scholarship. I was first introduced to Dolores Delgado Bernal's (1998) groundbreaking piece "Using a Chicana Feminist Epistemology in Educational Research" as a student in Danny's class during my PhD program. Although I had read work in Chicana feminisms as an undergraduate and early graduate student, Delgado Bernal's work on Chicana feminist epistemology allowed me to see how Chicana feminist approaches could be used in educational research. I began exploring the ways that CRT and Chicana feminist approaches aligned, and how they were distinct. I found that bringing together these approaches was particularly useful in developing humanizing research methodologies, and specifically in developing *testimonio* as a methodology in critical race research (Pérez Huber, 2008, 2009b). I then began to use Chicana feminist theories to examine the detrimental psychological and physiological effects microaggressions had on students, as well as the ways in which these students engaged strategies of healing from the trauma of racism (Pérez Huber & Cueva, 2012). Since this time, Chicana feminisms have been critical to my journey in CRT research and for theorizing racial microaggressions. Chicana feminist approaches provided insight into the ways racism and racist nativism marked the minds, bodies, and spirits of Latina/o students, and particularly women. However, these approaches also opened opportunities to understand how Chicanas and Latinas engage in powerful strategies of resistance and healing (Delgado Bernal, Pérez Huber, & Malagon, 2019).

This work led me to want to further theorize the relationship between racial microaggressions and institutional racism, those policies I found reinforced and (re)produced microaggressive experiences that negatively affect the minds, bodies, spirits, and well-being of Chicana/Latina women, and particularly undocumented women. Indeed, there was a need in the literature for deeper theorizing around racial microaggressions to understand how everyday racism was in fact linked to institutional racism and ideologies of white supremacy.

OUR STORIES COMING TOGETHER
TO FURTHER THEORIZE RACIAL MICROAGGRESSIONS

By summer of 2013, we (Danny and Lindsay) wrote an encyclopedia entry on racial microaggressions for the *Encyclopedia of Diversity in Education* (Solórzano & Pérez Huber, 2012), but because of limited space allotted to our contribution, we were not yet able to tackle this conceptual link. However, the entry began our collaboration on several studies in the next few years that attempted to show how CRT could be utilized to make connections to systemic racism. In the first paper we began working on, we developed a "racial microaggressions analytic framework" that could be used to explain the systemic relationship between racial microaggressions, institutional racism, and macroaggressions, or ideologies of white supremacy that reinforce racism (Pérez Huber & Solórzano, 2015a). In this framework, we showed how these experiences are perpetuated and (re)produced by institutional racism. We also developed the framework to show how ideologies of white supremacy played a foundational role in justifying the subjugation that racial microaggressions employ. We worked on revising and refining this framework for more than a year, until its final publication in the journal *Race, Ethnicity, and Education* in 2015 in an article titled "Racial Microaggressions as a Tool for Critical Race Research" (Pérez Huber & Solórzano, 2015b). We will continue to discuss this model later in this book.

In the second paper that summer, we began to theorize one type of racial microaggression we called visual microaggression.[23] This paper began with an experience I (Lindsay) had with my then 8-year-old daughter Layla, one night while reading a book together. The book was titled *Don't Tell Lies, Lucy!: A Cautionary Tale* and, as the title implies, is a story about a little girl who had a bad habit of telling lies (Cox, 2004). Midway through the book, Lucy borrows her friend's bike and crashes into a tree. Her friend's bike is shown in the illustration, scattered in pieces, strewn across the page. When Lucy explains to her friend what happened to the bike, she says that a "bandit" jumped in front of her. The corresponding illustration portrays Lucy riding down a path with a surprised, perhaps fearful expression on her face, a bandit standing in her way. The "bandit" image was a brown man wearing a large sombrero, a serape, and sandals—a stereotypical image of the "Mexican bandit." The image stunned me and I stopped reading, until Layla asked, "What happened,

Mommy?" Through a series of questions, I asked her about what she thought the image conveyed. She replied, "It's telling us that Latinos are bandits!" A few minutes later, she began crying, telling me, "I'm Latino, so they are saying I'm a bandit," feeling personally hurt by the image and the message that was conveyed to us that night in the book.

Soon after that night, I related this experience to my coauthor, Danny, during a research meeting. Danny encouraged me to include this story in our work and involve Layla as a research assistant. We eventually told this story as an example of a visual microaggression and further theorized the concept in an article titled "Visualizing Everyday Racism: Critical Race Theory, Visual Microaggressions, and the Historical Image of Mexican Banditry," that was published in the journal *Qualitative Inquiry* (Pérez Huber & Solórzano, 2015a). We used this experience to further build on the racial microaggressions analytical framework that we were writing about at the time (described previously). Shaped (in part) by this story with Layla, we added new dimensions to the framework to show how People of Color experience microaggressions through examining types of microaggressions, the contexts in which they occur, the effects they have on psychological and physiological well-being, and the ways in which People of Color respond to them.

Shortly after we began writing these papers, in October 2013, UCLA Chancellor Gene Block announced the release of an investigative report documenting the Faculty of Color's experiences with racial microaggressions on campus. The report was titled "Independent Investigative Report on Acts of Bias and Discrimination Involving Faculty at the University of California, Los Angeles," and became known as the Moreno Report—named after the chair of the committee, retired California Supreme Court Justice Carlos Moreno (Moreno, Jackson-Triche, Nash, Rice, & Suzuki, 2013). Chancellor Block mentioned the Moreno Report contained some sobering and disturbing accounts of bias and discrimination that some faculty had experienced at UCLA. The report references some of our work on microaggressions. It stated:

> Several faculty members referenced the notion of "microaggressions," which researchers have defined as "subtle verbal and nonverbal insults directed toward non-Whites, often done automatically and unconsciously. They are layered insults based on one's race, gender, class, sexuality, language, immigration status, phenotype, accent, or surname." It is not clear to us whether any workable definition of discriminatory conduct is capable of capturing every such microaggression experienced by a minority faculty member . . . Heightened awareness of the issue of racially insensitive conduct may help to reduce microaggressions or other subtle behaviors that degrade the work environment for faculty of color. (Moreno et al., 2013, pp. 20–21)

In response to the Moreno Report, the University of California Office of the President (UCOP) established a committee and issued their report in late December 2013 called the "UC Senate-Administration Work Group on the Moreno Report: Report to the President, Academic Council, and Chancellors" (UC Senate-Administration Work Group, 2013). Their report stated that "Systemwide P&T [Promotion and Tenure] has been concerned about *low level discriminatory actions* that occur over a long period of time—things such as undervaluation, *microaggression,* and *marginaliza-tion*—that never as a single instance reach the threshold for filing a formal grievance" (UC Senate-Administration Work Group, 2013, p. 10, empha-sis added). One of the UCOP responses was to initiate a UC system–wide seminar for university leaders at each of the 10 campuses. The UC created the *Faculty Leadership Seminar Series* titled "Fostering Inclusive Excellence: Strategies and Tools for Department Chairs and Deans." The stated goals of the 4-hour seminar were to: (1) help participants gain a better understand-ing of implicit bias and microaggressions and their impact on departmental/school climate; (2) increase participants' effectiveness at recognizing and interrupting/addressing microaggressions when they occur; and (3) discuss tools and strategies for developing an inclusive departmental/school climate. I (Danny) was invited to give the seminar lecture on microaggressions titled, "Using the Critical Race Tools of Racial and Gender Microaggressions to Examine Everyday Racism in Academic Spaces" at the first UCOP semi-nar series, which took place at the University of California, San Diego, in December 2014. These seminars took place at 10 UC campuses for depart-mental chairs, deans, and other campus senior leadership throughout the 2014–2015 academic year. I participated in the UCOP seminar series at five of the campuses, while Lindsay participated in the remaining four.[24]

As we traveled throughout California to participate in these seminars at the UC campuses, we noticed something happening. Racial microaggressions began to gain traction in public discourse. One hopeful example during that time was the 2014 multimedia campaign titled "I, Too, Am Harvard" led by Harvard University student Kimiko Matsuda-Lawrence. The campaign documented the experiences of Students of Color with racism at Harvard, and specifically racial microaggressions (see Bernhard & Delwiche, 2014). The campaign drew national attention to the concept and sparked similar campaigns in universities across the country. However, with this national at-tention also came criticism. During the same time, a series of opinion edito-rials were published in the *Los Angeles Times* (Volokh, 2015a), *Chronicle of Higher Education* (Gitlin, 2015), *The Atlantic* (Lukianoff & Haidt, 2015), and the *Washington Post* (Volokh, 2015b). Nearly all of these editorials (authored by white males) mentioned the UCOP faculty seminar series, making ill-informed and misconstrued arguments questioning the concept of racial microaggressions and, in some cases, attacking UCOP for creating the seminars. For example, UCLA law professor Eugene Volokh (2015a)

used the name "UC's PC Police" to describe UCOP efforts to raise awareness about racial microaggressions. Columbia University communications
professor Todd Gitlin (2015) argued that making faculty aware of racial
microaggressions was fueling "a plague of hypersensitivity" on college campuses. In 2015, we wrote the first policy brief on racial microaggressions
for the UCLA Chicano Studies Research Center (Pérez Huber & Solórzano,
2015c). We chose to publish in a policy brief format—similar to that of an
opinion editorial—to reach an audience beyond academicians. In the brief
we addressed some of these critiques by explaining what racial microaggressions are, and why they matter in the lives of People of Color.

To date, we have given more than 150 public lectures, presentations,
and workshops at public and private universities and in professional and
community settings. We have spoken to high school students, undergraduate, graduate, and professional students (from various departments/
schools), teachers and teacher candidates, principals and principal candidates, counselors, university leaders, civic leaders and community activists.
In these spaces, we have engaged in critical dialogues about racial microaggressions, and grappled with important questions that have pushed our
thinking about the concept. Our initial conversations about this book began
because we believed there was a need for a book explicitly theorizing racial
microaggressions that could be used as a conceptual tool located within the
broader theoretical framework of CRT in education. However, we believe
that this book will prove useful for audiences across disciplines and spaces
outside of education, because of our interdisciplinary approach (one tenet
of CRT). The conversations, questions, and critiques we have engaged in
collectively across these multiple audiences have shaped the way we decided
to write this book.

OVERVIEW OF THE BOOK

We have organized this book into seven chapters. Our introduction chapter
tells our stories about how each of us came to this work on everyday racism in
the form of racial microaggressions. The first chapter presents stories of racial
microaggressions from the perspectives of People of Color to center the lived
experiences of Communities of Color with everyday racism. This chapter also
outlines majoritarian stories of racial microaggressions—the dominant discourses that attempt to dismiss everyday racism. We provide a brief history to
illustrate the significance of race and racism in the United States, our working
definitions of these concepts, as well as our theoretical perspective, Critical
Race Theory (CRT) in education, which guides this book.

In Chapter 2, we use *critical race hypos* as a pedagogical tool to explain the types, contexts, effects, and responses to racial microaggressions
that are experienced by People of Color, and how racial microaggressions

are connected to institutional racism. Chapter 3 continues this discussion, engaging an in-depth analysis of the role of systemic racism in racial micro-aggressions that operate within our social institutions. We use examples to illustrate our analysis.

Chapter 4 examines everyday racism that can occur within (intragroup) and between (intergroup) Communities of Color through forms of inter-nalized racism. We provide models and examples to show how internalized racism can create intragroup and intergroup conflict, which functions to maintain racial hierarchies and (re)produce institutional forms of racism and white supremacy.

Chapter 5 shifts our analysis to the strategies Communities of Color can use to challenge everyday racism through the concept of racial microaffirma-tions—those everyday forms of affirmation and validation used by People of Color in a variety of public and private settings to express acknowledgment, respect, and self-worth, and to affirm a shared humanity. Chapter 6 is our conclusion chapter, where we summarize our analyses and offer recommen-dations for future research and praxis for racial microaggressions and racial microaffirmations.

CHAPTER 1

Laying the Conceptual Groundwork for Understanding Racial Microaggressions

COUNTERSTORIES OF EVERYDAY RACISM

We begin this chapter with the stories of People of Color. These stories provide a window into the realities of everyday racism that People of Color frequently experience in their daily lives in schools, universities, professional settings, and other public spaces. Richard Delgado (1989) writes, "For stories create their own bonds, represent cohesion, shared understandings, and meaning" (p. 2412). These stories reflect experiences with racial microaggressions, the language we use and have theorized to describe this form of everyday racism (see Essed, 1991). Over the course of this book, we will explain the concept of racial microaggressions, our related research, and the analytical models we have developed to better understand this everyday phenomenon. But first, we begin with the stories that give meaning to this work.

Esmeralda Bermudez is a journalist for the *Los Angeles Times*, writing narratives of Latinas/os in Los Angeles, California. She was born in El Salvador and raised in Los Angeles. This excerpt is from her personal story for the *Los Angeles Times* recounting her experience one day while speaking Spanish to her daughter as they played in the park (Bermudez, 2018).

I felt her staring at me on the playground as I called out to my daughter. She must be someone's grandmother, I thought. She must be curious, as people often are. Then she took one step toward me—pink fingernails, dark blond hair—and opened her mouth, e-nun-ci-a-ting each word.

"Speak English," she commanded. "You're confusing the poor girl."

My stomach dropped. I rose from the grass and braced myself to respond. And I did. But not before an old, familiar feeling washed over me, a mix of fear and shame I used to carry like a knapsack in grade school. I was 7 years old, just two years older than my daughter is now.

You wetback. Dirty beaner. Go back to Tijuana. You sound like Ricky Ricardo.

So many days at Lake Marie Elementary School ended the same way for me: angry and broken, waiting by the rosebushes for my mom's beat-up blue Datsun, wearing my knockoff sneakers and cheap, ruffled dresses from the swap meet. I thought I would never catch up.

—Esmeralda Bermudez, 2018

Grace Lin is a children's book author and illustrator. She is the daughter of Taiwanese immigrant parents. She was born and raised in upstate New York. Her story is transcribed from an independently organized 2016 TEDx talk, in Natick, Massachusetts (Lin, 2016).

In 5th grade, my class decided to put on the play *Return to Oz*, and all the girls wanted to be Dorothy, me included. So every day at recess, all the girls that wanted to be Dorothy, we would stand in a circle, and we would all sing "Somewhere Over the Rainbow" over and over again, practicing for the audition. Until the day of the audition, I turned to the girl next to me and I said, "Today's the audition! Do you think they might choose me to be Dorothy?" And she looked at me, and she said, "But you can't be Dorothy! Dorothy is not Chinese!" And when she said this, I felt so stupid. It was that horrible embarrassment where you get hot, and red, and sticky, as if your skin is crying tiny, boiling tears. It's that feeling when someone says to you, "Who do you think you are?" And you feel like you're nobody. I felt like I was nobody.

—Grace Lin, 2016

Claudia Rankine is an African American poet, playwright, and professor. She was born in Kingston, Jamaica, and is the Frederick Iseman Professor of Poetry at Yale University. This story is from Rankine's (2014) book of poetry, *Citizen: An American Lyric*.

Certain moments send adrenaline to the heart, dry out the tongue, and clog the lungs. Like thunder they drown you in sound, no, like lightning they strike you across the larynx. Cough. After it happened I was at a loss for words. Haven't you said this yourself? Haven't you said this to a close friend who early in your friendship, when distracted, would call you by the name of her black housekeeper? You assumed you two were the only black people in her life. Eventually she stopped doing this, though she never acknowledged her slippage. And you never called her on it (why not?) and yet, you don't forget.

—Claudia Rankine, 2014, p. 7

Stephanie Zywicki Masta is an assistant professor in curriculum at Purdue University. She is an Indigenous scholar who specializes in critical qualitative and Indigenous methodologies, experiences of racialized youth in schools, and the influence of colonialism in educational spaces. In her study titled, "'I am Exhausted:' Everyday Occurrences of Being Native American," Masta (2018) includes this experience from a Native American graduate student, Robert. Robert is studying in a STEM field at a predominantly white institution in the Pacific Northwest:

I wasn't really aware that I was [a] minority, until I got here. . . . It's weird sometimes, because I get things called at me . . . just those little things that add up after a while . . . sometimes, if I'm waiting for the bus at night, people will yell racist things, like "Go back to your country." One time I engaged them, I was like, "I'm already here, man!" Someone said that to me, like, really close to me, and they're like, "Go back to where you're from," and I was just like, "Phoenix?" You get those people constantly asking what you are. Once they're finding out you are Indian, the jokes about blankets and canoes, and just about anything they can think. The nickname Chief . . . It's just ha ha ha. Don't get me wrong, I have very thick skin, and I can take a joke as well as anyone else, but it's just, when it's a consistent thing with a lot of people here, even with fellow grad students. Like sometimes I don't want to be just a stereotype. It's a reality that I've come to accept, that that's just the way things work here. I'm what you would call a cultural oddity. I mean, how many Indians are really here in the sciences?

—Stephanie Zywicki Masta, 2018, p. 829

Through these stories, we see the "cohesion" that Delgado (1989) describes in storytelling. Across these four accounts, we read the experiences of four different People of Color whose stories are joined by the pain of everyday racism. These stories can be considered a specific form of storytelling in Critical Race Theory (CRT), what Delgado (1998) calls counterstories (see Solórzano & Yosso, 2002). The counterstories of Communities of Color open a discursive space to disrupt the normativity of whiteness and allow for the recognition of race and racism, when in so many spaces, racism is often dismissed. Delgado (1989) states that counterstories can "shatter complacency and challenge the status quo" (p. 2414). We believe that these stories speak directly to the ways People of Color experience racial microaggressions that have instant and lasting effects on the body, mind, and spirit. This chapter begins with the majoritarian stories of everyday racism. We respond to these ahistorical and aracial (raceless) stories with a short history of racism along with an historical narrative to document everyday racism. We then show the history of how Chester Pierce developed the concept of racial microaggressions over a 30-year period. We conclude with our use of CRT to understand and examine racial microaggressions.

MAJORITARIAN STORIES OF EVERYDAY RACISM

Dominant groups have their own stories (Delgado, 1989). These stories, what Solórzano and Yosso (2002) (and others) call the "majoritarian stories," function to maintain dominant group status over People of Color. Majoritarian stories (re)construct and justify systems of subordination that lead to inequitable social arrangements and, consequently, disparate outcomes for Communities of Color in nearly every sphere of social life, including education, health, wealth, and politics. There are countless majoritarian stories of racism. We have found majoritarian stories directly related to racial microaggressions. The stories that follow emerged during and after the 2014–2015 University of California Office of the President (UCOP) Faculty Leadership Seminar Series (discussed in the Introduction), which provided UC administrators training on racial microaggressions and implicit bias in academia. Those majoritarian stories went something like this:

This concept [microaggressions] is now being used to suppress not just, say, personal insults or discrimination in hiring or grading, but also ideas that the UC wants to exclude from university classrooms. . . . Well, I'm happy to say that I'm just going to keep on microaggressing. . . . It's about suppressing particular viewpoints.

—Eugene Volokh, 2015

Eugene Volokh is a professor at the UCLA Law School. He outwardly expressed his opposition to the UCOP Faculty Leadership Seminar Series in several opinion editorials, including the *Washington Post* editorial we have excerpted here. His argument hinged on the claim that training students, faculty, and administrators on racial microaggressions was a form of censorship, and a threat to academic freedom.

A similar argument came from Todd Gitlin, professor of communications at Columbia University, who also expressed his opposing views on the UCOP seminar series. He began his piece in the *Chronicle of Higher Education* (2015) with the question, "Are we living through a plague of hypersensitivity?" He states:

Most readers will be aware of campaigns to dampen hateful speech, to stop "microaggressions," and to get professors to supply students with "trigger warnings" . . . when anticipating visual and verbal disturbances. . . . Insofar as arguments about the need for trigger warnings, speech-muffling, and runaway squeamishness rest on beliefs about the practical consequences of speech, they fail. No one knows the effects of nasty talk. Slurs can be denounced as disgusting without requiring censorious policy. Cherry-picked surveys and anecdotes cannot overcome the principle that liberty of speech is too precious to cancel, most especially on campus. . . . Discomfort drives education.

Gitlin attempts to frame everyday racism as a form of "hypersensitivity" of "vulnerable people who need to be protected from upset." Here, Gitlin uses racially coded language of "hypersensitivity" and "vulnerability" to distance his argument from his central claim—that no institutional protections (policies or practices) should be afforded to "hypersensitive" People of Color who experience everyday racism. He implies that 50 years of racial microaggressions research (what he calls "surveys and anecdotes") is not enough to "overcome the principle" of free speech.[1] He concludes with a somewhat puzzling statement about discomfort driving education. It is unclear whether Gitlin's assertion refers to the discomfort of whites caused by engaging discussions of racism and white supremacy, because this would contradict his central argument of censorship and free speech. Or, could he mean that the discomfort experienced by People of Color who are targeted by everyday racism will somehow enhance their education? Majoritarian stories can be difficult to interpret because race is often discussed through linguistic proxies and codes that attempt to veil racist claims.

This line of argument becomes clearer with Greg Lukianoff and Jonathan Haidt's (2018) book *The Coddling of the American Mind*, which they explain emerged from the same concerns Volokh (2015a, 2015b) and Gitlin (2015) held about censorship and free speech. The majoritarian story of everyday racism they construct continues where Gitlin leaves off. They argue that increasing awareness of racial microaggressions contributes to a larger psychological phenomenon among youth in the United States that causes "cognitive distortions" that can lead to anxiety, depression, and even suicide. Their claim rests upon three "untruths" that youth are supposedly learning on college campuses. These "untruths" are: (1) "Fragility"—employing the "what doesn't kill you makes you stronger" dictum; (2) "Emotional reasoning"—that the offended are overly emotional and let those feelings guide their perceptions, and (3) "Us versus them"—that some young people construct "a battle between good people and bad people" (p. 4). These "cognitive distortions" lead to "safetyism." They state:

> Safetyism is the cult of safety—an obsession with eliminating threats (both real and imagined) to the point at which people become unwilling to make reasonable trade-offs demanded by other practical and moral concerns. Safetyism deprives young people of the experiences that their antifragile minds need, thereby making them more fragile, anxious, and prone to seeing themselves as victims. (Lukianoff & Haidt, 2018, p. 32)

Of course, the "victimhood" mentality that Lukianoff and Haidt (2018) imply here in their concept of "safetyism" is not a new idea when it comes to racism. The same deficit construct serves as the foundation for other white majoritarian stories about race and education, including affirmative action, which was also viewed as "spawning a victim mentality" (Woodson, 1996, p. 115). To trace this argument even further, it is connected to the myth of meritocracy, or the "bootstraps" myth, which predicates the belief that any-one who demonstrates intellect and hard work, no matter their social posi-tion, will overcome all barriers to success (Guinier, 2015). Years of research on systemic oppression generally, and on U.S. institutional racism in partic-ular, has proved this idea indeed a myth (Kendi, 2016). Going back further, the concept of meritocracy is supported by cultural deficit theory, which places blame on people, families, and communities who cannot overcome structural barriers to achieve educational success (Valencia & Solórzano, 1997). Cultural deficit theory has historically been used to explain academ-ic underperformance, and low educational outcomes among Students of Color in the United States (Solórzano & Solórzano, 1995; Valencia, 2010). According to this theory, African American, Native American, Latina/o, and certain Asian American parents are often framed as apathetic toward, or not valuing education. In turn, their families are assumed to have values and cultures that contrast with those necessary for academic success (Solórzano & Solórzano, 1995; Valencia & Solórzano, 1997). So, what is important about Lukianoff and Haidt's (2019) work is not so much what they say, but what they don't say. We can see cultural deficit theory playing out in their attempt to center the student as the "problem," that is, *those people* with their "cognitive distortions" about race that make them so fragile as to not be able to withstand everyday racism.

What these arguments also say, without saying it, is that the "problem" of racism is one that is not theirs (whites'). Lukianoff and Haidt (2019) state, "Wouldn't our relationships be better if we all did a little less blaming and dichotomous thinking, and recognized that we usually share responsi-bility for conflicts?" (p. 39). The authors believe that People of Color share in the responsibility of microaggressions because, after all:

> If you accidentally say or do something that a member of the group finds offen-sive, but harbor no dislike or ill will on the basis of group membership, then you are not a bigot, even if you have said something clumsy or insensitive for which an apology is appropriate. A *faux pas* does not make someone an evil person or an aggressor. (p. 44)

Lukianoff and Haidt (2019) seem to arrive at the same conclusion as Volokh (2015a, 2015b) in their majoritarian story, that racial microaggres-sions should be dismissed, and that they are going to keep on "microag-gressing." In effect, they claim that we should avoid teaching about racial microaggressions in higher education because it would "create an environ-ment of perpetual anger and intergroup conflict" (p. 46). To which, we believe, James Baldwin (in Baldwin et al., 1961) would have responded, "to be a Negro in this country and to be relatively conscious is to be in a rage almost all the time" (p. 205).[2] The majoritarian stories of these authors about racial microaggressions are in stark contradiction to the countersto-ries of People of Color we presented at the beginning of this chapter. These majoritarian storytellers dismiss and/or ignore the research on racial micro-aggressions that we present throughout this book. The majoritarian stories of Volokh, Gitlin, Lukianoff, and Haidt are also problematic because they are presented as ahistorical—problems of today's "hyper-sensitive" young people—with no connection to the history that got us to where we are. Here is a brief reminder of that history.

RECOGNIZING HISTORY TO NAME EVERYDAY RACISM

When studying both everyday and institutional racism, we need to recog-nize how these forms of racism have played out in history (Pérez Huber & Solórzano, 2015b). To tell the counterstory of everyday racism, we begin by sharing a short history of racism in the United States (see Figure 1.1). As one historical starting point, we could begin in 1619 when the first en-slaved Africans were brought to the shores of what is now the United States at Jamestown—156 years before U.S. independence.[3] From 1619 to 1865 African Americans were "legally" held in bondage and served as chattel or property for slaveowners. That period represents 246 years of "legal" slavery in what is now the United States—about 62% of U.S. history.[4] From 1865 to 1965 African Americans lived in an era of Jim Crow.[5] This period represented the "legal" separation and subsequent disenfranchisement of African Americans in all walks of social life—representing 25% of histo-ry and, combined with legal enslavement, 87% of U.S. history. Under Jim Crow, by law or by custom, African Americans were barred from living in the same neighborhoods as whites, attending the same schools as whites, working in the same jobs and factories as whites, going to the same churches as whites, going to the same restaurants as whites, participating in the ev-eryday political, civic, or social life as whites, or even being buried in the same cemeteries as whites. The period from 1965 to the present represents the "modern" era of civil rights in the United States—this 55-year period is sometimes referred to as the New Jim Crow, and covers about 13% of U.S. history (see Alexander, 2010). In this period, we have civil rights laws which decree that People of Color cannot be legally segregated in schools, at the workplace, or in other parts of social and political life. However, because of housing segregation and discriminatory social policies and prac-tices, the vast majority of People of Color attend schools that have fewer resources, are kept out of the highest-paid and most secure occupations, and have less access to quality health and wellness opportunities (Jones, 2000; Williams & Purdie-Vaughns, 2016; Williams, Priest, & Anderson, 2016). While education and economic indicators for People of Color are improving, the opportunity and outcome gaps with whites remain very wide (Pérez Huber, Vélez, & Solórzano, 2018). When we begin to talk about institutional or everyday racism, we need to acknowledge this 400-plus–year history of racism—both structural and everyday. We need to show that for African Americans, 87% of that history was spent in "legal" bondage or "legal" separation. We need to show how the accumulation of that history still impacts the everyvday lives of African Americans and other People of Color.[6] In order to maintain these conditions over these four centuries you need an ideology that justifies this arrangement—first as slave, then as *de jure*—and now as *de facto*—second-class citizens. That ideology is white supremacy. We define white supremacy as the assigning of values to real or imagined differences in order to justify the perceived inherent superiority of whites over People of Color that defines the right and power of whites to dominance. The short history we have laid out is the evidence that Volokh (2016a, 2016b), Gitlin (2015), Lukianoff and Haidt (2018), and others are unaware of, ignore, or erase in their majoritarian stories of everyday racism.

To continue to tell the counterstory, we examine the historical texts, looking for examples of everyday racism or racial microaggressions in the lives of People of Color. Here we center on the lived experiences of African Americans during the Jim Crow era in the early 20th century using the writings of W. E. B. Du Bois (1920, 1940): the books *Darkwater: Voices from Within the Veil* and *Dusk of Dawn: An Essay Toward an Autobiography of a Race Concept.*

Figure 1.1. An Abridged History of Racism in the United States

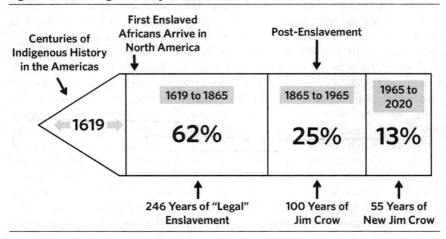

Everyday Racism in a White World: Circa 1920

The problem of being Black in the early 20th century and navigating a world in which one is subjected to a myriad of slights and dangers due to racism was critical to early race scholars (Lacy, 2007). Du Bois and his contemporaries documented and challenged the manifestations of these slights throughout the late 19th and early 20th centuries (Du Bois, 1899, 1920/2004, 1940/1984). During this period, the formal instruments of institutionalized white supremacy began to evolve and expand (Roediger, 1999). De jure segregation and the restrictive Black Codes characterized the South, while de facto rules of racial separation typified the North. There was also a simultaneous growth in white supremacist violence (Kendi, 2016).

Although Du Bois and other Black leaders worked to document and denounce these brazen practices of white terror, Du Bois also spoke eloquently about the more innocuous, mundane slights against African Americans living along the color-line (Du Bois, 1920/2004, 1940/1984). For instance, despite the hostile racial climate, African Americans sought out entertainment venues where they might gain some reprieve. Through a Black male protagonist in his book *Darkwater: Voices from within the Veil*, Du Bois (1920/2004) takes us to an encounter that leads eventually to a movie theater:

> My friend, who is pale and positive, said to me yesterday, as the tired sun was nodding:
> "You are too sensitive."
> I admit, I am—sensitive. I am artificial. I cringe or am bumptious or immobile. I am intellectually dishonest, artblind, and I lack humor.
> "Why don't you stop all this?" she retorts triumphantly.
> You will not let us.
> "There you go, again. You know that I—"
> Wait! I answer. Wait! (p. 171)

Du Bois then describes his character's everyday experiences of racism—on the streetcar, with the milkman, his white neighbor, children on the street, women on the streetcar, the policeman, the elevator man, the labor union, the lunch counter, at church, the science laboratory, the arts, in literature. The man's friend asks if this happens each day. The man replies:

> They do happen. Not all each day,—surely not. But now and then—now seldom, now, sudden; now after a week, now in a chain of awful minutes; not everywhere, but anywhere—in Boston, in Atlanta. That's the hell of it. Imagine spending your life looking for insults or for hiding places from them—shrinking (instinctively and despite desperate bolsterings of courage) from blows that are not always but ever; not each day, but each week, each month, each year. Just,

perhaps, as you have choked back the craven fear and cried, "I am and will be the master of my—"

"No more tickets downstairs; here's one to the smoking gallery."

You hesitate. You beat back your suspicions. After all, a cigarette with Charlie Chaplin—then a white man pushes by—

"Three in the orchestra."

"Yes, sir." And in he goes.

Suddenly your heart chills. You turn yourself away toward the golden twinkle of the purple night and hesitate again. What's the use? Why not always yield—always take what's offered,—always bow to force, whether of cannon or dislike? Then the great fear surges in your soul, the real fear—the fear beside which other fears are vain imaginings; the fear lest right there and then you are losing your own soul; that you are losing your own soul and the soul of a people;

That millions of unborn children, black and gold and mauve, are being there and then despoiled by you because you are a coward and dare not fight!

Suddenly that silly orchestra seat and the cavorting of a comedian with funny feet become matters of life, death, and immortality; you grasp the pillars of the universe and strain as you sway back to that befrilled ticket girl. You grip your soul for riot and murder. You choke and sputter, and she seeing that you are about to make a "fuss" obeys her orders and throws the tickets at you in contempt. Then you slink to your seat and crouch in the darkness before the film, with every tissue burning! The miserable wave of reaction engulfs you. To think of compelling puppies to take your hard-earned money; fattening hogs to hate you and yours; forcing your way among cheap and tawdry idiots—God! What a night of pleasure! (pp. 172–173).

In the excerpt above from Du Bois's (1920/2004) *Darkwater*, the central character provides a powerful narrative illuminating the mundane or everyday racism and stress endured by Blacks living their everyday lives, responding to whites, and seeking entertainment in 1920. Like other commercial venues (e.g., streetcars, department stores, restaurants, transportation centers), the movie theater was a unique geopolitical space that eluded complete racial segregation due to practical and fiscal constraints (Weyeneth, 2005). Hence, Du Bois's tormented, Black male protagonist, after all that he has experienced in the everyday, is permitted to purchase admission tickets for the same show as his white peers. However, his money was acceptable only to a certain point, as the attendant immediately offers the balcony as the only available seating option. Such Jim Crow or separate accommodations were typical for Blacks in movie theaters, athletic gymnasiums, public swimming pools, and municipal auditoriums across the country throughout the Jim Crow era (Weyeneth, 2005).

These malleable spaces were marked by impermanent and improvised partitions (sometimes no more than a single rope) in order to maintain racial inequity (Solórzano, 2016; Weyeneth, 2005). For example, where segregation was mandated, Blacks were allowed to shop at certain white-owned convenience stores but could not eat at the conjoined restaurant. In Northeast cities and Midwest regions, Black consumers experienced everyday racism through ill-defined, geographically specific, and ambiguous white supremacists' social customs (Larsen, 1928; Pierce, 1970). Thus, although shopping and entertainment were less (formally) racialized[7] in places such as New York, Chicago, or Los Angeles, Blacks faced potentially grave consequences in the event that they initiated conversation with whites or attempted to purchase items ahead of them. Additionally, as Du Bois's story illustrates, African Americans in Northern cities in the 1920s were often targets of random, spontaneous, coded, dehumanizing, and everyday racialized practices, as shown in the movie theater example (Weyeneth, 2005).

Although the movie theater in Du Bois's story is clearly operating within a white supremacist framework, the organization accepts money from African American community members and begrudgingly accommodates Black agitators who may undermine its carefully constructed semblance of order. Conversely, Blacks are permitted to "enjoy" their night out on the town and access "good seats" within a popular entertainment venue. Unfortunately, the steep cost of this convergence falls squarely on the cumulative tab of the African American male who endures yet another painful form of everyday racism. Consistent with contemporary research on mundane and extreme environmental stress (Carroll, 1998; S. Smith, 2004), Black people seeking entertainment in the early 20th century navigated deceivingly innocuous, as well as cumulative and racially hostile, climates during their leisure time.

Everyday Racism in a White World: Circa 1940

Twenty years after *Darkwater*, Du Bois (1940/1984) wrote *Dusk of Dawn: An Essay Toward an Autobiography of a Race Concept*. In "Chapter 6: The White World," Du Bois speaks personally to the experiences of racism he encountered in everyday life. We, however, interpret the narrative below as Du Bois speaking of the everyday racism he was forced to endure. Indeed, he speaks to the types, contexts, effects, and responses to these forms of everyday racism. He tells this story:

> I lived in an environment which I came to call the white world. I was not an American; I was not a man; I was by long education and continual compulsion and daily reminder, a colored man in a white world; and that white world often existed primarily, so far as I was concerned, to see with sleepless vigilance that I was kept within bound. All this made me limited in physical movement and provincial in thought and dream. I could not stir, I could not act, I could not live, without taking into careful daily account the reaction of my white

environing world. How I traveled and where, what work I did, what income I received, where I ate, where I slept, with whom I talked, where I sought recreation, where I studied, what I wrote and what I could get published—all this depended and depended primarily on an overwhelming mass of my fellow citizens in the United States from whose society I was excluded. (pp. 135–136)

In the same chapter, Du Bois tells another story of everyday racism:

...[A] lady in a Pullman car ordered me to bring her a glass of water, mistaking me for a porter, the incident in its essence was a joke to be chuckled over; but in its hard, cruel significance and its unending inescapable sign of slavery, it was something to drive a man mad. (pp. 136–37)

In these stories, Du Bois is speaking personally of the everyday racism he encounters and how it affects him, how it controls his everyday life, how it affects his physical and psychological well-being. Indeed, how it was "something to drive a man mad." We need a concept to understand everyday racism in both history and in the contemporary context. That concept is racial microaggressions, and the scholar who brought it to us was Chester Pierce.

CHESTER PIERCE AND THE CONCEPTUAL DEVELOPMENT OF RACIAL MICROAGGRESSIONS

What is needed for example is a sweeping new theoretical concept. . . . The poor black may need care based on other models such as the negotiation of "offensive mechanisms." (Pierce, 1969, p. 308)

Pierce first described the subtle forms of everyday racism experienced by African Americans as "offensive mechanisms" in a 1969 book chapter titled "Is Bigotry the Basis of the Medical Problem of the Ghetto?" As a medical doctor and psychiatrist, he explored tools to support the psychiatric needs of African American communities. In this 1969 chapter Pierce suggested that existing theories used to address these needs were inefficient and that new frameworks be developed to consider the role of race and racism in the everyday lives of African Americans. As a result, Pierce (1969) develops the concept of offensive mechanisms. He explained:

To be black in the United States today means to be socially minimized. For each day blacks are victims of white "*offensive mechanisms*" which are designed to reduce, dilute, atomize, and encase the hapless into *his "place."* The incessant lesson the black must hear is that he is insignificant and irrelevant. (p. 303)

In the 1970 book chapter "Offensive Mechanisms," Pierce extends this concept and first introduces the term *microaggression* to explain these "subtle and stunning" forms of racism. He states:

> Most offensive actions are not gross and crippling. They are subtle and stunning. The enormity of the complications they cause can be appreciated only when one considers that these subtle blows are delivered incessantly. Even though any single negotiation of offense can in justice be considered of itself to be relatively innocuous, the cumulative effect to the victim and to the victimizer is of an unimaginable magnitude. Hence, the therapist is obliged to pose the idea that offensive mechanisms are usually a *micro-aggression*. (pp. 265–266, emphasis in original)

Here we see Pierce begin to extend and transition from the term "offensive mechanisms" he uses in earlier work, to the concept he names "microaggressions." Although all his work was on African Americans, it is not until 1980 that Pierce explicitly uses the term "racial microaggression." In the chapter, "Social Trace Contaminants: Subtle Indicators of Racism in TV," Pierce (1980) tells us:

> The subtle, stunning, repetitive event that many whites initiate and control in their dealings with blacks can be termed a *racial microaggression* [emphasis added]. Any single microaggression from an offender to a defender (or victimizer to victim) in itself is minor and inconsequential. However, the relentless omnipresence of these noxious stimuli is the fabric of black-white relations in America. (p. 251)

Pierce doesn't use the term again in his writing until 2000, when he and his colleagues explicitly use race and microaggression in an encyclopedia entry on "Blacks, Stress in" (Profit, Mino, & Pierce, 2000). Pierce and his colleagues explain:

> The chief energy demand on Blacks is how to recognize, evaluate, anticipate, and dispose of *race-inspired microaggressions* [emphasis added]. These are automatic, subtle, stunning, seemingly innocuous messages, often non-verbal, which devaluate the Blacks; e.g. a Black man and a White man enter an elevator whereupon the single White female passenger clutches her handbag as she moves as close as possible to the White man. Microaggressions, the major and inescapable expression of racism in the United States, take a cumulative toll on Black individuals. As such they enter into the formation of Black group stress. What may be more important is that these cumulative, minor but incessant put-downs often remain as psychopollutants in the social environment. Their lingering intractability is a major contributor to the continuing traumatic stress suffered by Blacks as individuals and as a group. (pp. 327–328)

We borrow from and extend this rich conceptual history provided by Chester Pierce to develop the framework for understanding and analyzing racial microaggressions. First however, we define race and racism as central concepts to our theorizing.

DEFINING RACE AND RACISM

Over the course of 4 decades as educators and researchers, we have been searching for ways racism manifests in the everyday lives of People of Color. Before we explain the theoretical approach we take to do this, it is first necessary to explain how we define race and racism. Most agree that race is a socially constructed and contested term, fluid in meaning across time and space (Gillborn, 2006; Marable, 2002; Omi & Winant, 1994; Solórzano, 1997). Race as a social construction should not detract from its saliency in the daily realities of People of Color. Omi and Winant explain, "we consider race to be real because it is real in its consequences" (Omi & Winant, 2013, p. 963). Indeed, race has been used as a social marker on the bodies of People of Color today and historically to justify structures of domination in the United States and abroad (Gómez, 2018; Omi & Winant, 1994; Pérez, 1999). In the United States, race has been strategically used to create racial hierarchies where whites are placed above non-whites, according to their perceived alignment to whiteness (Harris, 1993; Roediger, 1999). In turn, these hierarchies are maintained by ideologies of white supremacy that reproduce a perceived superiority of whites over People of Color that over time becomes a normalized social fact (Bonilla-Silva, 2001; Gillborn, 2006).

Racism is a concept that is separate from but inextricably linked to the concept of race. Without race, racism could not exist. Albert Memmi (1968) states that a key element of racism is that it is based on perceptions. Memmi argues that perceived real and "imagined" differences between racial groups assign values that benefit one group at the expense of others. Thus, power is distributed according to real and/or perceived racial differences, creating structural inequities that benefit the perceived superior group. Similarly, Audre Lorde (1992) explains that racism is the belief in the "inherent superiority" of one group over another that justifies power and the "right to dominance" (p. 496). In previous work, we have used these scholars to identify three elements central to an understanding of racism: There is a perceived superiority of one group over others; the perceived superior group has the power to carry out racist acts; and various racial/ethnic groups are affected by those acts (Solórzano, 1998a). This definition of racism underlines the power of the "superior" group to maintain their domination over others. In the United States, historically, whites have occupied this perceived superior status within a racial hierarchy that is justified by ideologies of white supremacy and have, over time, distributed power and resources inequitably to People of Color (Du Bois, 1920/2004; Gillborn, 2008).

USING CRITICAL RACE THEORY
TO THEORIZE RACIAL MICROAGGRESSIONS

We define CRT as the work of scholars and practitioners who are attempting to develop an explanatory framework that accounts for the role of race and racism in education and that works toward identifying and challenging racism as part of a larger goal of recognizing and disrupting all forms of subordination (Solórzano, 1997, 1998a).[8] The following five tenets of CRT help guide the research, teaching, and policymaking in education and other fields:

1. CRT foregrounds race and racism and challenges separate discourses on race, gender, and class by demonstrating how racism intersects with these and other forms of subordination (e.g., sexism, classism, eurocentrism, monolingualism, ableism, and heteropatriarchy), and how they impact People of Color.
2. CRT challenges traditional research paradigms and theories, thereby exposing deficit notions about People and Communities of Color and educational practices that assume "neutrality" and "objectivity."
3. CRT focuses research and practice on experiences of People and Communities of Color and views these experiences as assets and sources of strength.
4. CRT offers a transformative response to racial, gender, class and other forms of discrimination by linking theory with practice, scholarship with teaching, and the academy with Communities of Color.
5. CRT challenges ahistoricism, acontextualism, and aracialism,[9] expanding the boundaries of the analysis of race and racism in education by using contextual, historical, and interdisciplinary perspectives to inform praxis.

These five tenets are not new in and of themselves, but together they represent a challenge to traditional modes of scholarship and practice. These five tenets form the basic perspectives, research methods, and pedagogy of CRT in education (see Solórzano, 1997, 1998a).

Using the tools of CRT, our search led us again to the work of W. E. B. Du Bois (1903) and what he called the "color-line." In 1897, Du Bois wrote an article in the *Atlantic Monthly* called "Strivings of the Negro People," in which he first introduced the early elements that would help us understand the concept of the color-line (i.e., the veil, second-sight, double-consciousness, and twoness).[10] Three years later, at the 1900 World's Fair in Paris, France, Du Bois curated a collection of photos and other artifacts in an exhibit called "The American Negro" (see Battle-Baptiste & Rusert, 2018; S. Smith, 2004). One of these artifacts—a social study—was called "The Georgia Negro." In this multimedia installation, Du Bois first used the phrase "The problem of the twentieth century is the problem of the color-line." In 1903, Du Bois, in *The Souls of Black Folk*, once again reminded his readers that the single greatest problem of the 20th century would be the problem of the color-line. Perhaps inspired by the article *The Color Line*, written by Frederick Douglass in 1881, Du Bois (1910) often reflected on the color-line in "Along the Color Line," a regular feature in *The Crisis*, the official magazine of the NAACP (National Association for the Advancement of Colored People), which was established in 1910. Du Bois observed the growing mountain of evidence surfacing both within and beyond the United States and constructed the following, now-famous question through which the Black experience had come to be defined: "How does it feel to be a problem?" (Du Bois, 1903, p. 7). We extend Du Bois's question to ask: "How does it feel for People of Color to experience and respond to the color-line in their everyday lives?"[11]

In order to address these questions, we return to Chester Pierce in defining racial microaggressions. Borrowing from, and extending Pierce's work (1969, 1970), we define racial microaggressions as one form of systemic, everyday racism used to keep those at the racial margins in their place. Racial microaggressions are (1) verbal and nonverbal assaults directed toward People of Color, often carried out in subtle, automatic, or unconscious forms; (2) layered assaults, based on a Person of Color's race, gender, class, sexuality, language, immigration status, phenotype, accent, or surname; and (3) cumulative assaults that take a psychological and physiological toll on People of Color (Pérez Huber & Solórzano, 2015a, 2015b). Throughout this book, we will provide examples of each of these elements of microaggressions to illustrate our definition.

We use the model provided in Figure 1.2 to illustrate how the five guiding tenets of CRT can help us understand the everyday racism that People of Color experience in the form of racial microaggressions. CRT is the framework, and its five tenets are the tools to examine and understand everyday racism in the form of racial microaggressions.

Another colleague who has advanced Pierce's work on racial microaggressions is Derald Wing Sue (and colleagues). Sue's work on microaggressions is widely cited in the fields of psychology and education and beyond. In this work, Sue and his colleagues (2010) provide a "taxonomy" of microaggressions that articulates how they are delivered (verbal, behavioral, environmental) and the various forms they take (i.e., microassaults, microinsults, and microinvalidation; Constantine, 2007; Constantine &

Figure 1.2. A Critical Race Theory Model to Understand Racial Microaggressions

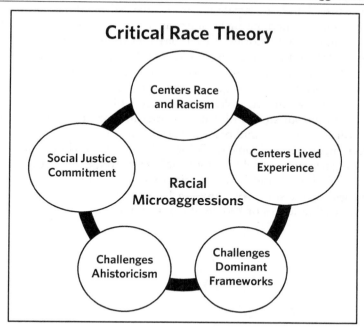

Sue, 2007; Sue, Bucceri, et al., 2007; Sue, Capodilupo, et al., 2007; Sue & Constantine, 2007; Sue, 2010). Sue (2010) argues that white supremacy serves as the foundation for the individual and institutional racism People of Color experience, and thus examines how the unconscious participation in microaggressions is harmful to all, including whites.[12] Theorizing microaggressions from a CRT perspective does not focus the analyses on how whites experience racial microaggressions. Rather, a CRT analysis centers on the lived experiences of People of Color, those targeted by microaggressions. Moreover, we challenge dominant ideologies of meritocracy and colorblindness prevalent in education by acknowledging how white supremacy has historically mediated, and continues to mediate, the everyday experiences of People of Color. Finally, our approach is interdisciplinary, building from Chester Pierce's work in the health sciences. Moreover, we do this to honor the Scholars of Color, like Pierce, who had the courage and took the risks to engage this research, particularly at times when critical perspectives on race were unpopular and delegitimized (Griffith, 1998).

As Paulo Freire (2000) argues, the ability to name oppression is a powerful tool, and is one of the first steps toward liberation for oppressed groups. Indeed, we believe also that the practice of naming racial microaggressions disrupts the normalized existence of racism and white supremacy in everyday life and calls attention to the structural inequities and individual pain they cause. This is a central reason we have dedicated our careers—and now, this book—to naming racial microaggressions. In line with CRT, we began this chapter with stories of everyday racism in the lives of People of Color to centralize their lived experiences as the springboard for our theorizing and for the discussions we will undertake in the remainder of this book. These stories are, in fact, counterstories—those stories that challenge dominant majoritarian narratives about the role of race and racism in U.S. society. Majoritarian stories of race and racism (such as those we shared here) are often dismissive and paternalistic, created to shift the responsibility of racial inequities to People of Color and away from whites and the ideologies and structures of white supremacy. However, knowing the history of People of Color is critical. We use history to confirm our position on the pervasiveness of racism across time—a history that most certainly shapes the everyday experiences of People of Color today.

Understanding the Types, Contexts, Effects, and Responses to Racial Microaggressions Using Critical Race Hypos

Derrick Bell (1999) once used the pedagogical tool he termed "racism hypos," or racism hypotheticals, to engage law school students in the "contradictions and dilemmas faced by those attempting to apply legal rules to the many forms of racial discrimination" that exist in U.S. society (p. 316). Like Bell, we are concerned with effective pedagogical strategies to teach race and racism. Honoring Bell's work in this area, we extend his pedagogical tool to what we call *critical race hypos,* to show the ways racism emerges in the everyday experiences of People of Color. In past work together we have theorized critical race hypos to build a bridge between theory and practice—the conceptual framework of racial microaggressions and the realities of People of Color—to teach about everyday racism (Pérez Huber & Solórzano, 2018). This hypo is different from the counterstories we presented in the last chapter. Our counterstories in Chapter 1 were first-person accounts of experiences with racial microaggressions. Our critical race hypos are composite hypotheticals based on our research.

A CRITICAL RACE HYPO

Melinda is a Latina PhD student in sociology of education at a major research university in New York. She is a 1st-year student taking the seminar course Introduction to Sociology of Education, which is taught by a white female instructor. The class is engaged in a discussion about how teachers and administrators often hold deficit perspectives of their Students of Color—perspectives that lead to the belief that low educational attainment is a consequence of the "cultural apathy" Students of Color and their families have toward education. The class is discussing the prevailing discourses that support those deficit views. During the discussion, Melinda makes a comment

in which she cites political theorists Ernesto Laclau and Chantal Mouffe.[1]
The instructor comments to Melinda with surprise, "You've read Laclau and
Mouffe?" Melinda's face becomes flushed with embarrassment, and she
suddenly feels hot. Her stomach drops. She holds her breath for a moment,
until she is able to find her words. With her heart pounding, she quickly
responds, "Yes, I have read them." Her peers stare at her, then each other,
uncomfortably. The class ends and she approaches the instructor outside the
room, after class. Melinda tells her that she did not appreciate her comment
and how she seemed so surprised that she had read such a theoretically dense
text. The instructor tells her, "Oh, I didn't mean anything by it. Good for you
for being able to get through a dense text like that. See you next week!" The
instructor turns away. Melinda walks away feeling angry and frustrated. For
the next week, she relives the moment over and over again, thinking about the
things she should have said to the instructor.

The next week, the assigned readings are on racial microaggressions,
and a group of Melinda's peers are facilitating a discussion. Melinda
arrives to class with her stomach in knots, knowing that this is exactly
what happened to her last week, and angry with the instructor's inability
to recognize how she perpetrated a microaggression against her. With her
heart racing and slightly out of breath, she shares with the group that she
believes the interaction that happened between herself and the instructor
was a racial microaggression. She looks at the instructor as she makes the
comment. The instructor looks at her with another surprised expression,
and responds, "No, no, I told you that I didn't mean anything by it. That's
not what I meant." Melinda continues to challenge her dismissal. "Would
you have made that comment to Paul if he told you he had read Laclau and
Moufee?" [Paul was a white male peer in the class.] She looks at Paul, who
remains silent. Melinda continues to share the numerous other interactions
she has had on campus with her instructors, peers, and staff who have
made similar comments, and begins to cry and says, "This really hurts."
The instructor becomes flustered and continues to maintain that she did
not mean anything by her comment; she begins to get emotional, also
near tears. The class becomes silent. Angela (an African American female
peer) says, "I've been thinking about that exchange all week, and wished
I would have said something; I did feel like that was a microaggression."
Several other students agree. Some remain silent. The instructor struggles
to explain, reiterating the claim, "That's not what I meant, I would never . . . "
Melinda interrupts her. "All you had to do was apologize."

We use this hypo to explain two models we have developed to understand
and analyze the racial microaggressions that Melinda experienced in her
classroom. Figure 2.1 is the first model. This figure shows that there are (1)
Types of racial microaggressions, or *how* one is targeted by a microaggression; (2) *Contexts* where and how the microaggressions occur; (3) *Effects*

Figure 2.1. A Model for Understanding the Types, Contexts, Effects, and Responses to Racial Microaggressions

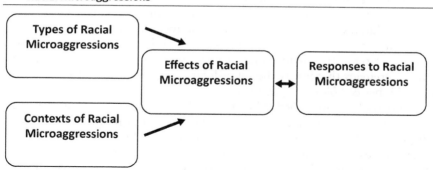

of microaggressions on the body, mind, and spirit of People of Color; and (4) *Responses* to racial microaggressions when they occur (Pérez Huber & Solórzano, 2015a). Here, we explain each of these components of the model and how Melinda's experience with microaggressions can be explained using it.

TYPES OF MICROAGGRESSIONS

There are various types of microaggressions People of Color experience based on race and/or ethnicity, gender, class, language, sexuality, immigration status, phenotype, accent, surname, and culture (Kohli & Solórzano, 2012). From a CRT perspective, we know that racism often occurs at intersections with other forms of oppression. Thus, in analyzing "types" it is important to acknowledge that a microaggression may be based on multiple characteristics and positionalities that define the identities and experiences of People of Color.[2] In the critical race hypo above, the type of microaggression was Melinda's perceived intellectual ability.[3] We see this perception enacted when the instructor expressed her surprised that Melinda had read such a theoretically complex text. Indeed, our research has found that lower academic expectations of Students of Color is a common type of racial microaggression (Pérez Huber, Johnson, & Kohli, 2006; Pérez Huber, 2011; Solórzano, 1998a; Solórzano et al., 2000; Yosso et al., 2009).

There are other types of microaggressions we have found. For example, we have found visual imagery that conveys racist stereotypes, perceptions, and/or beliefs about People of Color and can be described as one type of racial microaggression, what we call visual microaggressions (Pérez Huber & Solórzano, 2015a). Visual racial microaggressions have the same fundamental elements as racial microaggressions in general: They are layered, often subtle and unconscious, and cumulative. Visual microaggressions are often nonverbal, visual representations of racist ideas and beliefs about People of Color. These visual assaults can emerge in various mediums such as textbooks, children's books, advertisements, photos, film and television, dance and theater performance, and public signage and statuary.[4] Visual microaggressions reinforce institutional racism and perpetuate the ideologies of white supremacy that justify the subordination of People of Color by whites (Pérez Huber & Solórzano, 2015b).

Scholars have identified other types of racial microaggressions in education. For example, in 2009, Yosso and colleagues found that Latina/o college students frequently encountered racial joke-telling on predominately white campuses as "offensive verbal remarks with questionably humorous intentions" (p. 669). Race-themed college parties—those that encourage attendees to wear racist, stereotypical attire—represent another type of microaggression that is not uncommon in higher education, particularly at predominately white institutions (PWIs; Garcia, Johnston, Garibay, Herrera, & Giraldo, 2011). Vega (2019) names maternal microaggressions as those that target Women of Color mothers in higher education. Finally, Pérez Huber has explored racist nativist microaggressions as a type. She found Latina/o students are often targeted by these types of microaggressions, a form of racist xenophobic discourse that influences educational practice and policies, assigning a non-native status to Latina/o students (Pérez Huber, 2011; Gomez & Pérez Huber, 2019).

Related to race and higher education, Supreme Court Justice Sonia Sotomayor describes types of racial microaggressions in her dissenting opinion in the *Schuette v. Coalition to Defend Affirmative Action BAMN* case (2014). The ruling upheld a state ballot initiative, named Proposal 2, that Michigan voters passed in 2006 banning consideration of race in higher education admissions. In her dissent, Justice Sotomayor emphasized the importance of race (and racism) in the lives of People of Color, despite the majority opinion of the court. She starts by telling us why race matters:

> Race matters in part because of the long history of racial minorities' being denied access to the political process . . . Race also matters because of persistent racial inequality in society—inequality that cannot be ignored and that has produced stark socioeconomic disparities . . . Race matters for reasons that really are only skin deep, that cannot be discussed any other way, and that cannot be wished away. Race matters to a young man's view of society when he spends his teenage years *watching others tense up as he passes*, no matter the neighborhood where he grew up. Race matters to a young woman's sense of self when she states her hometown, and then is pressed, *"No, where are you really from?"*, regardless of how many generations her family has been in the country . . . Race matters because of the *slights, the snickers, the silent judgments that*

reinforce that most crippling of thoughts: "I do not belong here" [emphasis added]. (pp. 45–46)

Here, Sotomayor (*Schuette v. BAMN*, 2014) gives other examples of everyday racism—the change in body language when young Men of Color pass whites in public spaces, the questions about country of origin, or the "slights," "snickers," and "silent judgments" that insinuate People of Color do not belong in this country. In these last two examples, we would argue that the type of racial microaggression Sotomayor refers to are racist nativist microaggressions, underlined by both racist and nativist assumptions about People of Color (Pérez Huber, 2011). It is ironic that in the moment we write this chapter (July 2019) the same type of racial microaggression is being used by President Donald Trump to target four Democratic Congresswomen of Color—Representatives Alexandria Ocasio-Cortez (NY), Ayanna S. Pressley (MA), Ilhan Omar (MN), and Rashida Tlaib (MI)—all U.S. citizens. He tweeted that the Congresswomen should "go back" to the "crime infested places from which they came." To respond, Congresswoman Pressley (2019) retweeted Trump's post with her own tweet: "THIS is what racism looks like. WE are what democracy looks like. And we're not going anywhere. Except back to DC to fight for families you marginalize and vilify everyday" (Pressley, 2019). Since then, the *New York Times* has collected the stories of 16,000 readers who say they have been targeted by a similar verbal assault (Takenaga & Gardiner, 2019).[5] Indeed, all 16,000 stories are powerful examples of types of racial microaggressions.

CONTEXTS OF MICROAGGRESSIONS

There are contexts of racial microaggressions—*where* and *how* they occur. The context of the racial microaggression in Melinda's case was her graduate school seminar, with her instructor, and with her peers. Microaggressions can often occur in schools, classrooms, on the play yard, in laboratories, at meetings, and on college campuses.[6] The context of the microaggression refers not only to the location or space where the microaggression occurred but also to the larger circumstances and conditions present that allowed it to happen. In 1970, Chester Pierce explained a powerful example of how context is important to understand one type of racial microaggression he experienced while a professor at Harvard. Pierce stated:

I notice in a class I teach, after each session a white, not a black, will come up to me and tell me how the class should be structured, or how the chairs should be placed, or how there should be extra meetings outside the classroom, etc. The student is on the initiative and sees as his usual prerogative with a black, that he must instruct me and order me about and curb my own inclinations and independence. One could argue that I am hypersensitive, if not paranoid, about what I know every black will understand, that it is not what the student says in this dialogue, it is how he approaches me, how he talks to me, how he seems to regard me. I was patronized. I was told, by my own perceptual distortions perhaps, that although I am a full professor on two faculties at a prestigious university, to him I was no more than a big black n . . . .r [changed from original]. I had to be instructed and directed as to how to render him more pleasure! (p. 277)

Here, Pierce points to the important contextual clues that allow a reader to better understand how this experience is a racial microaggression. He explains that it was not so much what the white student said, but *how* he said it—the patronizing tone, the unapologetic stance, the demanding demeanor—all important subtextual context to understanding how the white student attempts to diminish the status of Pierce's position as a Harvard professor. This example shows the complexity of understanding context: Context encompasses much more than a physical or spatial location, but also important subtexts—what is understood, but remains unsaid.

Returning to the context of the hypo, the political theorists that Melinda referred to, and the space of her graduate seminar, were both contextual pieces important to understanding the racial microaggression that targeted her. The instructor was surprised that Melinda had read a particular kind of dense academic text. The context also prompts us to ask questions about others in the space that may have been targeted or affected by the microaggression. For example, we would argue that Melinda's peer, Angela, was a secondary target in the microaggression that occurred in the hypo—she was affected by the microaggression although she was not the primary target (we further describe the effects Angela experienced in the next sections).[7]

EFFECTS OF MICROAGGRESSIONS

Through years of research, Chester Pierce (1970, 1974, 1988) found that there are negative psychological and physiological effects of microaggressions. Moreover, the effects can be cumulative and take a toll on the bodies, minds, and spirits of People of Color over time. For example, those targeted by everyday racism can become angry or frustrated and develop feelings of self-doubt; their blood pressure may rise and their heart rate may increase (Clark, Anderson, Clark, & Williams, 1999; Gravlee, Dressler, & Bernard 2005; Smith 2004; Watson, 2019). Over time, they may develop more serious symptomatic conditions such as hypertension, depression, and anxiety (Hill, Kobayashi, & Hughes 2007; Pérez Huber & Cueva 2012; Williams & Purdie-Vaughns, 2016; Williams, Priest, & Anderson, 2016). Mundane extreme environmental stress, or MEES (Carroll, 1998), racial battle fatigue

(Franklin, Smith & Hung, 2014; Smith 2004; Smith et al., 2006; Smith, Allen, & Danley, 2007), and racial trauma (Truong & Museus, 2012) are conditions researchers use to describe such race-related health consequences. Some studies have attributed more fatal conditions such as cardiovascular disease and even increased morbidity to race-related stressors such as microaggressions (Adelman 2008; Gee, Ro, Shariff-Marco, & Chae, 2009; Geronimus, Hicken, Keene, & Bound, 2006; Pierce 1969). In the critical race hypo, Melinda experiences some of these effects. She physically feels her face become flush from embarrassment, her heart rate increases, and she feels her stomach "drop." According to the research we discuss here, these effects, when experienced persistently and over time, can lead to self-doubt, imposter syndrome, and negative health outcomes.

While most of the research on effects of racial microaggressions examines the psychological impact of everyday racism, the work of education scholar Kenjus Watson (2019) has examined the physiological. Biospecimens as well as data from surveys and focus groups with Black male college students were collected to examine the ways everyday racism impacted their physiological health. Using DNA samples from his participants, Watson examined the length of participants' telomeres, which are coverings at each end of a human chromosome that protect the chromosome from deterioration. Telomere length is an indicator of chronological aging; the longer the telomere length of the human chromosome, the longer the lifespan of the human body. Those with shorter telomere lengths have shorter lifespans. Watson (2019) found that 30% of Black male students in his study, all whose ages ranged from 18–26, had telomere lengths similar to or shorter than those of middle-aged female stage 4 breast cancer survivors twice their age.[8] Indeed, his study highlights the negative physiological consequences racial microaggressions can have on young Black men, consequences that will last throughout their lifetimes. These findings align with those of public health researchers who examine race-related stress, although these researchers do not explicitly use the term racial microaggressions (Jones, 2000; Williams & Purdie-Vaughns, 2016; Williams, Priest, & Anderson, 2016).

In previous work, Pérez Huber examined the effects of racist nativist microaggressions on undocumented Latina college students (Pérez Huber & Cueva, 2012). She found that these students experienced negative psychological effects of microaggressions they had encountered throughout their educational trajectories, many tracing back to early childhood. For example, one Latina participant, Alicia, discussed the academic self-doubt she experienced as an undergraduate political science major. It is important to note that Alicia could recount the racist nativist microaggressions she experienced in school beginning in preschool, shortly following her arrival in the United States. These microaggressions persisted throughout her education. Alicia shared:

Poli Sci classes can be intimidating sometimes because I would say 90 percent are male, white students. It's really intimidating when the professor asks you a question, and you're expected to know, and you're supposed to be really articulate. For me, I was actually a little bit sad this week because I don't feel like I'm very, I don't know, it's kinda sad to say, but I think I have problems with my speech. Sometimes [the professor] wants us to argue in class and make good points and like this girl that was sitting in back of me . . . she was bringing some good arguments, I mean, words I never even heard of, like from a Poli Sci dictionary. And I was like, "Damn, why can't I do that?" I can't be argumentative like that and articulate. And I got really sad . . . like, "Why can't I have good speech like that?" I don't know if you understand [what] I'm trying to tell you . . . They bring out these smart words in like every sentence, and I'm like, "Wow! I don't even know what that word was." So I feel intimidated a lot.

As Alicia shared this experience, she became very emotional. It was clear that the re-telling of this story caused her emotional pain. She described feeling as if something was psychologically "wrong" with her ability to express her thoughts and ideas in class. Following the interview, Alicia shared with me that she was planning to make an appointment at the university student disability services office to get tested for a possible learning disability.

Alicia's story illustrates the long-term and cumulative effects of racist nativist microaggressions when undocumented students experience lower academic expectations, when their home language is not valued, and when they are not expected to attend college, nor prepared by their educators and schools to attend (Pérez Huber, 2009a, 2011; Pérez Huber & Cueva, 2012). She describes a common effect many People of Color experience when faced with persistent racial microaggressions. That is, the internalization of the negative perceptions they are consistently targeted with through various types of racial microaggressions pervading everyday life. Today, Alicia has moved well beyond this difficult moment, has graduated from college, earned a master's degree in social work and continues to be active in improving the conditions of undocumented communities. Her story teaches us about the negative effects of microaggressions, both psychological and physiological. However, it also teaches us about Alicia's resistance and resiliency, the ways that she has responded to microaggressions. We discuss responses in the next section.

This research on racist nativism and Latina college students, documented prior to the 2016 election of Donald Trump, indicates that anti-Latina/o racism was a serious problem then, and continues today (Gomez & Pérez Huber, 2019; Pérez Huber, 2016). Indeed, as we discussed in Chapter 1, the forms of racism that we see today are a consequence of the racism that has existed in the United States for centuries. As we witness a more potent form of racist nativism targeting Latina/o communities, and Latina/o immigrants in particular, research is beginning to document its effects. For example, the Kaiser Family Foundation (2018) has found that Latina/o immigrant families experience increased levels of fear and uncertainty related to President Trump's anti-immigrant policies, as well as increased levels of racism and discrimination. These experiences are shaping unhealthy psychological and physiological changes, particularly in children, such as sleeping and eating problems, headaches, stomach aches, depression, and anxiety. Doctors in this study note a concern about long-term health consequences for children who are currently experiencing these symptoms, as research has found the effects of "toxic stress" to have physical and mental health consequences throughout one's lifetime.

RESPONSES TO MICROAGGRESSIONS

Pierce (1995) explained, "The most baffling task for victims of racism and sexism is to defend against microaggressions. Knowing how and when to defend requires time and energy that oppressors cannot appreciate" (p. 282). Pierce highlights the significance of developing responses to racial microaggressions. Such responses can vary, according to the type and context of the microaggression, as well as the effect it had on the individual. Moreover, one's response can be influenced by the effect, and vice versa. These responses can include engaging in counterspaces, or places located within or outside of educational institutions where People of Color develop strategies for healing, empowerment, and building a sense of community (Grier-Reed, 2010; Morales, 2017; Solórzano & Villalpando, 1998; Solórzano et al., 2000; Yosso et al., 2009). In the hypo, Melinda responds in several ways.[9] She informs her instructor that she indeed has read complex theoretical material. She responds again after class by confronting the instructor and bringing the incident up at the next class meeting.

However, there was another response in the hypo by Melinda's peer, Angela, an African American student in the class. In the hypo, Angela shares that she was also affected by the microaggression because it had also bothered her, and she had thought about the exchange during the week that followed. Angela shared she felt she *should* have responded. We have developed another model to better understand *how* this racial microaggression occurred, and how it impacted both Melinda and Angela.

In Figure 2.2 we continue to draw from the hypo and show how it provides deeper insight into racial microaggressions. The racial microaggression is positioned at the center, as the focus of the model. This would be the exchange Melinda had with her instructor, where the instructor was the perpetrator of the microaggression and Melinda was the target. When Melinda responded to this racial microaggression by confronting her instructor, her instructor claimed that she "didn't mean anything by it." This response meant that the instructor did not *intend* to perpetrate the microaggression. There are other theories used to explain unconscious or automatic forms of discriminatory behaviors. For example, implicit bias is a concept that explains the "unconscious mental processes" that can influence discriminatory biases a perpetrator unknowingly acts out (Greenwald & Krieger, 2006; Kang et al., 2012). Implicit bias seeks to understand the intent of the perpetrator, which is no doubt significant. However, as critical race theorists, our theorizing of racial microaggressions does not focus on the intent of the perpetrator, but on its impact or effects on the Person of Color targeted by them. Thus, we study the effects that racial microaggressions have on People of Color. In the hypo, we focus on Melinda as the primary target. However, there was also a secondary target, Angela. Angela explained that she was also troubled by the microaggression as someone who was in the room. The microaggression was not directed toward Angela, yet Angela also experienced effects.

The final components of the model are "institutional racism" and "white supremacy." In our definition we explain microaggressions to be a *systemic* form of racism. In this model, we illustrate racial microaggressions as inextricably linked to a system of institutional racism and white supremacy (see definition in Chapter 1) that has historically marginalized and excluded People of Color in the United States. We define institutional racism as "formal

Figure 2.2. A Model of Intent vs. Impact on Primary and Secondary Targets of Racial Microaggressions

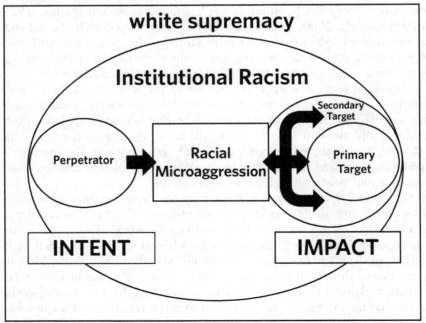

or informal structural mechanisms, such as policies and processes that systematically subordinate, marginalize, and exclude nondominant groups and mediate their experiences with racial microaggressions" (Pérez Huber & Solórzano, 2015b, p. 303). In the hypo, institutional racism is what leads to Melinda's and Angela's being the only People of Color in a cohort of 20 doctoral students. Institutional racism is also what leads to Melinda's having no structured recourse in her department for the racial microaggression she experienced. As in many departments and other academic units in U.S. higher education institutions, there is a lack of institutional policies addressing incidents of racism. In fact, many campus administrators have dismissed, and continue to dismiss, even blatant acts of racism (e.g., white nationalist posters and propaganda) as "free speech" (Lawrence, 1993).[10] However, this does not need to be so. There are clear policies implemented in educational institutions to protect against gender-based discrimination, namely the federal law known as Title IX of the Education Amendments Act of 1972. Title IX explicitly prohibits gender-based discrimination in any educational institution that receives federal funding. Title IX also requires all public school districts and higher education institutions to hire someone to oversee Title IX complaints and the investigation process. To date, no such policies exist to protect against race-based discrimination, despite the model Title IX has provided since it was first introduced as law in 1972. Thus, People of Color in educational institutions who are targeted by racism are left with no formal complaint process, let alone the ability to pursue an investigation into racist incidents. We argue that the absence of a policy to provide some protections against racism is an example of institutional racism. This absence only further perpetuates racism. We articulate the relationship between racial microaggressions and systemic racism in the following chapter. However, before moving on to this discussion we wish to offer an alternative critical race hypo. This hypo begins the same, but ends differently, to show how Melinda's experience could have had a different outcome:

Melinda is a Latina PhD student in sociology of education at a major research university in New York. She is a 1st-year student taking the seminar course, Introduction to Sociology of Education, which is taught by a white female instructor. The class is engaged in a discussion about how teachers and administrators often hold deficit perspectives of their Students of Color—perspectives that lead to the belief that low educational attainment is a consequence of the "cultural apathy" Students of Color and their families have toward education. The class is discussing the prevailing discourses that support those deficit views. During the discussion, Melinda makes a comment in which she cites political theorists Ernesto Laclau and Chantal Mouffe. The instructor comments to Melinda with surprise, "You've read Laclau and Mouffe?" Melinda's face becomes flushed with embarrassment, and she suddenly feels hot. Her stomach drops. She holds her breath for a moment, until she is able to find her words. With her heart pounding, she quickly responds, "Yes, I have read them." Her peers stare at her, then each other, uncomfortably. The class ends and she approaches the instructor outside the room, after class. Melinda tells her that she did not appreciate her comment and how she seemed so surprised that she had read such a theoretically dense text. The instructor tells her, "Oh, I didn't mean anything by—"(pause). The instructor stops for a moment and looks off into the distance as she thinks about the comment that she made to Melinda in class. Her eyes come back into contact with Melinda, who is visibly shaken and nervous. The instructor suddenly realizes that her comment has produced these feelings in Melinda. The instructor tries to find her words, and says, "You know what, I'm not going to tell you that I didn't mean anything by my comment because that would be dismissive." She continues. "I am sorry that my words made you feel that way. Thank you for bringing this to my attention." Melinda suddenly feels some relief and acknowledgment from the apology. Melinda replies, "Well, I thought you should know, considering our readings next week will focus on racial microaggressions. I felt like that comment was a microaggression." This time, it was the instructor whose face flushed red with embarrassment. Melinda noticed this and began to get nervous again waiting for the instructor's response. "I think you are right, Melinda. My comment was wrong and I am sorry. I will use the readings for next week as an opportunity to educate myself about racial microaggressions and hope that I can understand how I can avoid doing this again to my students in the future." Melinda thanks the instructor and tells her that she looks forward to the discussion next week. She leaves the interaction feeling some relief again, but also wishing that the instructor's comment had never been made.

We realize that this alternative hypo presents an ideal outcome not often experienced by People of Color when challenging perpetrators of racial microaggressions. However, the hypo represents four strategies discussed by Dr. Melanie Domenech Rodríguez (2014) for addressing everyday racism—acknowledge, apologize, thank, and offer amends. In this version of the hypo, the instructor stops herself from telling Melinda that she "didn't mean anything" by her comment. The instructor realizes that in doing so, she would be dismissing Melinda and her concerns. Instead, the instructor chooses to acknowledge Melinda by taking a moment to listen and think about what she had said in class to make Melinda feel this way. She then realized that her comment was the reason that Melinda seemed shaken— that she was indeed harmed by the instructor's words. Legal scholars use the term "racial harm" to describe the psychological and physiological injuries incurred by People of Color who face racial stigmatization, stereotypes, insults, and other forms of racial microaggressions (Delgado, 1982; Matsuda, Lawrence, Delgado, & Crenshaw, 1993). Here, we would extend Domenech Rodríguez's (2014) strategy of acknowledgment to be even more specific in recognizing the harm caused by racial microaggressions. Perpetrators may not be able to acknowledge a racial microaggression, even when a Person of Color names it. For example, in the hypo above, the instructor begins to tell Melinda that she didn't mean anything by her comment, but then realizes that Melinda was hurt by what she said. In this case, the instructor was not necessarily acknowledging the racial microaggression, but the way her words had harmed Melinda. For this, she was sorry, and she apologized. Unfortunately, perpetrators more often respond in other ways. In our research, we have found these comments (or some similar version of them) to be frequent responses from perpetrators when their racial microaggressions are challenged:

- "That's not what I meant."
- "It was just a joke."
- "You're taking this too seriously."
- "You're being too sensitive."
- "Don't act like a victim."
- "But I meant it as a compliment."

These responses function to dismiss the racial microaggression committed by perpetrators. In doing so, the perpetrator also dismisses the effects the Person of Color experienced as a result of the racial assault. In the critical race hypo that opened this chapter, this is exactly what the instructor did to Melinda. In the alternative hypo, the instructor acknowledged the harm she caused Melinda, apologized, and thanked her.

When Melinda called out the instructor's comment as a racial microaggression, the instructor responded by turning the situation into a learning opportunity.[11] She hoped that educating herself would prevent her from making the same mistake again. This strategy can be understood as the instructor's attempt to make amends with Melinda, and to demonstrate the sincerity of her apology. In this hypo, the amends the instructor attempted to make would have been an appropriate strategy. However, making amends can take on different meanings for different perpetrators. Making amends could be construed by some as shaking a hand, offering to take someone to coffee, or some other superficial gesture that would not address the microaggression. In other cases, well-intentioned perpetrators may perceive making amends as, for instance, asking questions like "What can I do?" or "How can I make this right?," relying on People of Color to advise them in remediating their racial assaults and seeking to make amends. It is important for perpetrators to understand that in asking these questions (and others like them) they discursively shift the responsibility of remediation to People of Color, rather than keeping that responsibility where it belongs, with themselves (Domenech Rodríguez, 2014). Such questions may make the perpetrator feel better about themselves, but most likely will have no effect on the Person of Color who was targeted by the racial assault. People who are the targets of racial microaggressions want to see that something is being done for themselves and for others. More productive questions that could be asked by perpetrators could be, "How did I come to consciously or unconsciously hold deficit beliefs about _____?" This question opens the opportunity to reflect on how institutional racism and white supremacy have shaped our socialization processes and influenced our beliefs and behaviors (see Figure 2.2).

Too often in educational institutions, white people look to People of Color for solutions, answers, and strategies to address issues of racism, and other racially coded issues such as "diversity," and "equity." Oftentimes, this type of work exceeds the workload of white colleagues, and is typically undervalued by the institution itself (Flores Niemann, 2012). Perpetrators of racial microaggressions should own the responsibility of dismantling everyday racism, whether it be the racism that they carry out themselves or the racism perpetuated by institutions. For this reason, we would argue that the final step in this process calls for perpetrators to take more specific action in addressing everyday racism—to educate themselves. To do this, perpetrators of racial assaults must do the work necessary for them to understand why their words and/or actions are microaggressive. This work could include reading and researching, but could also mean engaging in antiracist praxis. We discuss examples of this work in the conclusion chapter.

These four strategies we mention here—acknowledge harm, apologize, thank, and educate—do not erase the effects of racial microaggressions. At the end of this alternative hypo, Melinda no doubt remains disappointed and hurt by the instructor's comments. However, the instructor's strategies for acknowledging Melinda and the racial microaggression she perpetrated offer some relief. Moreover, the hypo does not allow us to see the long-term effects that these comments have on Melinda. What we hope both of these hypos demonstrate is how perpetrators can take a proactive role in taking responsibility for the racial microaggressions that they may unconsciously engage with People of Color. We also hope our discussion facilitates an understanding of how targets and perpetrators are impacted by structures of institutional racism and white supremacy.

CHAPTER 3

Examining the "Micro" Versus the "Macro" in Researching Racial Microaggressions

White supremacy is a crime and a lie, but it's also a machine that generates meaning.

—Ta-Nehisi Coates, 2017, p. 215

Racial microaggressions could not exist without the policies and processes that allow them to happen, or the ideological beliefs in white supremacy that justify them. In this chapter, we dedicate further attention to the ways racial microaggressions are intricately tied to institutional racism, and to the ideologies of white supremacy that justify and (re)produce microaggressions—a term we call the *macroaggression*. In the epigraph above, African American journalist Ta-Nehisi Coates (2017) describes white supremacy as an unending and persistent "machine" that has created meanings of race throughout U.S. history to justify racism. Indeed, white supremacy is "a crime" and "a lie," a violation of humanity that is based on nothing but abstractions of socially constructed ideas about race. Yet, it makes meaning. This meaning is so profound that it mediates the material conditions of life for People of Color and, ultimately, alarming and significant gaps in education, wealth, and health (Alexander, 2010; Ansell, 2017; Shapiro, 2017). In the first part of this chapter, we provide a framework that illustrates the inextricable and complex relationship between everyday microaggressions, institutional racism (i.e., structures and processes), and ideologies of white supremacy that maintain racial subordination. In the second part of the chapter, we provide examples of how the framework can be used to analyze historical and contemporary forms of racial microaggressions. We illustrate how this framework, *A Tree Model of the white supremist Roots of Racial Macroaggressions,* can be a robust conceptual tool to understand how People of Color experience racial microaggressions and how those everyday assaults emerge from ideologies of white supremacy.

THEORIZING THE MACROAGGRESSION: A TREE METAPHOR

Theorizing racial microaggressions from a CRT perspective challenges us to more clearly articulate the structural and systemic forms of racism that operate in everyday racist acts. To meet this challenge, we offer a model (Figure 3.1) we call a *Tree Model of the white supremist Roots of Racial Macroaggressions* to help researchers analyze how everyday experiences with racism are more than an individual experience, but part of a larger systemic racism that includes institutional and ideological forms. Our model uses the image of a tree to represent what we will define in the following sections as the macroaggression, institutional racism, and racial microaggressions. We use this image because it illustrates how each of these concepts are relationally structured and interrelated.

MACROAGGRESSION: THE ROOTS OF RACISM

We begin our explanation at the roots, where the foundation of the tree begins. In the model, the roots represent the ideological foundations of white supremacy that reproduce and perpetuate institutional (structural)

Figure 3.1. A Tree Model of the white supremist Roots of Racial Macroaggressions

Political System

Everyday Racism
(Racial
Microaggressions)

Criminal Justice
System

Educational System

Economic System

Mass Media

Health System

Institutional Racism

Racial
Macroaggression

white supremacy

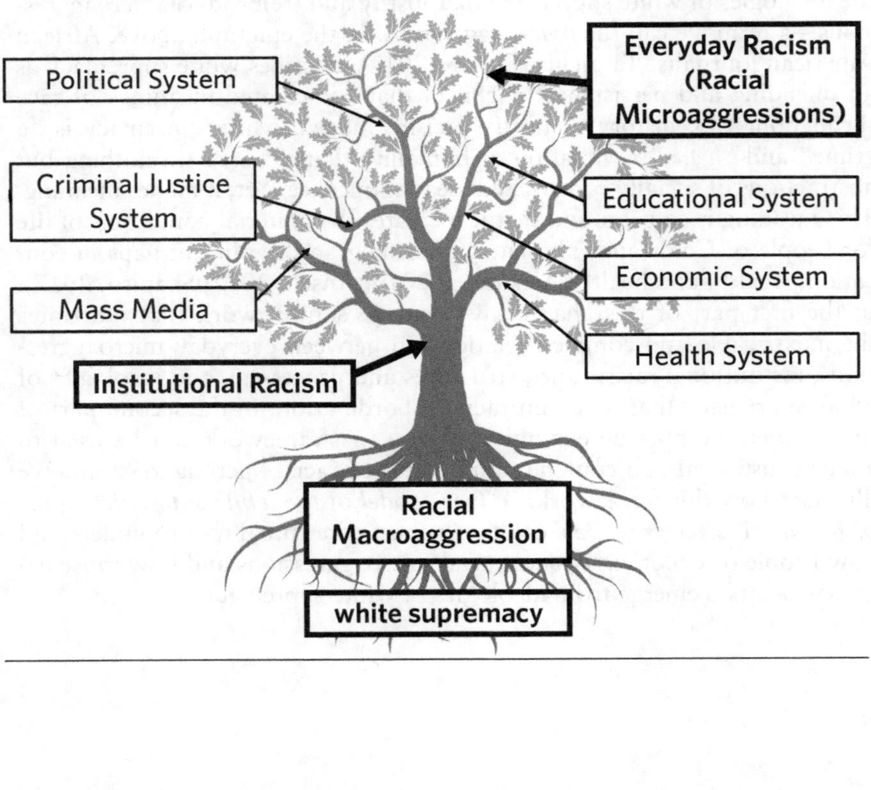

and everyday forms of racism. As we mentioned earlier, we define white supremacy as the assigning of values to real or imagined differences in order to
justify the perceived inherent superiority of whites over People of Color that
defines the rights and power of whites to dominance. White supremacy is an
insidious disease that upholds the conscious and unconscious acceptance of
a racial hierarchy where People of Color are consistently placed in a subordinate position to whites. This hierarchy structures the ideologies necessary
for racism to persist. It is the disease at the core of structural and everyday
racial inequity. Judge Robert Carter[1] (1988) used the metaphor of "disease"
to explain the failure of the landmark *Brown v. Board of Education* (1954)
U.S. Supreme Court decision to bring an end to racial segregation. In his
reflections on the case, Carter stated:

> . . . [T]he NAACP lawyers erred. The lawyers did not understand then how
> effective white power could be in preventing full implementation of the law;
> nor did it realize at the time that the basic barrier to full equality for blacks was
> not racial segregation, a symptom, but white supremacy, the disease. (p. 1095)

Carter argues that the NAACP lawyers overlooked the role of white
supremacy in their legal efforts to desegregate the nation's public schools.
Carter's reflection urges an analysis of white supremacy and how it plays
a central role in the examination of racism—to understand that racism is
a "symptom" of a larger "disease" of white supremacy. The concept of
the macroaggression allows for exactly this. We define the macroaggression
as the set of beliefs and/or ideologies that justify actual or potential social
arrangements that legitimate the interests and/or positions of a dominant
group over nondominant groups, which in turn lead to related structures
and acts of subordination (Pérez Huber & Solórzano, 2015b). Thus, macroaggressions provide the ideological foundations that justify the actions of
racism in the many forms they take, including institutional racism and racial
microaggressions. These ideologies provide the "mental frames" or "common sense" (Lakoff, 2006) understandings and perceptions of dominant
and nondominant groups needed to justify the oppression experienced by
the latter.[2] Referring back to the model, what emerges from the roots is the
trunk, the tree's structural support. The tree trunk represents institutional
racism.

INSTITUTIONAL RACISM: THE TRUNK AND BRANCHES

Institutional racism can be understood as formal and/or informal structural
mechanisms, such as policies and processes that systematically subordinate,
marginalize, and exclude nondominant groups and mediate their experiences with racial microaggressions (Pérez Huber & Solórzano, 2015b).

Institutional racism is a key component to understanding the function and permanence of racism in the United States.[3] Indeed, systemic racism is embedded within social institutions that, in turn, serve as structural mechanisms that perpetuate racism (Marable, 2002). Without a structural understanding of the racism that manifests in the everyday lives of People of Color, it remains an elusive concept that becomes difficult to "see" in any tangible way. However, when institutional racism is understood as a mechanism that strategically guides policies and processes in education, government, politics, and the law, the depth and breadth of institutional racism's significance in the everyday lives of all (People of Color and whites) emerges. The concept of institutional racism, then, articulates the larger structural conditions that exist and allow racial microaggressions to occur.

Manning Marable (2002) uses the term *structural racism* to explain how racism is embedded within U.S. social institutions. In this work, Marable (2002) states "[I]t is not the objective reality of difference between 'races' that produces disparities and social inequality between groups; it is structural racism that reproduces 'races'" (p. 28). Here, Marable highlights a critical function of institutional racism and its relationship to what we call macroaggressions. He explains that the *objective* perceptions—the dominant set of ideologies or beliefs—about racial groups cannot alone produce actual inequalities in the lives of People of Color. It is the structural forms of racism that (re)produce the actual and/or perceived social arrangements that legitimate the inequitable positions between People of Color and whites in U.S. society.

As the trunk provides structural support for the tree, institutional racism provides the structural mechanisms that perpetuate racism. To do this, the policies and processes of our social institutions systematically subordinate Communities of Color in our model. The branches that grow from the tree trunk are those social systems. As illustrated in Figure 3.1, education, economic, health care, mass media, criminal justice, and political institutions each function to produce racial inequities in nearly every outcome of social life—from income inequality to unequal educational opportunities, from health disparities to disproportionate criminalization, and from inadequate political representation to negative media portrayals, Communities of Color have historically and consistently been marginalized. These systems, however, could not solely perpetuate racism if not for the everyday practices that reinscribe it. Racial microaggressions are those everyday practices.

RACIAL MICROAGGRESSION: THE LEAVES

The remaining components of the tree in Figure 3.1 are the leaves. The leaves emerge from each system where institutional racism is embedded. These leaves represent the everyday practices of racism carried out by individuals and groups. As we have defined previously, racial microaggressions are (1) verbal and nonverbal assaults directed toward People of Color, often carried out in subtle, automatic, or unconscious forms; (2) layered assaults, based on race and its intersections with gender, class, sexuality, language, immigration status, phenotype, accent, or surname; and (3) cumulative assaults that take a psychological and physiological toll[4] on People of Color. Microaggressions allow us to "see" and "feel" those tangible ways racism emerges in everyday interactions. At the same time, they have a purpose. Whether conscious or not, microaggressions perpetuate larger systems of institutional racism. Microaggressions are the layered, cumulative, and often subtle and unconscious forms of racism that target People of Color. They are the everyday reflections of racist systems and ideological beliefs that impact Peoples of Color's lives. As illustrated in Figure 3.1, racial microaggressions are inextricably linked to institutional racism and macroaggressions. The ideologies of white supremacy provide the foundation for institutional racism, which in turn perpetuates racial microaggressions. One could not exist without the other.

Before continuing to explain how we apply these concepts to real-life examples, it is important for us to acknowledge the ways our theorizing departs from others'. Our conceptualization of racial macroaggressions is different from that of many other scholars, who define macroaggressions as the overt, "large scale" acts of racism (i.e., state-sanctioned racism) experienced by People of Color (Gildersleeve, Croom, & Vasquez, 2011; Levchak, 2018; Smith, Allen & Danley, 2007). In his early work, Chester Pierce (1970) also differentiated microaggressions from the "gross, dramatic, obvious macroaggression such as lynching" (p. 266). We argue that the terms "micro" and "macro" do not define acts of racism as minor or consequential. On this note, we believe Pierce would agree, as he later advocated that the "micro" in microaggression was not an attempt to minimize everyday racist acts, "since their very number requires a total effort that is incalculable" (p. 520). We concur with Pierce that we are limited by the terms we use to describe the complexities of racism and the harm they can cause.[5] Like Pierce, we do not intend to depreciate everyday racism by using the term "micro." Thus, in our definition of microaggressions, we state that they are "often subtle," but can also be blatant. As a result, we define racial microaggressions as taking on both covert and overt forms. Our major departure from Pierce (and others) is in how we identify the distinctions among everyday racism, the policies and processes that (re)produce it (via institutional racism), and the ideologies of white supremacy that justify racism. Despite these differences, we believe that our theorizing of racial microaggressions remains in alignment, not in contention, with Pierce and the trajectory of his work on microaggressions. We make a strategic effort to reappropriate the power of the term "microaggression" that has endured throughout the decades to capture a historically situated meaning for everyday racism.[6]

APPLYING THE FRAMEWORK

Now that we have explained the model and defined its components, we apply it to three examples of racial microaggressions that span historical and contemporary contexts. We do this to demonstrate the conceptual use of the model. Furthermore, with both historical and contemporary examples, we also demonstrate its utility to analyze microaggressions across time. The first example utilizes an historical artifact, an archival photograph to illustrate an example of a racial microaggression, institutional racism, and macroaggression in the 1930s Jim Crow state of North Carolina. In the second example, we use the 2013 class-action lawsuit *Floyd et al. v. City of New York*. This case challenged the New York Police Department's (NYPD) racial profiling practices and the unconstitutional stop-and-frisk program in predominately African American and Latina/o communities in New York City. The final example brings us to date in 2019 (as we write this chapter) to explore the inhumane treatment of Latina/o, and specifically Central American migrants in the United States and along the U.S.–Mexico border.

Example 1: John Vachon, "A Drinking Fountain on the County Courthouse Lawn" (1938)

Photography, particularly historical photography, provides an insightful view to America's racist past (Gates, 2019). Scholars such as Abel (2010) and Smith (2004) recognize the significance of visual photography to capture historically situated meanings of race. We agree such historical images are powerful and that is why we chose to use a photograph as our first example of racial microaggressions. Figure 3.2 is a 1938 photograph catalogued by the Library of Congress titled, "A Drinking Fountain on the County Courthouse Lawn," that was taken in Halifax, North Carolina. Photographers working for the Farm Security Administration, Historical Section, were charged with visually documenting "continuity and change" in America during the 1930s and 1940s, with a particular focus on visual signage (Vachon, 1938). This photograph is included in a collection titled, "Photographs of Signs Enforcing Racial Discrimination."[7]

In the photograph, a young African American boy stands next to a water fountain located on the lawn of a county courthouse. The entrance of the courthouse can be seen in the background to the left. A sign is posted on a tree to the left of the water fountain that reads, "COLORED." The boy seems to gaze at the photographer as the photo is taken.

We argue that the racial microaggression in the photo is the "colored" water fountain that the boy stands next to. Although the "COLORED" sign would not be considered subtle today, this was an everyday form of de jure racism (Jim Crow) experienced by this young boy at this particular historical moment (1930s), and in this particular geographic location (Southern United

Figure 3.2. "A Drinking Fountain on the County Courthouse Lawn"

Photograph by J. Vachon, 1938

States). Separate public facilities for African Americans in the South were an everyday experience in 1938.[8] We argue that consistent with our definition of racial microaggressions, the separate water fountain was a form of systemic everyday racism used to keep those at the racial margins in their place. Separate facilities for People of Color in the South in the 1930s were normative in dominant society, practiced and enforced accordingly in automatic and unconscious ways by many whites and accepted as a "natural" way of life (Alexander, 2010). If we could speak to this young boy as a grown man, he might very well describe the cumulative psychological and physiological toll he had experienced during his life, subjected to this form of everyday racism.

Where a racial microaggression occurs, institutional racism operates to enforce it. The institutional racism we identify in this photo is the Jim Crow de jure policy that maintained separate public facilities for whites and People of Color upheld at the time in the South—the Jim Crow "Colored Only" law. We argue that the "COLORED" sign posted on the tree in the photo represents Jim Crow. Jim Crow law is the institutional racism that functioned as a structural mechanism to systemically subordinate, marginalize, and exclude People of Color through policies like separate public facilities. In effect, Jim Crow laws were the forms of institutional racism that enforced and maintained the everyday racial microaggressions we see in this photo. If we would have been able to talk to the young boy in the photo as an adult, he most likely would tell us about the many ways his life has been limited by Jim Crow.

Although ideologies remain unseen to the eye, there are powerful ideologies at play that justified Jim Crow laws and mediated this young boy's everyday experience with racial microaggressions. Thus, the macroaggression we identify here is ideologies of white supremacy. These ideologies justified the social arrangements maintained by Jim Crow (institutional racism) that systematically subordinated People of Color at the time, and mediated experiences with racial microaggressions. Without the ideological foundations of white supremacy, neither institutional racism nor racial microaggressions could be justified or sustained.

With this historical artifact we identified the various ways racism manifests, from the everyday to the institutional to the ideological. Drawing from Figure 2.1 (A Model for Understanding the Types, Contexts, Effects, and Responses to Racial Microaggressions) in Chapter 2, we could also posit the psychological and long-term physiological effects the young boy suffered from microaggressions such as these. Returning to Carter's (1988) metaphor of symptom and disease, the water fountain and signage are symptoms of the disease of white supremacy that justify and allow for this racist signage and all that it represents. In the next examples we move to contemporary times to show how the Tree Model (Figure 3.1) can be used to analyze racial microaggressions that target People of Color today.

Example 2: Floyd v. City of New York (2013)

The federal class-action lawsuit *Floyd v. City of New York* (2013) challenged New York Police Department (NYPD) racial profiling practices and unconstitutional stop-and-frisks in predominately African American and Latina/o communities in the city. Stop-and-frisk persists in cities all over the nation, when police target mostly African American and Latino males for unlawful stops. As we write this book, an investigation by the *Los Angeles Times* has revealed that from 2015 to 2018, Black drivers were disproportionately stopped in "high crime" areas of Los Angeles by the city police department (LAPD; Chang & Poston, 2019). A civil rights attorney in the article described LAPD practices as "stop and frisk in a car," referring to the racial profiling that took place in the *Floyd* case. The Floyd case is a story of a community who sought to challenge these racist practices in the courts.

African American plaintiffs David Floyd, Lalit Clarkson, Deon Dennis, and David Ourlicht represented "hundreds of thousands" of New Yorkers stopped by NYPD officers for "suspicion-less" stop-and-frisks that disproportionately targeted African Americans and Latinas/os in the city (Fagan, 2010). According to an expert report presented in the case, African Americans and Latinas/os constituted 84 percent of stops from 2010 through 2012 under the city's stop-and-frisk policy, although these groups comprise only 50 percent of the city's total population. Nearly all of those stopped were released by officers who found no basis for summons or arrest (Fagan,

2012). From 2010 to 2012, there were over 1.6 million stops by police in New York City. Approximately 1.3 million of those stopped were African American and Latina/o, mostly male (Fagan, 2012). This would mean that NYPD stopped and frisked more African Americans and Latinas/os than the entire city populations of Buffalo, Rochester, Yonkers, Syracuse, Albany, and New Rochelle combined (New York State's six largest cities after New York City). The *New York Times* reported NYPD superior officers provided explicit orders for police to target "male blacks 14 to 20, 21" years of age under the same policy (New York Times Editorial Board, 2013).

In the opinion of the case, the court recognized that People of Color, and particularly African American and Latino males, were targeted by racial profiling practices such as stop-and-frisk "on the way to work, in front of their house or just walking down the street, without any cause and primarily because of their race" (Fagan, 2012, p. 3). We argue that the everyday and persistent practices of stop-and-frisk, which explicitly targeted Black and Brown men in New York City, were racial microaggressions. The routine practices of stop-and-frisk were layered microaggressions, based on race and gender. Thousands of police officers engaged these tactics automatically, and, perhaps, without being conscious of the racism they perpetrated. From report findings we know that those targeted by these microaggressions were negatively impacted by them. The Center for Constitutional Rights (2012) found that those stopped experienced trauma, humiliation, and endured "fear as a way of life" (p. 7). The report also found stop-and-frisks impacted not only individuals directly targeted by them, but entire communities, who reported feeling the presence of NYPD as a "military-style occupation" due to these everyday acts of racism consistently committed in their communities (p. 19). These findings illustrate how there were primary and secondary targets of this type of microaggressions, as we explained in Chapter 2.

Indeed, stop-and-frisks were everyday acts of racism endured by hundreds of thousands of People of Color in New York City. However, in order for NYPD to engage such widely used tactics, the tactics had to be institutionalized. The most obvious form of institutional racism is the stop-and-frisk policy itself, as a formal structural mechanism that systematically subordinated the plaintiffs targeted by racial microaggressions. The more conspicuous form of institutional racism operating within this example is what the court opinion called the "unwritten" policy of "targeting the right people for stops," or the informal structural mechanisms of institutional racism that subjected many members of the African American and Latina/o communities in the city to be held under suspicion of criminality.[9] According to the opinion delivered by U.S. District Court Judge Shira Sheindlin:

> [T]he City adopted a policy of indirect racial profiling by targeting racially defined groups for stops based on local crime suspect data. This has resulted in the disproportionate and discriminatory stopping of [B]lacks and Hispanics . . .

Both statistical and anecdotal evidence showed that minorities are indeed treated differently than whites . . . despite the fact that whites are more likely to be found with weapons or contraband. (*Floyd et al. v. City of New York*, 2013, p. 16)

In effect, the *Floyd* ruling acknowledged both formal and informal mechanisms of institutional racism that mediated police stop-and-frisk practices, or the racial microaggressions. Moreover, it was found that these racist practices disproportionately targeted African Americans and Latinas/os. What the *Floyd* ruling did not address is how the perpetrators of these racial microaggressions developed their racist beliefs and perceptions about African American and Latina/o communities. This is addressed by the final component of the Tree Model, the macroaggression (see Figure 3.1).

Identifying the macroaggression in *Floyd* exposes the powerful ideologies at play that articulate racist perspectives of Communities of Color. The *Floyd* case found police officers engaged racial profiling strategies based on racist perceptions of People of Color, and that these practices were formally and informally enforced by the city's written and unwritten stop-and-frisk policies. What the case does not explain is that, without widely held, normative, racist beliefs about People of Color maintained by many of the police officers that served in the NYPD, these stop-and-frisk policies and practices could not have emerged in such a pronounced way.

Based on the evidence presented in the *Floyd* case, the opinion revealed that African Americans and Latinas/os were (1) stopped more than whites "even when other relevant variables" were held constant, (2) were more likely than whites to be arrested for the same suspected crimes and, (3) were more likely than whites to be "subjected to the use of force" even when whites were more likely to require further enforcement action in a stop (liability opinion in *Floyd et al. v. City of New York*, 2013, pg. 12). Based on the facts of the case, we would argue that the macroaggression here is ideologies of white supremacy. Thus, the macroaggression that operates in *Floyd* is in fact the ideological beliefs in white superiority that led to actions of law enforcement to criminalize Men of Color through such policies (see Alexander, 2010).

Example 3: Immigration and the "Humanitarian Crisis"

The final example we provide in this chapter takes the analysis to what is happening in the everyday lives of some undocumented Latina/o immigrants in the United States. In February 2019, President Donald Trump declared a national emergency at the U.S.–Mexico border (Baker, 2019). The announcement was a response to an increase in the number of mostly Central American migrants arriving at the border seeking asylum. A rise in the violence and threat of death in their home countries has prompted the migration, which began in 2014 but has been given much recent attention by Trump (Carcamo, 2014). Building "the wall" at the U.S.–Mexico border has been one of the top priorities of the Trump administration and one that he built his presidential campaign around.[10] In 2016, when Trump announced his presidential bid, his speech focused mostly on further vilifying undocumented Mexican immigrants, calling them "rapists" and "criminals," and later, "bad hombres" (Mendoza-Denton, 2017; Pérez Huber, 2016). Trump's racist rhetoric became clear, quickly.

Throughout his election and his presidency, Trump has characterized undocumented communities as dangerous "animals," associating them with gangs, violence, and drugs (Davis, 2018). As a result, research has found that his rhetoric has directly led to increases in hate crimes throughout the nation (Miller & Werner-Winslow, 2016) as well as more hostile environments in schools and universities (Gomez & Pérez Huber, 2019; Muñoz & Vigil, 2018; Rogers, Ishimoto, Kwako, Berryman, & Diera, 2019). As we will explain in this chapter, the targeting of Latina/o undocumented communities is nothing new, and has a longstanding history in the United States. Here, we return to the concept of racist nativism introduced at the beginning of the book to explain how we position an analysis of the anti-Latina/o racism we have seen emerge during the Trump administration.

LatCrit & Racist Nativism

In the Introduction, I (Lindsay) told a story of how the concept of racist nativism evolved through a series of collective research projects with Danny and other colleagues. As explained in the Introduction, our theorizing of racist nativism began with a specific branch of CRT, Latina/o critical theory (LatCrit). LatCrit is a theoretical branch of CRT and serves as the foundation for unmasking the particular forms of racism that have emerged in recent immigration debates. LatCrit enables researchers to better articulate the specific experiences of Latinas/os through a more focused examination of the unique forms of oppression this group encounters. (Montoya & Valdes, 2008; Solórzano & Delgado Bernal, 2001). LatCrit is guided by the same tenets as CRT (see Figure 1.2), but also acknowledges issues specific to Latina/o communities, such as immigration status, language, ethnicity, culture, and phenotype. LatCrit allows for a more refined research focus and has led to the development of racist nativism.[11]

Racist nativism explains how People of Color have historically experienced racialized constructions of non-nativeness in the United States, regardless of their actual origin (Pérez Huber et al., 2008). Specifically, racist nativism examines the "inextricable" link between race and immigration status, contextualized by the historical racialization of Immigrants of Color, and allows for an analysis of the current moment of increased anti-immigrant sentiment (Sánchez, 1997). This conceptual framework explains how perceived racial differences construct false perceptions of People of Color as "non-native," and not belonging to the monolithic "American" identity—an identity that has historically been tied to perceptions and constructions of whiteness (Acuña, 1972; Haney López, 2006; Johnson, 2012). Historically, immigration law has been intricately tied to legal constructions of racial categories used to regulate those arriving in the United States and excluding those already residing in the country. Since the late 19th century, legal strategies have been used to restrict immigration and the rights of various immigrant groups perceived to misalign with constructions of whiteness (and American-ness), including Southern and Eastern European, Chinese, and Japanese immigrants. Today, legally sanctioned strategies of racist nativism target Latina/o communities both immigrant and non-immigrant, particularly Mexicans and Chicanas/os (Gómez, 2018; Ngai, 2004; Saito, 1997).

As explained in the Introduction, we have defined racist nativism as

> the assigning of values to real or imagined differences, in order to justify the superiority of the native, who is to be perceived white, over that of the non-native, who is perceived to be People and Immigrants of Color, and thereby defend the rights of whites, or the natives, to dominance. (Pérez Huber et al., 2008, p. 43)

This understanding of racist nativism builds upon the definitions of race and racism provided in Chapter 1. It also highlights the functionality of racist nativism to assign subordinate values to People of Color generally, and Latina/os especially. It does this by assigning a perceived differential status from whiteness that characterizes U.S. nativeness and belonging. In effect, racist nativism discursively assigns real and/or perceived subordinate values to Latina/os generally, and Latina/o immigrants in particular, in order to justify a perpetual non-native status to this group and to reinforce perceived white superiority. Racist nativism has been used as a concept to understand the discursive functions of racist nativism that shape the educational trajectories of Latina/o students, and particularly undocumented Chicana/Latina women (Pérez Huber, 2009a, 2011; Pérez Huber & Cueva, 2012). It has also been used to explore how the Trump administration has utilized racist nativism in current debates about undocumented immigration, and how they are linked to the discourse about changing demographics of the United States (Pérez Huber, 2016). In this section, we utilize racist nativism to explore the types of racial microaggressions that target undocumented Latina/o immigrants, and especially those from Central America, who are arriving in the United States seeking asylum.

Figure 3.3 is a scene from Linda Freeman's short film, *Unaccompanied: Alone in America* (2018). The image is of a young Latino boy sitting in an immigration courtroom before a judge with oversized headphones placed on his small head to receive translation services. This image, and the film

Figure 3.3. *Unaccompanied: Alone in America* (2018) by Linda Freeman[12]

it comes from, was meant to be representative of real-life events taking place every day in federal U.S. immigration courts. Here, mostly Central American migrant children who arrive in the United States without parents (or have been separated from them) are categorized as "unaccompanied alien children" (UAC's) and required to appear in immigration court without the right to an attorney or an interpreter. Freeman created the short film in hopes it would "galvanize the general public" to take action against unaccompanied children, some as young as toddlers, being subjected to court hearings by themselves.[13] The film is based on Freeman's research in federal U.S. immigration courts, including interviews with pro bono attorneys who had represented unaccompanied children in court hearings.

We argue that what this photo represents is a type of racial microaggression, a racist nativist microaggression. Similar to racial microaggressions, as defined earlier, racist nativist microaggressions are a form of systemic everyday racist nativism used to keep Latina/o communities in their place. This type of microaggression can be verbal or nonverbal, can be layered, and can take a cumulative toll on those who are targeted by them. This little boy represents so many Latina/o migrant children being required to appear in immigration court without understanding any of its proceedings, or even the language being spoken. Like many other unaccompanied children, he was most likely detained for some period of time in a holding cell or camp with living conditions that some reporters have compared to concentration camps (Pitzer, 2018). Dr. Colleen Kraft, President of the American Academy of Pediatrics, has called the separation of migrant children "government sanctioned child abuse" (Alvarez, 2018). These children have been held here without a trial and without guilt of any crime. This has become an unfortunate and everyday reality for tens of thousands of unaccompanied Latina/o children in the United States in recent years. The racism that characterizes this inhumane treatment is intricately tied to their status as undocumented immigrants. This example is different from the others we have provided in this chapter thus far, where the racial microaggression is isolated to one action or event. In this example, the ways that Latina/o unaccompanied minors are targeted by racist nativist microaggressions happens when they are arrested, when they are detained, when they are required to appear in court without representation or translation, and in their interactions with officials who remain complicit in their treatment. It has been reported that by the end of 2018, the number of unaccompanied children in government custody was over 14,000, the highest number ever reached in the United States (Kopan, 2018). While the image represents the experiences of unaccompanied minors, there are thousands of adult Latina/o migrants who faced the same treatment.[14]

The institutional racism that supports the racist nativist microaggressions so many Latina/o migrants have been subjected to are the policies that have facilitated this treatment. In May of 2018, the Trump administration unveiled a zero-tolerance policy that mandated the prosecution of every individual who entered the United States illegally. In the months that followed this announcement, Central American migrants continued to arrive at the U.S.–Mexico border seeking asylum to escape the violence and death that threatened them at home (Morrissey, 2018). Many of the migrants traveled thousands of miles through Central America and then Mexico, in a group for safety, in what the Trump administration and news media called "migrant caravans." The Trump administration's response was to first deny asylum to those who enter the country without documentation (Miroff, 2018). However, when those efforts were blocked by a federal judge, the administration formed an agreement with Mexico to allow for the migrants to wait in Mexico instead of in the United States to apply for asylum (Dinan, 2018; Partlow & Miroff, 2018). These events led to Trump's claim of a national emergency, referencing the unfounded "humanitarian crisis."[15]

The macroaggression in this example, as in the other examples we have provided in this chapter, are the ideologies of white supremacy that justify and maintain the unjust and inhumane treatment of Latina/o undocumented migrant children and adults. The Trump administration's inhumane immigration policies continue to propagate fear and trauma among immigrant communities across the United States (see O'Toole, 2020). The Kaiser Family Foundation (2018) reported that key health implications related to family separations: (1) compound existing trauma experienced by children and their families in their home countries and in their journeys to the United States, and (2) can have short-term and lifelong negative impacts on physical and mental health. Research has shown that these inhumane perspectives and white supremacist ideologies that undergird the administration's stance on immigration have led to "a discursive opening for others with similar beliefs to . . . reinforce racist nativism, creating a space to more comfortably perform white supremacy" (Pérez Huber, 2016, p. 241).

As we explained in Chapter 2, racial microaggression is contextual. The context of the racial microaggression must be understood in its persistent and everyday forms. When this context is understood, there emerges an opportunity to examine the underlying systemic causes of microaggressions. When systemic racism is revealed, the white supremacist ideologies that uphold its perpetuation and maintenance can be seen. In these ways, we agree with Coates's (2017) use of the metaphor "machine" to describe white supremacy. However, our analysis of racial microaggressions takes one step further to address what Judge Robert Carter once urged us to understand about racial inequity—the difference between symptoms of racism and the disease of white supremacy.

CHAPTER 4

Racism Within and Between Communities of Color

Internalized Racism

> Too bad mi'jita was morena, *muy prieta*,[1] so dark and different from her
> own fair-skinned children. But she loved mi'jita anyway. What I lacked in
> whiteness, I had in smartness. But it was too bad I was dark like an Indian.
>
> "Don't go in the sun," my mother would tell me when I wanted to
> play outside. "If you get any darker, they'll mistake you for an Indian." And
> don't get dirt on your clothes. You don't want people to say you're a dirty
> Mexican."
>
> —Gloria Anzaldúa, 2002, p. 220

For many People of Color, this excerpt of Gloria Anzaldúa's (2002) essay, titled "La Prieta," about the preference for light skin will sound sadly familiar. In this work, Anzaldúa explains that the rough draft of the essay was shelved for a year because she was "terrified" to write about how racism and heteropatriarchy can be perpetuated within Families and Communities of Color (p. 220). She wrote, "I am still afraid because I will have to call us on a lot of shit, like our own racism, our fear of women, and sexuality" (p. 221). Yet, Anzaldúa took the risk, exposing many personal and painful experiences during her lifetime. Honoring her work, we take a risk in this chapter and attempt to theorize how Communities of Color can also participate in structures of oppression. We also found that this chapter was a difficult one to write. However, like Anzaldúa (2002) we believe it is an important discussion to have in order to better understand how racism and white supremacy operate in our own lives and relationships with each other. As we described in Chapter 1 and will reiterate here, we believe People of Color cannot be racist but can internalize racism. Our communities have never possessed the political or economic power to create or enact structures of oppression. However, as Anzaldúa (2002) writes, we are capable of "unwittingly passing on to our children and our friends the oppressor's ideologies" (p. 231). This chapter will examine how white supremacist ideologies can be internalized within our own communities and enacted upon each other. Indeed, the internalization of deficit perspectives, racist, and heterosexist stereotypes among People of Color are one way that systems of white supremacy are (re)produced and white dominance is maintained. In this chapter we introduce the concept of internalized racism to explain a form of everyday racism that occurs within our own communities and benefits white supremacy. But first, some history.

The preference for light skin over dark skin is one that is prevalent in many Communities of Color (Harris, 2008). It has also created conflict. It is a phenomenon that is uncomfortable to discuss, even among those with critical viewpoints. However, it is important to understand that it did not begin with us. Such preferences have endured for centuries in Latina/o and African American communities since Spanish colonization of the Americas in the 15th century. It was during this time that Spanish colonizers used skin color to create a caste system of racial hierarchy that ensured the subordination of dark-skinned African slaves and indigenous communities of the Americas by white colonizers (Acuña, 1972). Once the caste system was abolished, the hierarchy it created continued in the hearts and minds of many white Europeans. They brought these beliefs with them to colonize the West from the 16th through 21st centuries. Their pillage included destroying Native American communities, establishing an institution of slavery to build generational wealth from Black labor, annexing Mexican land to expand U.S. territory over the Southwest, and importing Mexican, Chinese, and Japanese labor to establish and maintain agribusiness in the United States (Acuña, 1972; Coates, 2017; Dunbar-Ortiz, 2014; Gómez, 2018; Roediger, 1999; Takaki, 2008).[2]

Although there is much more history to tell than what we can provide here (see Figure 1.1), we point to this brief historical legacy of racism and white supremacy as the origins of internalized racism, what Anzaldúa (2002) described above in "La Prieta." It is important to acknowledge these origins, and the centuries-old preference for whiteness that determines who deserves access to education, opportunity, success, health, wealth, and who does not. Institutional racism ensures that white life outcomes exceed those of People of Color (see Gaxiola Serrano & Solórzano, 2018; Pérez Huber, Vélez, & Solórzano, 2018). However, white supremacy also operates to shape the beliefs and viewpoints of People of Color, particularly when it comes to race. A preference for whiteness can be shaped by everyday environments, including through television, film, media, social media, and pop culture—all of which pervade life in contemporary society. For Women of Color, there are even more ways to be influenced by whiteness, when white standards of beauty and "good hair" define what is considered feminine and beautiful (Berry & Duke, 2011; Jerald, Ward, Moss, Thomas, & Fletcher, 2017; Montoya, 1994). We must be clear that when racism is reproduced within Communities of Color, as in Anzaldúa's example, it is because of the historical legacies of racism and perceived white superiority that have shaped our society. The preference for whiteness we may see shows up in our own families and communities and is bound by centuries-old narratives that white is better, good, civilized, virtuous, beautiful, etc. This chapter explains how racism can be perpetuated within Communities of Color, through what we call internalized racism. In this chapter, we first explain this concept, and then show how it manifests in Communities of Color. We offer a model to understand internalized racism, and how it can help explain how racism operates within a racial group (intragroup) and between racial groups (intergroup).

We define internalized racism as the conscious and/or unconscious acceptance of a racial hierarchy and its related ideologies and structures that positions and privileges whites above People of Color (Kohli, 2017; Pérez Huber, Johnson, & Kohli, 2006). This racial hierarchy reinforces white supremacy and is institutionalized through racist structures (i.e., mass media, criminal justice, education, economic system, political system—see Figure 3.1). Internalized racism is a learned process of socialization where one internalizes and acts out the negative perceptions of People of Color created by racism and white supremacy. These negative perceptions can be internalized and enacted through intragroup and intergroup conflict that reinforces institutionalized racism and the racial hierarchies it produces. Figure 4.1 illustrates how internalized racism operates.

The model begins at the outer frame of the figure, where we place white supremacy, the ideologies and structures that (re)produce all forms of racism generally, and internalized racism specifically. As we explained in the previous chapter, ideologies of white supremacy justify the structural mechanisms that systemically subordinate People of Color through institutionalized racism. Institutionalized racism creates a racial hierarchy, where whites are placed above People of Color. In turn, this leads People of Color to internalize those racial hierarchies in the form of internalized racism. Internalized racism can then be acted out against other Persons of Color within one's racial group, causing intragroup conflict. Internalized racism can also be acted out against a Person of Color from another racial group, causing intergroup conflict, which (re)inforces institutional racism and white supremacy. In the following sections, we provide examples, grounded in data, that explain how internalized racism is experienced, and how it emerges to create intragroup and intergroup conflict within and between Communities of Color.

Figure 4.1. Internalized Racism and Intragroup and Intergroup Racial Conflict

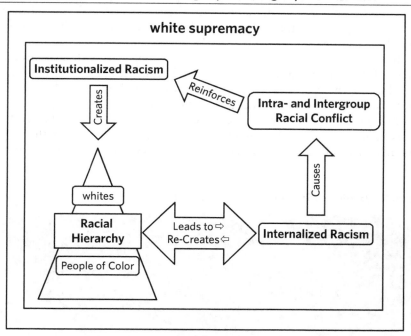

INTERNALIZED RACISM: THE CLARK DOLL EXPERIMENT

The landmark Supreme Court case *Brown v. Board of Education* (1954) was supposed to end state-sanctioned segregation that prevailed during the Jim Crow era. Key to this decision was the research of social psychologists Kenneth and Mamie Clark (Guinier, 2004). What became known as the Clark Doll Experiment was a study of the psychological effects of racial segregation on African American children. The study included Black children between the ages of 5 and 7 years old. In this experiment, children were shown two dolls—one Black and one white—and asked a series of questions that prompted them to identify which of the dolls was a "good" doll, which was a "bad" doll, which was the "nice" doll, and which doll they would prefer to play with (Clark, Chein, & Cook, 2004; Clark & Clark, 1947, 1950).[3] The study found that African American children typically preferred the white doll over the Black, associating negative characteristics with the Black doll and positive characteristics with the white doll. The findings provided evidentiary support for the plaintiffs in *Brown,* who argued that

African American children internalized the perceived inferiority most whites held about Blacks during the time.[4] The photo in Figure 4.2 was taken by the renowned photographer Gordon Parks, who documented the study in a special issue of *Ebony* magazine in 1947.[5]

In the photo, Dr. Clark stands before the young boy, with his arms outstretched, holding a Black doll in one hand and a white doll in the other. The child sits before him, pointing to the white doll, while looking at Dr. Clark. Because we know the context of this photograph, we believe that it reflects how the child has internalized racism. Using our model in Figure 4.1, we explain. In 1947 in the United States (particularly in the South) white supremacist ideologies were widely accepted. These ideologies were critical

Figure 4.2. Gordon Parks, "Untitled, Harlem, NY, 1947"

Photograph by Gordon Parks. Courtesy of and copyright The Gordon Parks Foundation.

in establishing institutional racism, in which many local and state laws were passed to segregate People of Color from whites, limit their voting rights, and prohibit marriage between People of Color and whites. As we have explained in earlier chapters, such laws became known as Jim Crow (Gates, 2019). In the photo, this young boy's reaction represents the internalization of the racial hierarchies that uphold principles of white supremacy. We can imagine that Parks is taking this photo while Dr. Clark asks the little boy a question, perhaps about which is the "good" doll, or the "nice" doll, as he points to the white doll. Because of white supremacy, institutional racism, and the racial hierarchies created by them, this little boy, no more than 7 years old, had come to believe in the superiority of whites over Blacks, leading to his own internalized racism. The little boy would experience in everyday life the manifestations of white supremacy, with whites in control of Black lives. Now decades old, the Clark Doll Experiment has been replicated multiple times in social science research (see Fegley, Spencer, Goss, Harpalani, & Charles, 2008; Spencer, 2008; Van Ausdale & Feagin, 2001) and in the media (see Ahuja, 2009; CNN, 2010). These replicated studies have found consistent results over time, showing that internalized racism is a persistent consequence of racism and white supremacy in society today. The next section will describe a form of internalized racism in Latina/o communities.

INTERNALIZED RACIST NATIVISM:
EL TEATRO CAMPESINO'S "EL CORRIDO"

In Chapter 3 we defined racist nativism. In this section we use the concept of racist nativism to show how People of Color can internalize the racist and xenophobic beliefs that define perceptions of U.S. belonging. We use Figure 4.3 to argue that white supremacy is the overarching ideology and related structures that subordinates People of Color generally and Immigrants of Color in particular. Within that overarching frame, institutionalized racist nativism creates racial hierarchies, with the native (i.e., white) on top and the perceived immigrant on the bottom. People of Color then internalize those racial hierarchies in the form of racist nativism. Internalized racist nativism re-creates those racial hierarchies within People of Color, or, in this case, between citizens and noncitizens. This leads to intragroup conflict, which in turn reinforces institutionalized racist nativism.

The following example of internalized racist nativism is borrowed from a 1976 play called *El Corrido* (*Ballad of a Farmworker*) (Teatro Campesino, 1976). The play was written by Luis Valdez and performed by El Teatro Campesino. The overall plot line for *El Corrido*[6] highlights the migration journey of the allegorical figure Jesus Pelado Rasquachi from a village in central Mexico to the agricultural communities of the United States, to the end of his life in an urban community in California. In this tale, Valdez

Figure 4.3. White Supremacy, Racial Hierarchies, and Internalized Racist Nativism

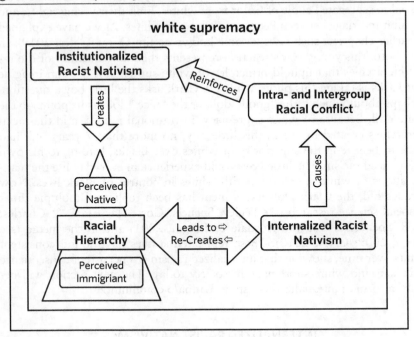

explores how Mexican migrants are controlled by poverty in both Mexico and in the United States, and how the state controls their daily lives, the power of agribusiness, and the social borders embedded in institutional and everyday racism and racist nativism. The play also uses the trope of hierarchies. For instance, the *Patron* (owner) is always on top, followed by the *Patroncito* (Mexican labor contractor), and, at the bottom, the *Pelado* (worker).

As we continue to theorize about how People of Color internalize racism, racist nativism, and heterosexism we return to a staple in ethnic studies readings in the 1960s and 70s—Albert Memmi's *The Colonizer and the Colonized* (1974). Here Memmi offers a useful tool to understand how the colonizer controls the colonized (a sort of internalized control)—how the owner controls the worker. He shares the concept of the "pyramid of petty tyrants." He describes it as

each one, being socially oppressed by one more powerful than he, always finds a less powerful one on whom to lean, and becomes a tyrant in his turn. . . . All have at least this profound satisfaction of being negatively better than the colonized. (p. 61)

In our examples we see how People of Color sometimes set up these "pyramids of petty tyrants"—racial hierarchical pyramids, racist nativist hierarchical pyramids, and at the intersection of each of these, gendered hierarchical pyramids. Borrowing Memmi's "pyramid of petty tyrants" and inserting it into the play *El Corrido*, we found that the playwright, Luis Valdez, set up 14 tripartite hierarchical examples of power and oppression. For example, in Scene Two of the play Valdez starts with the:

> American
>   Mexican
>   Bracero.

He continues with the:

> Patron
>   Patroncito
>   Mojado.

When speaking to gender dynamics he refers to:

> El Patron
>   El Hombre
>   y La Mujer.

When his children internalize the hierarchy and are becoming assimilated into U.S. society, they speak to:

> Americans
>   Mexican-Americans
>   Mexicans.

These four examples of the "pyramid of petty tyrants" show the importance of having someone to look down on, someone less than you. Derrick Bell (1992b) speaks to a similar hierarchical dynamic at work in Black/White relations in the beginning of his book *Faces at the Bottom of the Well*:

> Black people are the magical faces at the bottom of society's well. Even the poorest whites, those who must live their lives only a few levels above, gain their self-esteem by gazing down on us. Surely, they must know that their deliverance depends on letting down their ropes. Only by working together is escape possible. Over time, many reach out, but most simply watch, mesmerized into maintaining their unspoken commitment to keeping us where we are, at whatever cost to them or to us. (p. v)

The *New York Times* opinion writer Charles Blow (2019), when speaking on white supremacy, states that "white supremacy isn't necessarily about rendering white people as superhuman; it is just as often about rendering nonwhite people as subhuman. Either way the hierarchy is established, with whiteness assuming the superior position." So, being at the bottom of that racial pyramid, that racial hierarchy, is an important step in dehumanizing and rendering People of Color as subhuman.

To set the stage for our example of internalized racist nativism, the three main characters have been selected by a labor contractor to work in the agricultural fields of California. They are in the back of the truck heading to the fields. One of the characters is Alberto, an older *Mexicano* farmworker (the Old Man). The second character is Beto, a younger Mexican American from the city looking for work. The third character is Gonzalez, a young undocumented *Mexicano* farmworker. In the first scene of the play, we get introduced to the characters in the back of the truck as the Old Man brings out his guitar to sing a *corrido*—"The Corrido de Jesus Pelado Rasquachi." Scene two takes us through Jesus's journey from a small village in Mexico to the United States, where he travels working in the agricultural fields throughout the country. At the end of Scene Two, Jesus Pelado Rasquachi gets deported to Mexico. Scene Three, returning to the back of the truck, begins with the Old Man and Beto discussing Jesus Pelado Rasquachi getting deported and figuring out his next moves to return to the United States. As they discuss the various *movidas* (moves) that Jesus can use, the dialogue takes an unfortunate turn between Beto and Gonzalez:

SCENE THREE

GONZALEZ:
Oi es, ques sabes tu [Hey, what do you know]. You know so many *movidas* [moves].
What are you doing in this *troka* [truck]?
You're no better than the rest of us.

BETO:
Who said I was, man?

GONZALEZ:
Yo soy de Mexico. [I am from Mexico].

BETO:
I'm from *Califas* [California].
So what, man? We're all *Raza* here.
But if we are going to survive *ese*, we got be cool, we got to think, we got to let it slide.

If I can't get a job in the city, *esta suave hermano* [it's cool my brother], I'll work in the fields.
It's no skin off my nose.
As long as I get enough to breeze, I do what I please. *Mi entiendes* [You understand]?

GONZALEZ:
Esto es puros babozadas [This is a bunch of bull shit].

GONZALEZ:
Do you know who you are, *pocho* [assimilated Mexican American]?

BETO:
Hey, I'm a Chicano, OK?

GONZALEZ:
(Through his teeth)
Chicanooooo.

BETO:
(Turning to the OLD MAN)
Do you believe this guy?

GONZALEZ:
Do you know what the word means? *Chicaneria*?

BETO:
Yah, I know what it means.

GONZALEZ:
It means crook! *Ladron*! [Thief!].

BETO:
(Again, turning to the OLD MAN)
Can you believe this dude?

GONZALEZ:
Hablan totacha, pero no saben ni madres de español! [They speak street slang, but they don't know any Spanish!]

BETO:
What did you say, ese?

GONZALEZ:
Que no sabes ni madres de español, tapado! [That you don't know any Spanish, dumb ass!]

BETO:
Y que tu sabes, Chuntaro, hijo de tu chin . . . ! [And what do you know, wetback, son of a b . . . .!]
(BETO and GONZALEZ lunge at each other and the farmworkers intercede, trying to prevent a fight. Then they tell the OLD MAN:)
Go ahead with the corrido.

BETO:
Go ahead paisano [countryman].
(BETO and GONZALEZ eye each other carefully, but they calm down. The OLD MAN clears his throat)

OLD MAN:
Didn't I tell you? Sometimes we come across the border, but we take the border with us.
That's what happened to *Jesus Pelado Rasquachi*.
The border went into his *maseta* [head].

In Scene Three, Luis Valdez takes us into the back of the labor contractor's truck on the way to the fields. You get to know the character of BETO as a young urban Chicano just looking for work any way and anywhere he can find it. As a U.S. citizen (with that privilege), BETO also comes across as dismissive of what undocumented Mexican workers have to go through when they come to the United States in search of work. There is a point in Scene Three when BETO is trying to show the other workers on the truck how he uses his *movidas* [moves] both in work and in life that puts him in conflict with GONZALEZ, the Mexican undocumented worker. At that point in the scene GONZALEZ tells BETO that his talk is *"puras babosadas"*—pure bullshit—and goes on to challenge BETO's Mexican identity by stating "Do you know who you are, *pocho* [assimilated Mexican American]?" At this point, the re-created racial hierarchies are confusing, because it is GONZALEZ who is putting Mexicans or *Mexicanos* on top of Chicanos or *pochos* [derogatory terms for assimilated Mexican Americans]. He goes on to ask "Do you know what the word means? *Chicaneria . . .* It means crook! *Ladron* [Thief)!]." Clearly GONZALEZ doesn't understand the history and politics of the ethnic identifier *Chicano* but has come north from Mexico with stereotypes of what Chicanos or Mexican American are—and clearly has created a hierarchy that puts them in conflict with each other. BETO responds with *"Y tu, que sabes, Chuntaro, hijo do tu chin . . . !* [And what do you know, wetback, son of a b . . . .!]." It is at that point that they lunge at each other and the workers in the truck get in between them. The OLD MAN finally intervenes and brings the intragroup conflict back to the *corrido* and states: "Didn't I tell you? Sometimes we come across the border, but we take the border with us. That's what happened to *Jesus Pelado Rasquachi*. The border went into his *maseta* [head]." Using the tools of racist nativism and the "pyramid of petty tyrants," we see that two groups at the bottom of the socioeconomic ladder find ways through experience and language to place themselves one rung above the other and re-create racial hierarchies within groups.[7] This leads to the reinforcement of institutionalized racist nativism and white supremacy.

INTERGROUP CONFLICT: THE "BLEXIT" MOVEMENT

Now that we have explained examples of internalized racism, and internalized racist nativism, we present the final component of Figures 4.1 and 4.3, the intergroup conflict caused by internalized racism that emerges between Communities of Color. We use the Blexit campaign to show this type of conflict. In an interview with the *Washington Post Magazine*, African American conservative commentator Candace Owens described the emergence of Blexit (Nelson, 2019). She coined the term after a 2018 meeting of the Conservative Political Action Conference, where Owens met Nigel Farage, conservative British leader of the Brexit Party. In a manner similar to the way the Brexit portmanteau was used to signify the exit of Britain from the European Union (EU), Owens sought to create a campaign calling for African Americans to exit the U.S. Democratic Party. Thus, "Blexit" began. The Blexit campaign seeks to attract more African Americans to the Republican Party, and to disrupt the history of Black support of Democratic candidates and political views.[8] According to Owens, African Americans and other People of Color have been "used" by the Democratic Party to gain political power but received nothing in return (Nelson, 2019). She argues that the abysmal conditions of Communities of Color provide the evidence. Owens takes on other familiar tropes to argue that liberal values have done more harm than good for African American communities. Some of these racist tropes include: (1) That the focus on racism creates a "victimhood mentality" (also discussed in Chapter 1) and a "lack of personal responsibility" among African Americans; (2) that welfare programs are to blame for government dependence of Black families, and in particular, of single Black mothers; (3) that institutional racism does not exist; and (4) that institutional racism is not a problem in U.S. society, but rather, the problem is African Americans who believe it does. Owens claims that African Americans have been "mentally enslaved" on the Democratic "plantation" and that it is time they "Be Free" (Nelson, 2019). To signal these ideas, "Be Free" is the main tagline used on the Blexit website, and "Off the Plantation" is a slogan used by the campaign.[9] Yet, in the same interview Owens speaks to African Americans and states:

> It's because of racism, because of some imaginary white boogeyman, that you're never gonna be successful . . . if anything in this society, there's almost a level of Black privilege now. [Whites] can't say anything or else [they're] called a racist. I can say anything I want because I'm Black. So that's a whole new privilege, that Black people get away with saying things that white people could never say. (quoted in Nelson, 2019)

Owens uses yet another trope, reverse racism, to argue that white people have somehow lost their privilege, replaced by those "new" privileges gained by Blacks.

It is no surprise, then, that Owens and the Blexit campaign support President Donald Trump and many of his racist policies, particularly his anti-immigrant stance. At the inaugural event in January 2019 of Blexit in Los Angeles, California, many attendees donned red Make America Great Again baseball caps, one of Trump's signature campaign tools. At this rally, the Blexit campaign distributed posters that read "Build the Wall" and in small print below, "Americans before illegals" for rally attendees to wave during the event (see Figure 4.4). In fact, Owens has been clear that the Blexit movement is hinged upon a hard, anti-immigrant stance, similar to the Trump administration's.

Blexit has been especially successful in the use of social media and other technology platforms, where this rhetoric is launched into the public

Figure 4.4. Blexit "Build the Wall" Poster

discourse. In 2018, Owens tweeted: "Regarding #DACA: Send them ALL home!—Unlimited immigration has harmed the black community for decades. Put Americans first, not law-breaking illegal immigrants. In conclusion: WALL!"

In this tweet, Owens refers to Deferred Action for Childhood Arrivals (DACA), the federal program implemented by the Obama administration to provide certain eligible undocumented youth with protection from deportation and a permit to work legally in the United States.[10] The majority of DACA recipients are undocumented Latina/o youth, mostly from Mexico and Central America (Pérez Huber, 2015). In a 2019 podcast interview, Owens explained undocumented immigration as a threat to African American communities:

> I'm really focused on the Black community. The community that has been affected the most by illegal immigration is the Black community. It's just a fact. I mean, you talk about low-wage workers, the people that are the most unemployed in this country, are young Black men between the ages of 18 and 21. Right? So they have been negatively impacted by the influx of people running over the border. Because they come here and say, ok, well you were gonna pay this guy seven dollars, whatever the minimum wage is, we'll do it for less. And that directly impacts the Black labor force. (Rogan, 2018)[11]

In this interview, and in others, Owens reproduces two longstanding anti-immigrant narratives. The first is the perceived threat of undocumented immigrants to the livelihood and well-being of others, in this case, the African American community. The second is the myth that undocumented immigrants are a "resource-drain" on the U.S. labor market and the economy. Such narratives have pervaded immigration discourse in the United States since the early 20th century, and have been used to target Latina/o undocumented communities more recently (Chavez, 2008; Chomski, 2014; Ngai, 2004). These narratives reflect exactly what we described earlier in Chapter 3 and in the previous example of *El Corrido*—racist nativism, that is, a specific form of racism that targets Latina/o undocumented or immigrant communities. We argue, then, that this example shows how Owens has internalized racist nativist beliefs about undocumented immigrants. It also shows how Owens perpetuates racist nativism to explain the inequitable conditions that exist within African American communities. This claim would directly contradict Owens's argument for personal responsibility, and shows the instability of her position about the effects of racism on Communities of Color.

We now return to our model in Figure 4.3 to trace the process of internalized racist nativism. Candace Owens, the Blexit campaign she started, and many of its People of Color followers, are perpetuating narratives that hold strong foundations in white supremacy. Racist nativism is institutionalized through anti-immigrant policies, and it emerges more frequently during moments of heightened anti-immigrant sentiment. For example, in 1994 California voters passed Proposition 187 (the Save Our State initiative) to deny social services to the undocumented. In 2006, House Resolution 4437 was introduced to further militarize the border and criminalize the undocumented. In 2010, Arizona passed Senate Bill 1070, which requires immigration checks during local law enforcement stops. As we discussed in Chapter 3, in 2018 the Trump administration implemented a zero-tolerance policy on undocumented immigration that separated thousands of migrant children from their parents, and has led to the detainment of thousands more adults in federal detention centers.[12] Such policies justify a racial hierarchy, where whites are placed above People of Color, in this case undocumented Latina/o communities. People of Color internalize this hierarchy, where it becomes re-purposed to place some groups above others. In the case of Candace Owens and the Blexit movement, African American communities are placed above Latina/o un-documented communities in this re-purposed hierarchy. The internaliza-tion of such a hierarchy has led to intergroup racial conflict between these groups. This conflict can be seen across the Blexit website, as well as its social media platforms, where supporters often post their racist nativist views using the hashtag Blexit.

For example, one post we found was a photo (see Figure 4.5) of three smiling African American women, standing proudly as they held small U.S. flags.[13]

The woman in the middle wore a t-shirt that read, "I THINK, therefore I am a CONSERVATIVE." The three women held a handmade sign that stretched across their torsos. The sign read, "Democrats choosing illegal immigrants first means black lives come last." In this message, the women implicitly refer to Black Lives Matter, a movement to end police murders of African Americans specifically, and police violence in Black communities generally.[14] It shows the conflict that can arise when Communities of Color internalize racist nativism and repurpose racial hierarchies that ultimately pit one racial group against another. As scholar Carol Anderson (in Nelson, 2019) explains, "[Candace Owens] just appears to be one of a small coterie of black folks circling around Trump . . . trying to put a black face onto white supremacy."[15] Indeed, we would agree with Anderson's analysis, and we would add an additional dimension to this argument. That is, Derrick Bell's (1992a) concept of racial realism. According to Bell (1992a), racial realism is the premise that racism is a permanent aspect of our society, em-bedded in the lives of all persons in the United States, and destructive to all of society's institutions and structures. Bell argues that racial equality in the United States is an unobtainable goal, due to the permanence of racism. The institutional racism that our society was built upon has historically main-tained, and will continue to maintain, the subordination of Black people

Figure 4.5. #Blexit Social Media Post

(and we would argue other People of Color).[16] Thus, in the struggle for justice and dignity of Communities of Color, racial equality should not be the goal. Bell (1992) states:

> Black people will never gain equality in this country. Even those herculean efforts we hail as successful will produce no more than temporary "peaks of progress," short-lived victories that slide into irrelevance *as racial patterns adapt in ways that maintain white dominance* [emphasis added]. This is a hard-to-accept fact that all history verifies. We must acknowledge it and move on to adopt policies based on what I call: "Racial Realism." This mind-set or philosophy requires us to acknowledge the permanence of our subordinate status. That acknowledgment enables us to avoid despair, and frees us to imagine and implement racial strategies that can bring fulfillment and even triumph. (pp. 373–374)

A central premise of racial realism is that racism will never be overcome because it is adaptive, constantly changing form in efforts to "maintain white dominance." For Bell, racism is like a mythological shape-shifter.[17] It has the ability to change its own contours and configurations by shifting form. According to Bell, if history and the law can teach us anything, it is that racism has always been, and always will be.

Candace Owens exemplifies what Bell (1992) describes as "involuntary pawns in defining and resolving society's serious social issues" such as immigration. White supremacy uses People of Color to achieve its own goals of white dominance. Owens upholds white supremacy in her own beliefs, and in her use of power (e.g., political power) to encourage other People of Color to do so. In this way Owens indeed is a "pawn" of white supremacy, what Bell would also call a "race traitor" (1992b).[18] "Race traitors" are those People of Color who have betrayed the interests of their communities by perpetuating stereotypic and deficit perspectives of People of Color and supporting policies that ensure racial harm, thereby working toward maintaining the status quo.[19] Race traitors actively use their power to uphold white supremacy and justify institutional racism. These People of Color leaders have used their political, economic, and intellectual power to uphold white supremacy by undermining their own communities and/or other Communities of Color. They have perpetuated deficit perceptions and stereotypes of Communities of Color and supported anti-immigrant policies in their rhetoric and policymaking. Indeed, these race traitors have become "pawns" in the game to maintain white dominance. Through their political and intellectual influence, they have contributed to empowering institutional racism and ideologies of white supremacy. Bell's concept of "race traitor" is one example of the adaptation of racism that takes place within a process of racial realism, that is, structures of institutional racism adapting to allow some People of Color to have just enough power to keep their communities in their place within the racial hierarchy (see Figures 4.1 and 4.3).

In this chapter we have taken up an uncomfortable, but necessary, conversation about how racism manifests within Communities of Color. We believe that People of Color have agency to make decisions about how they do or do not participate in racism and white supremacy. However, white supremacy is embedded within all social institutions, which, in turn, influence the perspectives of all those who pass through them. As a result, deficit perspectives of Communities of Color often become normalized into widely held beliefs that blame these communities for social inequities and low educational outcomes. These deficit perspectives are so pervasive, they can infiltrate the ways that People of Color themselves view their own communities. Thus, People of Color can perpetuate racism and the ideologies of white supremacy that ensures its permanence. We have attempted to show this process in the models of internalized racism and internalized racist nativism that we have provided in this chapter. It is important to note that these models are simplified visuals of very complex processes and experiences. The models offer a conceptual beginning point to bring in the complexities and nuances of lived experience to understand how internalized racism occurs.

Historically, law, policy, and governance have protected white rights and white lives over those of People of Color (Bell, 1992a). Internalized racism and internalized racist nativism are symptoms of the disease of white supremacy that enables People of Color to believe the perceived inferiority of themselves and their communities, in a racial hierarchy where they take a perpetually subordinate status to whites. Institutionalized racism and racist nativism perpetuate this ugly cycle that can lead to conflict and even self-hate (Bagwell, 1994). The Clark Doll Experiment provided empirical evidence of internalized racism in the 1950s, while the race traitors of our society today and since show how internalized racism and racist nativism have persisted through time. Anzaldúa (2002) opened our discussion of internalized racism in this chapter, and we close it with her reminder of hope for our communities as she ended her essay "La Prieta." She states, "I believe that by changing ourselves we can change the world" (p. 232). Anzaldúa (2002) believed that, through our resistance, transformation was possible. We focus on these possibilities in the following chapter.

CHAPTER 5

Responding to Racial Microaggressions
Theorizing Racial Microaffirmations

We opened the first chapter of this book with the stories of People of Color to bring their lived experiences to the center of our analysis. We return to the stories of People of Color as our book comes to a close. However, the stories we highlight here are different. Rather than the recounting of painful experiences of everyday racism, these stories focus on affirmation, humanity, and joy. We argue that Communities of Color have always responded to racial microaggressions in powerful and transformational ways. One of those responses is a concept we call *racial microaffirmations* (Pérez Huber, 2018; Solórzano, Pérez Huber, & Huber-Verjan, 2020). We began theorizing this concept 5 years before the writing of this book (see Solórzano, 2014).[1] In this chapter, we explain how we came to define, and later theorize, this concept that moves our analysis from everyday racism and systems of oppression to the resiliency and hope of Communities of Color.

Before providing our definition, we begin with a story from the memoir of African American literary critic and historian Henry Louis Gates, Jr. (1994). For us, Gates's story highlights what racial microaffirmations look like in the experiences of People of Color. It was this story that became the starting point to theorize the concept of racial microaffirmations.[2] Thus, his story precedes our definition. Gates begins his 1994 memoir, titled *Colored People*, with a letter to his daughters, Maggie and Liza. He explains that, in part, the letter is prompted by a question posed by Liza, about why Gates would talk to African American "strangers" on the street. Gates writes:

> Dear Maggie and Liza. . . . Last summer, I sat at a sidewalk café in Italy, and three or four "black" Italians walked casually by. . . . Each spoke to me; rather, each *nodded* [emphasis added] his head slightly or acknowledged me with a glance, ever so subtly. When growing up, we always did this with each other, passing boats in a sea of white folk. . . . Which is why I still *nod* or speak to black people on the streets and why it felt so good to be acknowledged by the Afro-Italians who passed my table at the café in Milan. . . . Above all, I enjoy the unselfconscious moments of a shared cultural intimacy, whatever form they

take, when no one else is watching, when no white people are around. . . . And I hope you'll understand why I continue to speak to colored people I pass on the streets.

Love, Daddy. (pp. xi–xvi)[3]

In his story, Gates (1994) explains why he chooses "to speak to colored people" he passes in the streets, even though (according to his daughters) they may seem to be strangers. Gates explained that there were two purposes for why he does this. The first was to acknowledge other African Americans amid the "sea of white folks," as a strategy of acknowledgment in white-dominated space. The second purpose, he explained, was that this acknowledgment created a "shared cultural intimacy" among other African American people (p. xv). What Gates seems to suggest is that this "shared cultural intimacy" is an affirmative validation of Blackness amid white space, where People of Color often experience marginalization, exclusion, and erasure.[4]

We seek to name and theorize such moments in this chapter—those everyday forms of affirmation and validation that People of Color engage in a variety of public and private settings. The nods, smiles, embraces, use of language, and other actions that express acknowledgment, respect, and self-worth—what we call *racial microaffirmations*. We define racial microaffirmations as the subtle verbal or nonverbal strategies People of Color engage that affirm each other's dignity, integrity, and shared humanity. These moments of shared cultural intimacy allow People of Color to feel acknowledged, respected, and valued in a society that constantly and perpetually seeks to dehumanize them (Pérez Huber, 2018; Solórzano, Pérez Huber, & Huber-Verjan, 2020). We argue that racial microaffirmations can be one response to the everyday indignities posed by racial microaggressions (see Figure 2.1 in Chapter 2).

THEORIZING RACIAL MICROAFFIRMATIONS

Microaffirmations is a term that was first used, to our knowledge, in 2008 by economist Mary Rowe. Rowe (2008) used the term to describe effective mentorship practices for faculty and practitioners in academic and professional spheres. Rowe defined "micro-affirmations" as, "apparently small acts, which are often ephemeral and hard-to-see, events that are public and private, often unconscious but very effective, which occur whenever people wish to help others succeed" (p. 46). Rowe argued that "micro-affirmations" could improve professional environments and productivity when people's strengths were valued and acknowledged. Indeed, Rowe's (2008) idea is useful in naming everyday affirmations that make others feel validated. We were intrigued by this concept because Rowe explains how recognizing the strengths that people bring with them to the workplace can promote feelings of validation. We considered how such a concept could be used to develop a way to describe the strategies People of Color use to affirm each other. In 2014–2015, we began using the term *racial microaffirmations* in academic presentations to describe one way People of Color respond to racial microaggressions (see Pérez Huber & Huber-Verjan, 2015; Solórzano, 2014, 2015). Our conceptualization of racial microaffirmations is quite different from Rowe's. As we explained in our definition, and in the example we used from Gates's (1994) memoir, we focus on the everyday strategies of validation and acknowledgment People of Color utilize with and among each other. Our definition is more conceptually aligned with Jones and Rolón-Dow (2018), who also argue that racial microaffirmations "resist the impact of racism" through acts of affirmation and validation (p. 39). We extend the concept of racial microaffirmations from validation to naming strategies that seek to (re)claim the humanity and challenge the dehumanization of everyday racism (Pérez Huber, 2018; Solórzano, Pérez Huber, & Huber-Verjan, 2020).

Our conceptualization of racial microaffirmations led us to search the literature for theories that could help us ground an understanding of this concept. During this search, we found self-affirmation theory in psychology to be useful. Claude Steele first introduced self-affirmation theory in 1988 as a "self-system that essentially explains ourselves, and the world at large, to ourselves . . . activated by information that threatens the perceived adequacy or integrity of the self" (pp. 261–262). Steele (1988) explains that self-affirmation is a "coping process" used to maintain self-integrity when one experiences a cognitive dissonance that is "inconsistent with self-images of adequacy and integrity" (p. 277). In other words, when an individual has an experience that challenges their self-integrity (e.g., racial microaggressions), the person will engage in what Steele calls "adaptive reactions" to reduce the "sting-to-self" and eliminate the perceived threat in an effort to maintain their integrity. Steele (1988) examined this phenomenon in a series of experimental tests where people were exposed to some negative perception of themselves (e.g., being perceived as uncooperative). In responding to the threat, the individuals engaged in "self-affirming actions" (e.g., agreeing to help) that validated their overall self-integrity by affirming characteristics of the self that were important to their identities (e.g., being helpful and collaborative) (p. 267). It is important to note that Steele argues "self-affirming action" does not necessarily directly challenge a specific threat to self-integrity (p. 268). Rather, he states, "an individual's primary self-defensive goal is to affirm the general integrity of the self, not to resolve the particular threat" (p. 268). Steele continues,

> because of this overriding goal, the motivation to adapt to a specific self-threat of one sort may be overcome by affirmation of the broader self-concept or of

an equally important, yet different, aspect of the self-concept, without resolving the provoking threat. (p. 268)

In other words, one may engage in self-affirming behaviors to validate self-integrity, without the expectation that they can resolve the threat. This finding may explain why People of Color continue to engage in racial microaffirmations, regardless of the permanence of racism, or racial realism (Bell, 1992a).[5]

In 2006 (18 years after Steele), Sherman and Cohen (2006) expanded on the theory of self-affirmation. They explained:

People can be affirmed by engaging in activities that remind them of "who they are" . . . those qualities that are central to how people see themselves . . . In a difficult situation reminders of these core values can provide people with perspective on who they are and anchor their sense of self-integrity in the face of threat . . . A "self-affirmation" makes salient one of these important core qualities or sources of identity. (p. 189)

Similar to Steele (1988), Sherman and Cohen (2006) argue that self-affirmations can lessen the negative effects of threats to the self by affirming important aspects of one's own identity to maintain a sense of "self-worth" (p. 184). However, Sherman and Cohen extend Steele's theorizing of self-affirmation to emphasize the significance of social identities (e.g., race, gender) in coping with threats. Thus, rather than being exposed to negative information or events about an individual's personality or habits—as was the case for most of Steele's experiments in 1988—Sherman and Cohen underline the significance of threats to "collective aspects of self." They state, "People will defend against threats to collective aspects of the self much as they defend against threats to individual or personal aspects of self . . . even when these events do not directly implicate oneself" (p. 206). In fact, psychological research has supported this claim, particularly as it relates to stereotype threat for People of Color.[6] We argue that negative racial group threats (such as stereotype threat) are a form of racial microaggressions. Thus, according to this psychological research, People of Color will engage in strategies to affirm a collective racial group's worth, what we call racial microaffirmations. Moreover, Sherman and Cohen (2006) argue that self-affirmations can deter negative health outcomes related to stress, and that "it is plausible that repeated affirmations might help people cope with daily stressors" (p. 199), such as the stress of everyday racial microaggressions. Finally, these researchers and others have found that self-affirmation strategies can improve academic outcomes for Students of Color in schools and in institutions of higher education (Cohen, Garcia, Purdie-Vaughns, Apfel, & Brzustoski, 2009; Layous, Davis, Garcia, Purdie-Vaughns, Cook, & Cohen, 2017; Walton & Cohen, 2011).

It is clear to us that psychological research has already begun to theorize self-affirmations among People of Color by examining how they happen and how People of Color are impacted by them. We argue that the theorizing of self-affirmation in psychology provides evidence of the possibilities of racial microaffirmations. However, our theorizing of racial microaffirmations departs from this research through our focus on the explicit ways those affirmations are related to an individual and collective sense of worth, among racial groups. This is exactly what we believe Gates (1994) refers to in his description of "shared cultural intimacy" (p. xv) and exactly what we refer to in our explanation of racial microaffirmations as affirming the shared humanity of People of Color.

EXAMPLES OF RACIAL MICROAFFIRMATIONS: EXISTING LITERATURE

Once we found theoretical grounding for the concept of racial microaffirmations, our next step was to explore existing literature to find examples. As with Gates (1994), we knew that writers and scholars would not necessarily be using the term *racial microaffirmations* to describe their experiences. However, having a clear definition and a theoretical grounding provided a set of guidelines to see the multiple ways that racial microaffirmations could emerge in everyday life. We found several powerful examples that we will explain here. Thus, we began this next step in our research with the question, *what other examples of racial microaffirmations can we find in the literature?*

To begin this search, we returned to Gates's (1994) retelling of what we would argue is a racial microaffirmation. What Gates described was a complex and nuanced cultural understanding of a simple gesture, a head nod. Although we are not members of the African American community, we understood that the head nod is an important and culturally significant act within the Black community, demonstrating acknowledgment and respect. Thus, our next step was searching for literature that would explore the significance of the nod. Indeed, we found several important pieces that included a discussion of this type of racial microaffirmation. These works are important, because: (1) They show how a racial microaffirmation is distinct from race-neutral affirmations, such as those Rowe (2008) outlines, and (2) how racial microaffirmations are a response to everyday racism and systemic oppression.

Sociologist Michael Eric Dyson (2001) explains the historical significance of racial codes utilized by African Americans dating back to slavery. Dyson explains, "In slavery, our forebears had to devise a means of communication that slipped the notice of the majority culture, since what they had to say sometimes challenged the status quo . . . After slavery, the need for codes persisted" (p. 93). These codes persisted, Dyson argues, because

African Americans could not freely express themselves in "a hostile white world" (p. 93). The nod, then, has become one of these codes. For Dyson, the nod is also a gendered code. Dyson explains:

> At its root, the nod may be most useful for its affirming role in the politics of acknowledgment among black men. American society remains reluctant to recognize our humanity. Or more fundamentally, that we exist at all. The nod is a way of literally and figuratively saying, "I know you exist. I see you. I acknowledge your being." (p. 94)

In Dyson's explanation of the nod, he describes the act of acknowledgment and the recognition of humanity that we theorized in our understanding of a racial microaffirmation. In Dyson's explanation, the nod is also a gendered act, specifically affirming Black men. Other Black scholars, however, discuss the nod in more general terms, as a culturally significant gesture practiced by Black communities, regardless of gender. For example, sociologist Elijah Anderson (2018) explains what he calls the "the racial nod":

> Being generally outnumbered by white people, black people feel a peculiar vulnerability, and they assume that other black people understand the challenges of this space in ways that white people cannot. Since the white space can turn hostile at any moment, the implicit promise of support black people sense from other black people serves as a defense, and it is part of the reason that black people acknowledge one another in this space, with the racial nod—an informal greeting serving as a trigger that activates black solidarity in this space. (The Nod section, para. 2)

Like Anderson (2018), Black journalist Musa Okwonga (2014) reiterates the meaning of the nod to take on an element of unspoken community solidarity amid hostility. Okwonga states:

> The Nod is also so much more than that: It's a swift yet intimate statement of ethnic solidarity . . . That means it's always a privilege to receive The Nod, which is the closest thing to a secret handshake I will probably ever have. Sometimes, though, it's bittersweet, reflecting how far black people yet have to go to feel at home in their surroundings. (paras. 2, 6)

Finally, African American Studies professor James Jones (2017) examined how race is structured into the organization of the U.S. Congressional workplace. Among his findings was that Black staffers (men and women) utilized the nod as an adaptive strategy to feel seen in a white male–dominated environment where they are often rendered unseen. In Jones's (2017) study, the nod transcended professional rank, class, and age as a practice engaged by all levels of African Americans in Congress, from service employees to

Congress members. It was used to facilitate introductions between Black people on Capitol Hill, to acknowledge "a shared experience" among them, and to gauge shared viewpoints and value systems.[7]

Our research on the meaning of the nod practiced in African American communities solidified our initial cultural intuition[8] that this gesture could be considered a racial microaffirmation.[9] The scholars and writers we have mentioned here share deep and meaningful insights into this act found to be marked by a desire to build solidarity and empowerment within white space. As Gates (1994) first described in his memoir, this research confirmed for us that the nod is a powerful example of a racial microaffirmation practiced among the African American community. Our research on the nod prompted us to consider what kinds of racial microaffirmations we may encounter in our own Latina/o communities.

Our next example comes from previous research we have engaged with my (Lindsay) eldest daughter, Layla. For several years, we have worked with Layla to understand how racial microaggressions emerge in the everyday experiences of Youth of Color. Layla found that one of her first memories of a racial microaggression was an image she found in a children's book, with a racist depiction of a "Mexican bandit" (Pérez Huber & Solórzano, 2015a; Solórzano, Pérez Huber, & Huber-Verjan, 2020). As her work identifying racial microaggressions progressed, she began to develop an understanding of racial microaffirmations, a concept we were just beginning to explore. Layla found that children's literature could also be a place where racial microaffirmations could be found that empowered Youth of Color (Solórzano, Pérez Huber, & Huber-Verjan, 2020). Layla explained:

> I started thinking about what the opposite of a microaggression would be. I thought about the book I was reading at school during that time, *Esperanza Rising,* by Pam Muñoz Ryan (2002). I explained to my mom that the main character, Esperanza, was a young Latina girl from a wealthy family in Mexico. After her family experienced several tragedies, Esperanza and her mother lost their home in a tragic fire. Esperanza and her mother had no choice but to move to a migrant camp and work as laborers in the fields of the Central Valley in California. The book was an example of what the opposite of a microaggression is because Esperanza persevered through very hard times and is a great role model for other Latina girls, like me. I felt proud to be able to share the same race as Esperanza. (p. 204)

While in earlier research Layla had found children's literature to be an unfortunate source of racial microaggressions, she found that children's books could also be a place where children are empowered and affirmed by the stories and characters they read about. It has been found that Children of Color are far less likely to read books with characters that reflect their own racial identities (Pérez Huber, Camargo Gonzalez & Solórzano, 2018).

However, Layla's story illustrates the affirming power of children's books that include positive portrayals of People of Color.

Layla's example prompts another important question about racial microaffirmations: *What are the ways adults can engage microaffirmations with Children of Color?* This question led us to other examples of microaffirmations in the field of education. Janie Victoria Ward's (1996) research examined how Black mothers socialize their daughters to maintain self-esteem and self-worth through culturally specific parenting practices. In her work, she features the story of one Black mother, Lillian:

> When my daughter Patsy was four, I would sit her down between my legs and every morning as I combed and braided her hair I would have her reach up and run her hands through it. "Look," I'd say, "Look at how pretty your hair is . . . Look at how different it is from your little white friends and how special that is." (p. 85)

In Ward's research, this mother strategically engaged the practice of affirming her young daughter's beauty by complimenting her hair. This was an attempt to validate her daughter's beauty and worth, in a world where beauty is defined by whiteness.

In a similar education study about Latina mothers, Bianca Guzmán (2012) explained how the culturally specific practices of sharing *cuentos*, *consejos*, and *pláticas*[10] with daughters can create positive self-agency for Latina girls that enables them to challenge racism and other forms of subordination in their lives. In a separate psychology study, J. Parker Goyer and colleagues (2017) examined how positive affirmations of middle school Students of Color (Latinas/os and African Americans) led to increased levels of self-esteem and long-term positive academic outcomes. Such studies highlight the prevalence and significance of racial microaffirmations in the lives of Youth of Color.

We have found other examples of microaffirmations in existing literature. We would argue that legal scholar Margaret Montoya's (1994) use of the Spanish language (and storytelling) in her groundbreaking law article "Máscaras, Trenzas y Greñas: Un/masking the Self While Un/braiding Latina Stories and Legal Discourse" is a strategy to affirm her own "mestiza" identity, and that of other Latina/o readers (p. 32).[11] Montoya (1994) writes:

> The Euro-American conquest of the Southwest and Puerto Rico resulted in informal and formal prohibitions against the use of Spanish for public purposes. So by inscribing myself in legal scholarship as *mestiza*, I seek to occupy common ground with Latinas/os in this hemisphere and others, wherever situated, who are challenging Western bourgeois ideology and hegemonic racialism. (p. 32–33)

Montoya explains that her use of the Spanish language is a conscious strategy to express solidarity with other Latina/o scholars concerned with racial justice in legal writing. In this act of disruption of the traditional legal canon, Montoya utilizes language to signal recognition and affirmation to other critical Latina/o and Spanish-speaking scholars in the legal academy. Indeed, Montoya (1994) argues that, "incorporating Spanish words, sayings, literature, and wisdom can have positive ramifications for those in the academy and in the profession, and for those to whom we render legal services" (p. 34). Montoya shows us that racial microaffirmations in scholarship and literature can go beyond the politics of representation—beyond the *seeing* of others *like you* represented in writing—and toward a conscious strategy to subvert the discursive power that mediates what formats become "traditional" in academic scholarship. Montoya did this with her groundbreaking article in multiple ways. Her use of language was one, but her use of personal narrative and counterstorytelling were also unique and a strategic contribution to academic legal scholarship. These subversive strategies invite People of Color to engage with texts they have historically been excluded from. Indeed, Montoya's work suggests that there are pedagogical implications of racial microaffirmations.

EXAMPLES OF RACIAL MICROAFFIRMATIONS: OUR PERSONAL STORIES

When I think about racial microaffirmations, I (Lindsay) think about the moments spent with my daughters each year at their annual *baile folklórico* performances. This traditional Mexican dance performance has its roots in regional community dance forms in Mexico that were eventually adapted for stage performance (Najera-Ramirez, 2009). Each dance in the performance highlights the regional dance and music styles of the Mexican state from which it comes. This dance is always accompanied by music (and is even better with live music), and there are certain mariachi-genre songs that are very likely to be played at these performances. "Son de la Negra" and "La Madrugada" are almost always included in Mexican *baile folklórico* performances in the U.S. Southwest.[12] Although I did not necessarily listen to these songs growing up in my household, hearing them—particularly as they are accompanied by Latina/o dancers, and especially children—has an effect on me. When I see them dressed in their bright, colorful dresses, dancing to music that celebrates Latina/o culture, it is a sight of beauty inspired by cultural pride. Each time (they have performed for many years) I get goosebumps. Music in our communities (and in others) can be a powerful form of racial microaffirmation.[13] It can remind us of the beauty of the countries we are from, or the countries from where our elders/ancestors have come, of home. This has meaning particularly when you live in a place where your people are often demonized as criminals and economic burdens, and treated as second-class citizens (Chavez, 2008; Pérez Huber, 2016).

When I see and hear their dancing, I am reminded of the privilege I have to be able to engage in the (re)claiming of our culture and language with my daughters. From family stories passed down from my elders who lived in the U.S. Southwest for generations (Texas and California), I knew they constantly encountered racist nativist messages, particularly in schools—that Spanish was a "bad" language, not allowed to be spoken, that being Mexican meant being less than, and that it was necessary to make strategic moves toward whiteness to avoid some of the harshest discrimination. My mother, aunt, and uncle all changed their names as elementary students at their predominately white Catholic school, when nuns couldn't pronounce them, and their peers teased them. My grandparents did not speak Spanish to them, or to my sisters and me, as we later grew up with them. Today, I understand my family history and the choices they made to be mediated by racism and racist nativism. I also understand the consequences of this legacy of racist nativism. It has led to difficult moments in developing racial and cultural identities and an understanding and confidence in who I am and where I belong, and it has led to the linguistic terrorism[14] I have experienced. However, as a parent, I could play a role in taking back *some* of what was taken from us. There have been many choices and efforts made to do this; dancing *folklorico* was one of them. Their dancing is a type of racial microaffirmation that is a response to the generations of racism experienced by my family in the U.S. Southwest.

As I (Danny) reflect on how I came to racial microaffirmations, I'm reminded of my experiences growing up in neighborhoods to the east of Downtown Los Angeles. My father, Manuel Solórzano Sr., inculcated in me a love of our communities. Not just the Latina/o communities of the eastside, but the African American communities of the southside, and the Asian American communities of Little Tokyo and Chinatown near Downtown Los Angeles. Riding with my father through these neighborhoods delivering Mexican bread to small markets throughout the neighborhoods of East L.A., South Central L.A., and Downtown L.A. infused a knowledge of these communities, a respect for these communities, a love of these communities. It was my first introduction to the community cultural wealth that existed all through these communities. These journeys affirmed for me their beauty, their history, and my place in these communities.[15] My later coming to ethnic studies generally, and Chicana/o and African American studies in particular, was further affirmation of my history and others' histories—the stories of People of Color. And now, as faculty, every year I attend Chicana/o Studies departmental graduations and Raza graduations. These culminating events are further affirmations for students, their families, their communities, and for us, their faculty.

EXAMPLES OF RACIAL MICROAFFIRMATIONS: EMPIRICAL EVIDENCE

With the concept of racial microaffirmations being a recent development, studies have yet to examine the topic empirically. Thus, our next step in theorizing was to empirically investigate racial microaffirmations. Our most recent work was conducted with the assistance of my (Lindsay's) graduate students Tamara Gonzalez and Gabriela Robles. The study explores how Graduate Students of Color at a public 4-year university in California experience racial microaffirmations in schools, at home, and in their communities. This study confirmed our theorizing of racial microaffirmations and the existing literature that implicitly supports it, showing how students feel acknowledged, valued, and validated by these everyday acts. We also found that just as there are types and contexts of racial microaggressions (see Figure 2.1; Pérez Huber, 2015), there are types and contexts of racial microaffirmations.

Ariel was a 1st-year male-identified Latino graduate student. He shared that in one of his classes he was learning about former Mexican president Benito Juárez, and coincidentally encountered a mural of him on his university campus. Ariel shared:

> Being an activist, and also being in political science, I was learning about other leaders around the world. It just so happened that I was learning about Benito Juárez. Even though I'm from Ciudad Juarez, which [is named] after him, I really don't know much about him. So I was walking . . . and I pass by La Raza building and somebody was painting a portrait of Benito Juarez. When I saw that, I was just like, what? You have that here? I felt that connection and I was just like happy. The following week I went [back] and checked it out. And once I went inside [the building] and I saw that they had different photographs of other leaders, I felt I [could] identify, and I felt like all these are my [people]. (personal communication, October 24, 2019)

Ariel explains that although he is from the Mexican city named after this historic leader (Ciudad Juárez), he knew very little about Benito Juárez's life until he learned about him during his undergraduate career. Seeing the mural of Juárez on his campus was surprising, and he immediately felt a connection. The image prompted him to return to the building where it was displayed, and where the multicultural center was located. Here, he found more photos of Latina/o leaders. Seeing them made him feel connected to his community. The type of microaffirmation that Ariel describes is a visual racial microaffirmation experienced within the context of his university.[16]

Brittany is an Afro-Latina woman who recently completed her graduate program. She is a case worker at a nonprofit organization in Los Angeles focused on re-entry support for formerly incarcerated youth. In her example,

Brittany explains how music can play a role in racial microaffirmations. The context that she describes is her workplace. Brittany shared:

> Unfortunately, formerly incarcerated [people] are mostly Black and Brown. I think when they come into the office, it's kind of like a dual affirmation, where I feel like I can be myself and I'm not in a space filled with white people doing nonprofit work. I'm in a space filled with People of Color, and I'm playing hip hop music when they're coming by the office. I'm playing jazz and salsa. I feel that kind of makes them feel welcome because they are often pushed out of spaces, and led down a path that society forced them into. So the office space feels like the center of a racial microaffirmation, where you're providing services in an authentic way, and they feel comfortable being able to express themselves, and we get to know [them] on a deeper level. So that feels really good. (personal communication, March 7, 2019)

Here, Brittany explains how she utilizes music that has cultural relevance for the communities she works with as a way to discursively open her office door for the mostly African American and Latina/o youth she serves. She also explains that a racial microaffirmation can be a "dual" experience, being simultaneously affirming for the person giving and for the person receiving the microaffirmation. In this case, she is affirmed by the Youth of Color that she works with, and they are affirmed by her support as they share space and time in this predominately white nonprofit organization.

Teresa shares a similar experience, showing us that space can be a type of racial microaffirmation. Teresa is a 1st-year graduate student and full-time teacher who identifies as Latina. She teaches 2nd-graders at a predominately Latina/o elementary school in Los Angeles. In her example, Teresa describes a morning routine she engages each day with her students in the classroom.

> I try to affirm my students every day, all day because I'm a firm believer in a holistic approach to education, and especially [with] little ones. I think it's really important to build that foundation. So every morning before we walk in, we do a call. We do a lot of "call and response" and I say, "Hey there scholars!" They say, "Hey, Ms. Lozano." And then I say, "I'm here and I see you!" And then they respond, "It feels good to be seen!" So every day, they start their day knowing that their presence is valued and important. And then after we have breakfast, we stand up and we do a poem, an excerpt [from a TedTalk] that I got from an educator named Dr. Rita Pearson. We say, "I am somebody. I was somebody when I came. I'll be a better somebody when I leave. I am powerful. I am strong. I deserve

the education that I get here. I have things to do, people to impress and places to go." And we say that every morning no matter what. They don't know, but I'm also affirming myself when I say that. So I think it's important when you're affirming others, you're also affirming yourself as well. And I think that that really builds that community and that understanding of our shared humanity. (personal communication, March 7, 2019)

In Teresa's powerful example she explains a strategic pedagogical practice as a racial microaffirmation that she engages in her 2nd-grade classroom. She utilizes a call-and-response method, coupled with a poem excerpt, to ensure that her students begin each day feeling "seen" and "important," and reminding them that they are "powerful." Teresa's experience also confirms Brittany's idea of what she called a "dual" microaffirmation. That is, the mutual reciprocity that can be experienced by People of Color that engage in racial microaffirmations. Teresa builds on this idea by suggesting that it is the mutual reciprocity that can lead to solidarity and a sense of "shared humanity" in the act of a racial microaffirmation.

In this chapter we have just begun to scratch the proverbial surface of what we believe is a concept with great potential and depth. Indeed, racial microaffirmation is an everyday strategy of resistance. However, it is also something more. It is a particular form of resistance marked by the desire to affirm the dignity and humanity of People of Color—those qualities significant to all human beings—but often denied by institutional racism and white supremacy. Racial microaffirmations, then, are a (re)claiming of the dignity and humanity that everyday racism attempts to take from Communities of Color. We have only begun to explore the many ways that racial microaffirmations can emerge. We believe racial microaffirmations can be seen all around us, in everyday environments, if we pay attention. For example, spaces created by and for People of Color can be a racial microaffirmation, such as the Raza graduations Danny described in this chapter. Layla Huber-Verjan described how racial microaffirmations can emerge in texts (Solórzano, Pérez Huber, & Huber-Verjan, 2020). Lindsay described a type of racial microaffirmation experienced through music and performance. The participants in our focus groups described other examples in art and pedagogy. In the Introduction to this book, Danny described how a high school student once shared that learning about racial microaggressions gave her a way to "name" her pain. We believe that racial microaffirmations can provide a language for People of Color to name their humanity.

Racial microaffirmation is a concept that reminds us that our dignity is already within us, and that we affirm it every day with our families, in our communities, with colleagues, and with those whom we may not know, but with whom we share a "cultural intimacy" that binds us in our collective humanity. While this empirical research on racial microaffirmations has just begun, our research thus far has found that racial microaffirmations are already practiced in schools, communities, workplaces, homes, and many other spaces occupied by Communities of Color. If we were to look, we are sure racial microaffirmations could be found throughout history, in the struggles of People of Color for dignity and humanity in the face of racism.[17] Put simply, racial microaffirmations are those everyday reminders that we matter—and we believe Communities of Color have been telling each other this, in their own ways, since the beginning.

CHAPTER 6

Conclusion

This book has been an attempt to bring together the ideas, concepts, and theorizing around racial microaggressions that have developed from our critical race research projects conducted (collectively) during the past 2 and a half decades. Our intention was to bring together our work to provide a set of tools for those interested in engaging critical race research and praxis on racial microaggressions. We hope that these tools provide some readers with a language to "name" the pain of everyday racism, as one African American high school student once shared it did for her.

During our years of research, we have learned important lessons about studying everyday racism. First, a racial microaggressions analysis should always include an examination (or at the very least, an acknowledgment) of the structural conditions that lead to everyday racism. As we have discussed throughout the book, examining the structural conditions that lead to everyday racism is critical to understanding how racism is (re)produced over time. Moreover, this structural analysis shifts the focus from the people targeted by racial microaggressions, and toward the social conditions that limit the life opportunities of People of Color. Without this focus, culturally deficit perspectives of Communities of Color become more easily utilized to explain everyday racism and the social inequities that shape it.[1] Indeed, this is at the core of our argument, to delve beyond the symptoms of racism and to acknowledge the disease of white supremacy, as Judge Robert Carter (1988) once urged.

Second, history teaches us that resistance is born from struggle. As certain as we are that racism exists, we also know that it is and has been challenged and resisted every day by Communities of Color. It is critical to examine and understand the many forms racism takes on in our society. However, it is just as important to recognize and name the ways People of Color respond to it. In doing so, we honor the many forms of resistance Communities of Color have engaged and continue to engage that seek to challenge and transform racism (Solórzano & Delgado Bernal, 2001). In our theorizing we have tried to be intentional about acknowledging resistance to everyday racism for these reasons.

Third, we need to affirm the dignity and humanity of People of Color that this resistance demands. This means acknowledging, supporting, and valuing the presence and contributions Communities of Color bring with them to any public or private space. Recognizing the everyday strategies of racial microaffirmations People of Color engage is crucial for understanding responses and resistance to microaggressions. Moreover, it is important to also recognize the ways racial microaffirmations operate outside of the construct of racial microaggressions.

The concept of racial microaffirmations can stand alone conceptually because its existence lies in the agency of Communities of Color, rather than in systemic racism and white supremacy. Racial microaffirmations can move toward transformation of injustice by focusing analysis on the ways Communities of Color have, and continue to affirm, a shared humanity and collective self-worth. Thus, it is important to acknowledge those everyday strategies utilized by People of Color to let others know "I see you"—those small moments of affirmation that can get lost if we do not stop to acknowledge them.

We have discussed each of these lessons in this book, although we realize that our contributions are only a beginning. To our knowledge, this is the first book to theorize racial microaggressions from an explicit Critical Race Theory (CRT) perspective in education. We look forward to the work of other scholars who will continue to further theorize, critique, and build upon the models we have provided throughout this book. We believe that these models of racial microaggressions also provide important implications for practitioners in the field of education and others who serve Communities of Color. We hope that they can be used for implementing strategies to counter racial microaggressions, and to acknowledge racial microaffirmations in education and beyond. As we conclude, we offer a few beginning points for future research and praxis on everyday racism.

FUTURE RESEARCH ON RACIAL MICROAGGRESSIONS: PROMISING AREAS

One gap in racial microaggressions research is the study of everyday racism with Youth of Color, generally, and those in K–12 schools in particular. Much of the research on racial microaggressions in education focuses on higher education contexts with college-age students. However, scholars have found that preschool-age children have already developed an understanding of race and racism (Tatum, 1997; Van Ausdale & Feagin, 2001), and these perceptions mediate their peer preferences (Spencer, 1984), and how they differentiate themselves from others (Tronya & Hatcher, 1992). Yet educational research exploring race and racism with young children is sparse, and even more so with Children of Color. This work is especially urgent in the current moment. Research has found that Students of Color have experienced an increase in racially hostile school environments since the election of Donald Trump in 2016 (Huang & Cornell, 2019; Rogers et al., 2017; Rogers et al., 2019). This research suggests that the racist rhetoric perpe-trated by the Donald Trump presidency has had profoundly negative effects on Students of Color throughout the United States. Indeed, students across the nation will feel these negative effects long after his presidency. Thus, research on racial microaggressions in K–12 schools is particularly urgent now, and will continue to be far into the future. Findings in this area can lead to theorizing effective curricular and pedagogical interventions on rac-ism in elementary, middle, and high schools that could equip students with important tools they can use into adulthood. For example, Dolores Lopez's (2017) study on the experiences of Latina/o elementary school students and racial microaggressions found that, indeed, children understand how they are targeted by everyday racism in a dual-immersion instruction school. Her study suggested that a "critical pedagogy curriculum" that incorporates an asset-based perspective on the Spanish language and Latina/o culture could have been useful to help students mitigate racial microaggressions.

Another opportunity for the study of everyday racism is to explore what we call visual microaggressions. In Chapter 2, we briefly mentioned visual microaggressions as one type of racial microaggression that can be seen in everyday environments. We noted in that chapter that visual racial microaggressions are often nonverbal representations of racist ideas and beliefs about People of Color (Pérez Huber & Solórzano, 2015b). These visual assaults can emerge in various forms. For example, in Chapter 5, Layla Huber-Verjan described how we can see visual microaggressions in textbooks and children's books when People of Color are portrayed in ra-cially stereotypical ways, or erased from important historical events (Pérez Huber & Solórzano, 2015b). They can be seen in advertisements, photos, film and television, dance and theater performances, and public signage and statuary. Similar to the ways that microaggressions function, visual micro-aggressions reinforce institutional racism and perpetuate the ideologies of white supremacy that justify the subordination of People of Color. Visual microaggressions are an important type of microaggression to explore be-cause they often quietly convey implicit, deficit, and racist messages about People of Color. One powerful example is an image captured in 1956 by renowned African American photographer Gordon Parks (see Figure 6.1). The image, titled "Department Store," shows an African American wom-an with a young African American girl (maybe 6 years old), both dressed in their Sunday best, standing on a sidewalk in Mobile, Alabama (Parks, 1956). They stand under a sign with red neon lights that reads "COLORED ENTRANCE" with a blue neon arrow pointing toward the door right be-hind where they stand gazing across to the opposite side of the street.[2] Parks documented the everyday experiences of this woman and little girl and so many other African Americans during the segregation era in the South. It captures both the everyday subtlety and the racial violence experienced by

Figure 6.1. Gordon Parks, "Department Store, Mobile, Alabama, 1956"

Photograph by Gordon Parks. Courtesy of and copyright The Gordon Parks Foundation.

African Americans during the Jim Crow Era. In recent work we have documented visual forms of microaggressions in Latina/o communities. We found that stereotypical images of Mexican banditry have persisted for over 100 years in film, and are present today in children's books, advertisements, and school celebrations (Pérez Huber & Solórzano, 2015b). Many forms of visual microaggressions go unnoticed because they have become normalized within everyday environments, yet their racist messages are powerful.

Another promising area of racial microaggressions research is work that takes a quantitative approach to examine the negative health consequences of everyday racism. We would argue that research in the health sciences on racial discrimination indicates that there are measurable psychological and physiological effects of racial microaggressions (Beatty Moody, et al., 2019;

Chae et al., 2016; Chae, Lincoln, Alder, & Syme, 2010; Chae et al., 2012; Gravlee et al., 2005; Harrell, 2000; Hill, Kobayashi, & Hughes, 2007; Park, Du, Wang, Williams, & Alegria, 2018; Watson, 2019; Williams, Yu, Jackson, & Anderson, 1997; Williams, 2018; Zeiders, Doane, & Roosa, 2012). This research provides the quantitative evidence for Dr. Chester Pierce's argument decades ago—that everyday racism can lead to negative health outcomes for People of Color. Research on the effects of racial microaggressions is critical to our understanding of how everyday racism impacts the minds and bodies of Communities of Color. However, we also wonder how we can quantitatively measure other ways People of Color experience racial microaggressions. For example, quantitative research on campus climate in higher education informs an understanding of how Students of Color experience racist institutional cultures (Hurtado, Alvarado, & Guillermo-Wann, 2015; Hurtado, Milem, Clayton-Pedersen, & Allen, 1999). In turn, racially hostile campus climates can have negative consequences for Students of Color. One question for quantitative researchers interested in taking up this area of research would be: *How can we quantitatively measure experiences of everyday racism on college campuses? In schools? In the workplace, or in other spaces?*

Some of the current research on racial discrimination and microaggressions provides insight into how we could begin to answer such questions. For example, Franklin, Smith, and Hung (2014) examined the "racial battle fatigue" of Latina/o college students who experience racial microaggressions. Racial battle fatigue examines the psychological, physiological, and behavioral stress responses People of Color have to racial microaggressions. We found that the measures that this study used are borrowed from a more extensive body of research in public health that we would argue is directly related to racial microaggressions.

Public health scientist David R. Williams (2016) has developed the "everyday discrimination scale" to empirically investigate the effects of racial discrimination and socioeconomic status (SES) on the physical and mental health of People of Color compared to their white counterparts in the United States and South Africa (Sterthnal, Slopen, & Williams, 2011; Williams et al., 2008; Williams et al., 1997). The findings of these studies consistently indicate that Black communities (in the United States and abroad) experience higher frequencies of everyday discrimination than whites that can be correlated to negative health outcomes and, ultimately, to health disparities between these groups.

Williams (2016) uses several versions of the everyday discrimination scale, and we can adapt the measure to ask "In your day-to-day life, how often do any of the following happen to you?," followed by a series of statements, some including:

- You are treated with less respect than other people are.
- You are treated with less courtesy than other people are.

- People act as if they think you are not smart.
- People act as if they are afraid of you.
- You receive poorer service than other people at restaurants, offices, or bookstores.

These questions are then followed by possible responses to measure the frequencies of these experiences (i.e., every day, once a week, a few times a week or year, less than once a year, or never) (Williams, 2016). Although Williams and his colleagues do not use the term racial microaggressions to describe these experiences, we would argue—as we have throughout this book—that these everyday forms of discrimination are, in fact, racial micro-aggressions. Thus, Williams's research would be a beginning point for future researchers interested in quantifying racial microaggressions in school/university settings. In fact, Williams et al. (1997) recommend that future research include other non-Black racial groups. We would extend this suggestion to recommend that research on Latina/o communities is urgently needed, considering their population growth across the nation (U.S. Census Bureau, 2019). Even more specifically, future research could correlate heightened anti-immigrant sentiment since the 2016 election of Donald Trump, racist nativist microaggressions, and negative health outcomes.

Related to Williams's (Williams et al., 1997) everyday discrimination scale is the "heightened vigilance scale," which assesses how African Americans respond, or anticipate, everyday discrimination (William, 2016; Williams et al., 2012). This scale uses the measure "In your day-to-day life, how often do you do the following things?," followed by these items:

- Try to prepare for possible insults from other people before leaving home.
- Feel that you always have to be very careful about your appearance (to get good service or avoid being harassed).
- Carefully watch what you say and how you say it.
- Try to avoid certain social situations and places.

These responses gauge what Williams calls the "emotional responses" and "stressfulness" associated with racial discrimination (Williams et al., 2012, p. 977). Examples of some of the responses measured with the heightened vigilance scale are: anger, frustration, powerlessness, vulnerability, inferiority, and resignation. Similar to our Types, Contexts, Effects and Response Model (see Figure 2.1) for racial microaggressions, Williams's research on vigilance examines the range of responses African Americans have to racial discrimination, and especially those individuals from low-SES households. The research on vigilance provides a pathway for future research to quantitatively document responses to racial microaggressions. We would recommend that future research continue this line of inquiry but also seek to explore the more transformational responses People of Color have to everyday racism that we outline (Chapter 2), such as resistance, and, possibly, racial microaffirmations (Chapter 5).

As we explain in Chapter 5, future research on racial microaffirmations is much needed, as it is a relatively new concept in educational research. Quantitatively, we believe it is possible that the current scale instruments created by Williams and colleagues (1997, 2016) to explore racial discrimination could be adapted to capture racial microaffirmations. These scales could be used to examine racial microaffirmations in a range of contexts: in schools, universities, workplaces, and other spaces. Racial microaffirmation scales could also be used to examine collections of textbooks, artwork, and other textual and visual materials where Communities of Color are represented and affirmed. For example, if we adapted the Williams and colleagues's (1997, 2016) everyday discrimination scale outlined above to measure racial microaffirmations, we could first explore *how* People of Color feel affirmed in their everyday lives. Building from Willams's scale, we could ask, "In your day-to-day life how are you acknowledged, affirmed, or valued in your school/institution setting?" Drawing from our research thus far on racial microaffirmations, this question could be followed by these possible measures:

- Through the use of language (e.g., a language other than English, vernacular language/expressions)
- Through physical gestures (e.g., a nod, a smile, eye contact)
- Through the presence of other People of Color
- Through artwork, murals, paintings, photography, films, or other visuals
- Through books, textbooks, magazines, research articles, or other texts

Similar to Williams's (2016) scale, the recommended response categories could be: almost every day, at least once a week, a few times a month, a few times a year, less than once a year, or never. This scale could assess how racial microaffirmations are experienced, while another scale could be developed to understand the effects of these racial microaffirmations.

If we were to create a scale to capture the effects of racial microaffirmations, or, *how* a microaffirmation makes a Person of Color feel, then we could ask, "In your day-to-day life, how often do any of the following happen to you when you are with other (Latina/o, African American, Asian American, or Native American) students at your (institution type)?" This question could be followed by these measures:

- You feel acknowledged or valued.
- You feel more comfortable, relieved, or at ease.

- You feel seen.
- You feel appreciated.
- You feel respected.

These measures could then be followed by the same response categories as used by Williams (2016). Everyday racial microaffirmations scales, if we were to call them this, would focus on *how* a Person of Color experiences a racial microaffirmation and how it makes them *feel*. As renowned African American writer Maya Angelou said, "People will forget what you said, people will forget what you did, but people will never forget how you made them feel."[3] We believe this may be one powerful way that quantitative research could capture racial microaffirmations.

A qualitative approach for each of these areas of inquiry is also needed. For example, in a current study we are conducting with one of our graduate students, Lorena Camargo Gonzalez, we seek to engage what we call a Critical Race Content Analysis to examine the racial representations of Characters of Color in children's early reader books. A Critical Race Content Analysis (CRCA) utilizes the tenets of CRT to engage a critical reading of children's books that forefronts raced (and intersectional) representations within the narratives and images of children's literature (Pérez Huber, Camargo Gonzalez, & Solórzano, 2018; Pérez Huber, Camargo Gonzalez, & Solórzano, under review). CRCA functions to locate power within storylines, uncover dominant ideologies that circulate within the narrative, and examine cultural authenticity. We encourage this analysis to be approached from an interdisciplinary perspective and be guided by social justice goals. We have designed qualitative analysis rubrics to engage CRCA to examine racialized representations, as well as the ways resistance emerges through children's stories. One of the ways that resistance can emerge is through racial microaffirmations, as Layla Huber-Verjan (Solórzano, Pérez Huber, & Huber-Verjan, 2020) describes in Chapter 5. This project is one example of how critical race tools can be developed to examine racial microaffirmations in children's literature, but could also be adapted to examine other textual and visual forms of writing and images (i.e., textbooks, photography and visual arts, film and media, social media, literature for adults).

We believe there are other important areas of future research on racial microaffirmations to mention here. First, studies can more closely examine the interactional dimensions of racial microaffirmations. As our focus group data suggested in Chapter 5, college Students of Color mention what we call "mutual reciprocity" when engaging in a microaffirmation. However, we also do not assume that microaffirmations are *always* mutually reciprocal. In addition, we do not yet fully understand the meaning-making involved in the exchange of racial microaffirmations. For example, what role does a Person of Color's community and/or family history play in how they engage racial microaffirmations? In how a microaffirmation is received? In how it is delivered or given? In Chapter 5 we discussed the nod as one type of racial microaffirmation practiced within the African American community. Some scholars have argued that this microaffirmation is mediated by gender (Dyson, 2001), others not (Anderson, 2018; Okwonga, 2014). Thus, future research questions could also explore how intersectionality emerges through racial microaffirmations. In addition, there is a need to explore how microaffirmations are experienced across (intergroup) and within (intragroup) Communities of Color.

Second, as current literature and our focus group data indicated, there are pedagogical implications of racial microaffirmations that could be especially important for education. In Chapter 5, one focus group participant, a Latina teacher, shared a powerful example of how she engaged daily racial microaffirmations with her elementary school students. This routine microaffirmation was utilized each day, reminding students that they are important and powerful. Similarly, in Chapter 5 we discussed the work of legal scholar Margaret Montoya (1994) and her use of language and storytelling to discursively "invite in" Latina/o communities to engage legal scholarship. We would argue that this is indeed a pedagogical strategy. In fact, Montoya engages other pedagogical strategies specific to teaching that could also serve as examples of racial microaffirmations, for example her work (with colleagues) on name narratives. A name narrative is a classroom practice that prompts Students of Color to explore their family histories, acknowledge their cultural capital, and understand how their life experiences are mediated by social structures (Montoya, Vásquez & Martínez, 2014). Name narratives as pedagogy is a strategy to affirm the cultures and experiences of Students of Color in the classroom, a space where they are often marginalized. These examples of pedagogical racial microaffirmations are only a few of what we believe are many critical pedagogies used by educators within and beyond the field of education. Future research would further explore and name others.

PRAXIS: DISRUPTING RACIAL MICROAGGRESSIONS

Before we conclude, we also wanted to provide some future directions for praxis. As researchers we often receive the question, "what can I do?" about racial microaggressions. Our response can depend on the person (or people) asking the question. For example, engaging this question with a Person of Color who experiences racial microaggressions would be different from engaging it with a white person who realizes that he may have microaggressed. For People of Color, we would argue that the onus of responsibility to recognize and disrupt racial microaggressions should not solely rest with them.

Too often, People of Color are looked toward for answers about racism. In education, Teachers, Faculty, and Administrators of Color often become the institutional go-to people to lead discussions and trainings related to race. Much of this work is done above and beyond the responsibilities of white colleagues in the same professional positions. We argue that the responsibility to understand and disrupt racism should also lie with the institution. If an institution—whether it be a school, college, or university—is committed to equity and diversity (as most state they are), it should have institutionalized programs in place to ensure that those within the organization understand what this commitment means. For us, this commitment means that there is a widely recognized definition of equity and that it centers on strategies to provide more equitable access and opportunities for People of Color. It means that institutions are not asking whether racism exists, but *how* it operates through its systems, policies, and processes. Finally, it means the institution seeks to provide an understanding of the relevant histories that have led to the inequities we seek to remediate, and explicit steps toward that remediation. However, before we get to this point there must be a general understanding that racism, in all of its manifestations, is a problem in the first place. To begin a process of disrupting racial microaggressions, this fact must first be recognized.

Chester Pierce (1974) offered this statement about the disruption of racial microaggressions, stating African Americans "must be taught to recognize . . . microaggressions and construct his [and her, their] future by taking appropriate action at each instance of recognition" (p. 520). We would argue that all people, not only People of Color, should be trained to recognize everyday racism in order to take action against it, wherever and whenever it occurs. Figure 6.2 illustrates a model created from Pierce's argument.

Figure 6.2. Chester Pierce's Model of Recognition, Reflection, and Action

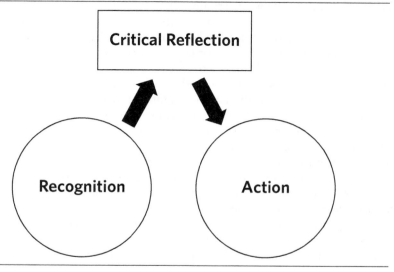

The figure begins with the recognition of racial microaggressions. Only after they are recognized can we begin a process of critical reflection to understand how and why the microaggressions happened. With this understanding, appropriate action can be taken.

We believe one promising possibility for praxis in the disruption of racial microaggressions is theater. Chicano actor and playwright Luis Valdez developed *Teatro Campesino* in the 1960s as a cultural branch of the Chicano Movement and the United Farm Workers Movement (UFW) in California.[4] *Teatro Campesino* was created to raise awareness about the plight of farm-workers in the UFW and of sociopolitical injustices suffered by Mexicans and Chicana/o communities in the U.S. Southwest more broadly. It was also used as an organizing tool, encouraging audiences to participate in the social change that these movements struggled for (see Broyles-González, 1994). Similarly, in the 1970s Brazilian theater scholar Augusto Boal (1979) developed *Theater of the Oppressed*, a range of Freirean-influenced performance techniques that encouraged audience members to become active participants in the storyline and in the analysis of real-life sociopolitical issues. The goal of *Theater of the Oppressed* was to engage audiences in a critical reading of instances of social and political injustice—those that could be seen in everyday realities. Indeed, scholars have borrowed the techniques from Teatro Campesino and Theater of the Oppressed to engage critical analyses of social issues in education and with Students of Color. For example, Sylvia Vega Rodriguez (2018, 2019) used these performance strategies in her work with Latina/o elementary school students from immigrant families in Los Angeles. Her work sought to explore how these children could use artistic expression to bring their own critical analysis and agency to the troubling moment of heightened anti-immigrant sentiment encouraged by the 2016 election of Donald Trump.

Another step that must be undertaken to disrupt racial microaggressions in education is institutional responsibility. The disruption of racial microaggressions should be a priority for institutional leadership. For example, Shaun Harper (2017) argues for *racially responsive leadership* in higher education that enacts proactive, rather than reactive, efforts and policies that challenge racism. At the same time, institutions must support the efforts of people and programs within their organizations that seek to do this work. For example, Harper (2017) explains that universities typically request consultation from a racial equity center or scholar only when there has been an incident of racism on campus. Having racially responsive leaders means that there is a concerted, consistent, and on-going effort to challenge racism regardless of the current climate or individual incidents. These racially responsive leaders would support these efforts, even in the midst of disagreement and potential hostility toward anti-racist work. We would argue that racially responsive leaders are needed just as much in K–12 schools, the workplace, labor unions, businesses, and community organizations.[5]

These are just some of the possibilities for future directions of research and praxis on racial microaggressions. At the moment this book is being written, the racist (and racist nativist) policies of the Trump administration have created a context of hate that targets Communities of Color in the United States and abroad. The racism we see today is certainly not new, as we have attempted to show in our references to the historical contexts of racism. History tells us that racial progress happens in waves, moving us forward, then back, and then forward again (Coates, 2017).[6] This has only been possible because of the resistance People of Color have engaged historically to challenge racial microaggressions and other forms of racism. Although we find ourselves in a moment of retrenchment for racial progress, we will most certainly find ourselves again riding a wave of progress forward, toward the betterment of our communities. We hope that this book acknowledges those courageous efforts to name the pain of everyday racism. Like Bell, we agree that racial realism is a reality (Bell, 1992a). Yet, also like Bell, we agree that our success is found in the struggle (Bell, 1992b). We hope this book provides new tools to support the efforts in that struggle as we collectively and continually push forward.

Notes

Introduction

1. Throughout this book, we write primarily in a collective voice (i.e., we) as coauthors. However, there are also moments in which we give individual perspectives, especially related to personal experiences. Daniel Solórzano indicates his voice with "Danny" and Lindsay Pérez Huber indicates her voice with "Lindsay" where appropriate.

2. From 1975 to 1985 I taught in the Chicano Studies Department at East Los Angeles College (ELAC).

3. The *Chronicle of Higher Education* is a weekly newspaper that addresses the latest news, information, and job listings in the field of higher education.

4. I credit Professor Laurence Parker, my colleague at the University of Utah, with this term.

5. For three seminal readers in Critical Race Theory and the law see Crenshaw, Gotanda, Peller, & Thomas, 1995; Delgado, 1995; and Matsuda, Lawrence, Delgado, & Crenshaw, 1993.

6. I am now exploring how CRT can be used in the science, technology, engineering, and math (STEM) fields.

7. For my story of that journey in race and ethnic studies and Freirean pedagogy see Solórzano, 1989; Solórzano 2013; Solórzano, 2019; Solórzano & Yosso, 2001.

8. I begin this work in MSE as an Educational Testing Service Postdoctoral Fellow in Educational and Social Policy in 1986.

9. "People of Color" is intentionally capitalized to reject the grammatical norm. This practice is part of a political move toward language use that reflects the values of social and racial justice. It also applies to "Students of Color," "Communities of Color," "Immigrants of Color," and "Men and Women of Color." For these reasons, we also chose to de-capitalize "white," particularly in the context of the term "white supremacy" where capitalization can discursively emphasize power and dominance.

10. In later work on Critical Race Spatial Analysis with my colleague, Veronica Vélez, we acknowledge that place and space have related but distinct meanings (Solórzano & Vélez, 2016; Solórzano & Vélez, 2017; Vélez & Solórzano, 2017). According to Friedland (1992), "place is the fusion of space and experience, a space filled with meaning, a source of identity" (p. 14). We have come to differentiate and utilize each term based on Friedland's (1992) definition.

11. Aldon Morris's (2015) *The Scholar Denied: W. E. B. Du Bois and the Birth of Modern Sociology* speaks of Parks's failure to reference Du Bois on this and other sociological constructs (see pp. 145–147).

12. This paper was my first professional CRT presentation. I presented it at the Annual Meeting of the Association for Studies in Higher Education, Orlando, FL, November 2, 1995. The title of my talk was "Critical Race Theory, Marginality, and the Experiences of Minority Students in Higher Education." I never published this paper, but, like a good backyard car with usable spare parts, the manuscript held ideas I could use in other papers on racial marginality (Solórzano & Villalpando, 1998), mentoring (Solórzano, 1998a), racial microaggressions (Solórzano, 1998b), and spatial analysis (Solórzano & Vélez, 2016; Solórzano & Vélez, 2017; Vélez & Solórzano, 2017).

13. In the 1969 chapter, Chester Pierce first introduces the concept of offensive mechanisms, which was the precursor to microaggressions. There are 13 articles where Pierce shares his developing ideas about the concept (see Pierce, 1969; Pierce, 1970; Pierce, 1974; Pierce, 1975a; Pierce, 1975b; Pierce, 1980; Pierce, 1988; Pierce, 1989; Pierce, 1995; Pierce, Carew, Pierce-Gonzalez, & Wills, 1978; Pierce, Earls, & Klineman, 1999; Pierce & Profit, 1991; and Profit, Mino, & Pierce, 2000). In addition, we have Ezra Griffith's 1998 biography on Pierce.

14. The initial team that conducted the data gathering consisted of Walter Allen, Grace Carroll, Daniel Solórzano, Miguel Ceja, and Elizabeth Guillory. In addition, the following people assisted in the preparation of the report to the court: Gniesha Dinwiddie, Gloria Gonzalez, and Tara Yosso, all doctoral or former education and sociology doctoral students at UCLA.

15. In one of the most comprehensive histories of racial microaggressions, Wong, Derthick, David, Saw, and Okazaki (2014) state that the Solórzano, Ceja, and Yosso (2000) article on African American students preceded the Sue, Capodilupo, Torino, Bucceri, Holder, Nadal, and Esquilin (2007) and Sue and Constantine (2007) articles by 7 years. However, the 1998 Solórzano article on Chicana and Chicano scholars was the first empirical piece on racial microaggressions.

16. Throughout this book, we continue to use the term "Latina/o" as a pan-ethnic description of people of Mexican, Central American, South American, Cuban, Dominican, and Puerto Rican descent. However, we acknowledge the move toward "Latinx" as a grammatical strategy for inclusivity of individuals who identify outside of the female–male gender binary. We use the term Latina/o because of the ongoing debate about the use of "x" and its meaning (de Onís, 2017). Latina/o honors the work of scholars like David Hayes-Bautista and Jorge Chapa (1987), who made the case for the importance of conceptually and operationally defining Latino populations, while situated within a historical context of changing terminology. Their 1987 article "Latino Terminology: Conceptual Bases for Standardized Terminology," explained the history that can help us understand the social and political contexts behind the terms we use as researchers. Their call in 1987 continues to have resonance as we engage in debates about ethnic identifiers such as "Latinx" and "Chicanx." We think there is a need for researchers to have this discussion to address the issue of using the "x" as more researchers move toward this term.

17. I would not be an academic if not for the mentorship and research experience I received as an undergraduate at UC Irvine. I have named two people who were mentors during my undergraduate career, my counselor Ramon Muñoz, and political science professor Dr. Lisa García Bedolla. In addition, I would like to acknowledge the mentorship of Dr. Jeanett Castellanos. These mentors have supported me—and continue to support me—in my academic pursuits. I would also like to

acknowledge the important undergraduate research programs that I participated in that encouraged undergraduate research and doctoral education, including the Summer Bridge Program, the Summer Academic Enrichment Program (SAEP), the Undergraduate Research Opportunities Program (UROP), and the Summer Research Opportunities Program (SROP). Through all of these I was introduced to research and to the PhD career pathway.

18. At the time it was introduced, this bill was unique in its framing—to protect national security and to contribute to antiterrorist efforts. It proposed that any undocumented immigrant residing in the United States be charged with a felony for his "illegal" presence in the country, effectively barring him from ever gaining legal status in the United States. The bill also sought to charge anyone, regardless of legal status, with a felony who assists or conceals the status of an undocumented immigrant from the U.S. government. H.R. 4437 also sought to expand the U.S.–Mexico border wall. It became known as the "Sensenbrenner bill" after one of its sponsors, Representative James Sensenbrenner (R-Wis.). The Senate passed an alternative bill, S. 2611 (Comprehensive Immigration Reform Act of 2006). Both bills died in conference committee.

19. The study was an unpublished manuscript titled "Beyond the direct impact of the law: Is Assembly Bill 540 benefiting undocumented students?"

20. The people, united, will never be defeated!

21. Racism targeting indigenous communities in Mexico can be traced back to Spanish conquest during the 16th century. In 1848, the Treaty of Guadalupe Hidalgo ended the Mexican-American war when the U.S. annexed over half of Mexico's territory, what is today the U.S. Southwest. Under the Treaty, Mexicans living in this territory had a choice to relocate to the newly established borders of their country or remain in the U.S. with full citizenship. Scholars have documented the racism and second-class citizenship Mexicans and Chicanas/os have historically been subjected to. See Acuña (1972) and Gómez (2018).

22. In 1968, in the aftermath of the 1967 summer uprisings across the United States, President Lyndon Johnson established the Kerner Commission. They issued their report called the *National Advisory Commission on Civil Disorders, 1968—The Kerner Report*. They begin the report by stating on the first page, "What white Americans have never fully understood—but what the Negro can never forget—is that white society is deeply implicated in the ghetto. White institutions created it. White institutions maintain it, and white society condones it" (p. 1). We would add that white society benefits from the "ghetto." As we write this book in June of 2020 (52 years later), we ask if "white Americans" still don't understand their implication in the "ghetto," and still don't understand their complicity in white supremacy (National Advisory Commission on Civil Disorders, 1968).

23. Tara Yosso (2000) first used the concept of visual microaggressions in her dissertation—A Critical Race and LatCrit Approach to Media Literacy: Chicana/o Resistance to Visual Microaggression.

24. UC Berkeley chose to create its own response to the UCOP faculty seminar series and excluded the racial microaggressions lecture.

Chapter 1

1. In 1993, the first authored book on Critical Race Theory in the law was titled, *Words That Wound: Critical Race Theory, Assaultive Speech, and the First*

Amendment (Matsuda et al., 1993). The title is illustrative in that its focus was on "Words That Wound"—racist hate speech on and off college campuses. The authors begin the book with the sentence "[T]his is a book about assaultive speech, about words that are used as weapons to ambush, terrorize, wound, humiliate, and degrade. Of late, there has been an alarming rise in the incidence of assaultive speech" (p. 1). Racial microaggressions in all their forms are also racially assaultive, injurious, and increasingly commonplace. In *Words That Wound*, Matsuda and colleagues identified these "polite and polished" colleagues (i.e., white male elites) as the chief spokespeople against those Academics of Color who dared to challenge the orthodoxy of "merit, rigor, standards, qualifications, and excellence" (p. 14). Matsuda and colleagues (1993) argue that the "first amendment arms conscious and unconscious racists—Nazis and liberals alike—with the constitutional right to be racists" (p. 15). They also state that "[W]e are in this fight about how to balance one individual's freedom of speech against another individual's freedom from injury" (p. 15).

2. Later in this chapter, we will see how W. E. B. Du Bois (1920, 1940) describes this rage. Another response to the majoritarian storytellers comes from Derrick Bell (1992a). He introduces us to Mrs. Biona MacDonald, a civil rights activist in the Mississippi Delta. When asked by Bell where she found the courage to continue working in civil rights in the face of intimidation, Bell wrote, "'Derrick,' she said slowly, seriously . . . 'I am an old woman. I lives to harass white folks'" (p. 378).

3. It should be noted that Indigenous peoples populated these lands for centuries before the first settler colonists came to what is now the Americas (North, Central, and South America). The settler colonists invaded and occupied Native lands and committed genocide against the Native People throughout the Americas. The Indigenous peoples' story of racism begins when the first European settler colonists came to the Americas. It should also be noted that subsequent African American, Chicana/o, Asian American, and other People of Color have stories of racism that also began when settler colonists made contact with the Americas.

4. These approximate percentages reflect the time at which we are writing this book. As time progresses, these percentages will change. However, the history of institutional racism and white supremacy remains.

5. We use the end of the Civil War as a point in time where explicit and implicit Jim Crow laws begin. We would argue that variations of Jim Crow existed in the Northern states before and after the end of the Civil War. The North used their version of Jim Crow to continue Black subjugation.

6. We recognize that African Americans and non-Black People of Color experience the consequences of slavery differently.

7. A racialized society, space, and/or subject are characterized by racial stratification, marginalization, and disparity that align with the ideology of white supremacy (Ladson-Billings, 1998).

8. Here, education is broadly defined as a process that occurs within and outside of formal schooling institutions. In effect, we recognize that racial microaggressions occur within these varied contexts, as is evident in the examples we present both earlier and later in the book.

9. We use the term "aracialism" to name an analysis that lacks, dismisses, or erases the consideration of race and racism.

10. These Du Boisean concepts were also a part of Solórzano's journey to the concept of marginality mentioned in the Introduction.

11. In his seminal work *The Souls of Black Folk*, Du Bois (1903) poignantly defined and articulated the intersection between space and race as the color-line. He stated: "Since then a new adjustment of relations in economic and political affairs has grown up . . . which leaves still that frightful chasm at the color-line across which men pass at their peril. Thus, then and now, there stand in the South two separate worlds; and separate not simply in the higher realms of social intercourse, but also in church and school, on railway and street-car, in hotels and theatres, in streets and city sections, in books and newspapers, in asylums and jails, in hospitals and graveyards" (p. 72). In 1897, W. E. B. Du Bois wrote an article in the *Atlantic Monthly* called the "Strivings of the Negro People." In this article he first introduces early elements that, in *The Souls of Black Folk* (1903), would help us understand the concept of the color-line: the veil, second-sight, double-consciousness, two-ness. These color-lines could be a street, a highway, a river, railroad tracks, or any other geographic or structural indicators that separate racial groups—the physical and non-physical divide between racial/ethnic groups that ensures that white people receive better treatment, services, and opportunities than People of Color.

12. Sue (2010) theorizes racial microaggressions within the context of the counseling psychology field, and specifically to provide counseling practitioners with strategies to address the unconscious racism that informs their practice with Clients of Color. In this context, the focus on the perpetrator is important and much needed. Here, we acknowledge these contributions. However, we differentiate a theory of racial microaggressions from a CRT perspective that explicitly focuses on the target of the racial microaggression: People of Color.

Chapter 2

1. See, for example, Laclau & Mouffe, 2014.

2. There are other types of microaggressions. See, for example, Solórzano (1998a) on gender microaggressions and Pérez Huber (2011) on racist nativist microaggressions. See also Nadal (2013) on sexual-orientation microaggressions.

3. It is important to note that our concern is for Melinda and how she experienced the racial microaggression, and not for the professor, who tried to explain away the behavior.

4. To find powerful examples of visual microaggressions, we would encourage readers to visit the Jim Crow Museum of Racist Memorabilia at Ferris State University in Big Rapids, Michigan. The museum displays various objects with racist depictions of African Americans during the Jim Crow era. A small display at the entrance to the museum has been added to the collection that shows objects with racist depictions of Native Americans. There are also several traveling exhibits that display racist objects from more contemporary pop culture with racist and heteropatriarchal imagery. See www.ferris.edu/jimcrow/, where many of these displays can be found.

5. The *New York Times* highlighted in this article 67 of the "most representative" experiences shared by their readers in which they experienced perceptions of not belonging.

6. For examples of types of microaggressions encountered in higher education institutions, see the important volume that documents the experiences of Women of Color in academia, titled, *Presumed Incompetent: The Intersections of Race and Class for Women in Academia* (Gutiérrez y Muhs, Niemann, González, & Harris, 2012).

7. See Truong, Museus, and McGuire (2016) for examples of secondary racism, or what they call vicarious racism. It is also important to note here that personal and community histories can provide contexts to understand the ways that primary and secondary targets can be affected by racial microaggressions.

8. Watson (2019) discussed a range of variables that are also important to consider when assessing and comparing telomere length of Black male college students. Socioeconomic status, prior health conditions, and racial group exposure (racial makeup of their home schools and communities) can all play a role in telomere length. He suggested further research examine the relationships of these variables (and others) to racial microaggressions, race-related stress, and telomere length.

9. Derrick Bell's use of racism hypos in the classroom did not include responses. Rather, the responses to and questions about Bell's hypos were prompted by his law students. In our critical race hypo, we provide responses of Melinda, her peers, and the instructor.

10. Again, Matsuda and colleagues (1993) state that "we are in this fight about how to balance one individual's freedom of speech against another individual's freedom from injury" (p. 15).

11. There are other possibilities for "making amends" in this hypo. For example, the professor could have approached the chair and/or dean of her department to request that all faculty have professional development opportunities to learn about recognizing, addressing, and disrupting racial microaggressions in classroom settings.

Chapter 3

1. Robert Carter joined the NAACP Legal Defense and Educational Fund in 1944 and became a legal assistant to General Counsel Thurgood Marshall. Many argue that Carter was the chief legal architect of the civil rights cases brought before the courts. Carter argued 23 cases before the U.S. Supreme Court and won 22 of them. He argued for using social science data in civil rights cases brought before the court. For instance, in *Brown v. Board of Education* (1954), Carter used the psychological research of Kenneth and Mamie Clark showing the deleterious effects of segregated schools on Black students' learning and development (i.e., Clark Doll Studies). In 1956, Robert Carter succeeded Thurgood Marshall as the general counsel of the NAACP. He resigned from the NAACP in 1968.

2. It is important to note that white supremacy is not the only form a macroaggression can take in the analysis of microaggressions. For example, gender microaggressions can be experienced by white women. The macroaggression in the analysis of these types of microaggressions would be patriarchy. Other forms of macroaggressions could be theorized located within other systems of oppression (e.g., heteropatriarchy, ableism, ageism, etc.).

3. Derrick Bell (1992a) uses the concept of *racial realism* to describe the permanence of racism in the United States. In his work, he cautions us against focusing intently on efforts that merely change racism's form. Rather, he argues, we must develop and implement "strategies that can bring fulfillment and even triumph" (p. 374). Institutional racism articulates a systematic positioning of race and racism in the United States that leads to racial realism. Racial microaggressions, then, become a tool, or "strategy" in understanding how everyday racism occurs in order to confront and dismantle structures of oppression.

4. We use the term *toll* as Chester Pierce (1974, 1989) used it, to describe the cumulative effects of racial microaggressions over time.

5. It is important to note that Chester Pierce argued that while the term "micro" was only "micro in name," he also considered "macroaggressions" as overt forms of racism. In 1970 Pierce distinguishes between microaggressions and the "gross, dramatic, obvious macro-aggression such as lynching" (p. 266).

6. Through this reappropriation of terminology, we engage a discursive shift of power that allows us to (re)create and (re)envision the meaning of microaggression. Historically, People of Color have engaged similar strategies with terminology, particularly for terms to describe racial/ethnic identity (e.g., Black, Chicana, Chicano).

7. Full title of the collection is "Photographs of Signs Enforcing Racial Discrimination: Documentation of Farm Security Administration—Office of War Information Photographers" (see www.loc.gov/rr/print/list/085_disc.html).

8. One could argue that de jure and de facto racism also occurred in other parts of the United States.

9. This could be an example of what Michelle Alexander (2010) refers to as the "New Jim Crow."

10. During his declaration, Trump admitted that invoking the national emergency was not necessary, but a faster way to get funding for construction of "the wall." This, after he was unsuccessful in negotiating with Democrats for border-wall funding during the longest government shutdown in U.S. history, from December 22, 2018, to January 25, 2019.

11. As we describe in this section, we use the term "native" to refer to the discursive values assigned to groups, shaped by constructions of whiteness that define belonging and not-belonging in the United States. We consider this use of the term "native" to be distinct from the use of the term "native" to describe indigenous communities such as Native Americans.

12. This photo is a screenshot from Freeman's 2018 documentary posted on Vimeo at https://www.unaccompaniedchildren.org/.

13. See the website for the film at www.unaccompaniedchildren.org/about, where filmmaker Linda Freeman tells her story about how she became involved in this project.

14. U.S. Customs and Border Patrol Protection reports that in 2018 over 500,000 apprehensions were made at the U.S. Southwest border (see www.cbp.gov/newsroom/stats/sw-border-migration). Of those, 48,325 were categorized as "unaccompanied alien children" coming from Mexico, Honduras, El Salvador, and Guatemala (see www.cbp.gov/newsroom/stats/sw-border-migration/usbp-sw-border-apprehensions).

15. We would argue that "the crisis" was not the migrants themselves, but the ways that they have been inhumanely treated, forced to sleep under roadways and tents in Tijuana, Mexico, for those being processed, or arrested and detained, for those who took the chance to cross the border into the United States. The most disturbing treatment was suffered by those most vulnerable, the children of migrants. Under this zero-tolerance policy, thousands of children who entered the United States with parents were taken away and sent to separate detention centers, often hundreds of miles away (Carcamo & Repard, 2018; Jordan, 2018). The Trump administration claimed that there were less than a few hundred children separated from their parents. Yet, the U.S. Department of Health and Human Services (HHS, 2020) reported that from April 2018 to March 2020 there have been 3,774 children separated from their parents. Officials have admitted that there was no structured system in place to reunite the separated children who were placed in shelters and foster homes

(Littlefield & Vasquez, 2018), conflicting with the information provided by the HHS. In the FAQ page for unaccompanied alien children (www.hhs.gov/programs/social-services/unaccompanied-alien-children/faqs/index.html) the agency claims that there has been "misinformation" about the agency's oversight of these children and explains a federal call center that is used in the system to reunite separated children and parents. The Kaiser Family Foundation reported that the number of unaccompanied children who were separated from their parents was over 2,342. It was estimated that during the implementation of this policy (May 5 to June 9, 2018), an average of 65 children per day were separated from their parents (Kaiser Family Foundation, 2018). Compounding the atrocities that are being committed against these children are reports of sexual abuse while in U.S. custody. Axios (2019) reports that in the 4 years from 2014 to 2018 thousands of unaccompanied children in U.S. custody have been abused. Axios reported data from the Department of Health and Human Services provided to the new media outlet by Rep. Ted Deutch's office (D-FL 22nd District). See www.axios.com/immigration-unaccompanied-minors-sexual-assault-3222e230-29e1-430f-a361-d959c88c5d8c.html. The Trump administration has been actively seeking to create new immigration policies and change current ones to deny these migrants the opportunity to seek better lives for themselves and their families in the United States.

Chapter 4

1. In the Spanish language *morena* refers to a dark-skinned woman. *Muy prieta* means a very dark woman, referring to skin color.

2. Even the islands surrounding the United States were not spared. Spain first colonized Puerto Rico before it was ceded to the United States, and the U.S. military overthrew the Kingdom of Hawaii in order to annex these islands (see Gonzalez, 2000, and Trask, 1999).

3. Clark & Clark (1947) reported that there were a total of eight questions the participants in the study were asked about these dolls. They were: (1) Give me the doll that you like to play with—(a) Give me the doll that you like best, (2) Give me the doll that is a nice doll, (3) Give me the doll that looks bad, (4) Give me the doll that is a nice color, (5) Give me the doll that looks like a white child, (6) Give me the doll that looks like a colored child, (7) Give me the doll that looks like you.

4. The study was footnoted in the Brown case (footnote 11), making *Brown* one of the first Supreme Court cases to utilize social science research as evidence for a case. See Guinier (2004).

5. The series of photos taken by Parks for the Clark doll study was a part of *Ebony* magazine's photo archives. In 2019, the Johnson Publishing Company, which owns the magazine, sold *Ebony*'s photo archives (more than 4 million images). The images will be donated to the National Museum of African American History and Culture and the Getty Research Institute. This photo was used with permission from the Gordon Parks Foundation.

6. The play begins with a prologue and continues with seven scenes (acts). The structure of the play's seven scenes moves between the farmworkers in the back of the labor contractor truck to a theater stage where the corrido is enacted. To view *El Corrido* and other Teatro Campesino plays, see cemaweb.library.ucsb.edu/ETCList.html.

7. At the end of the play, the undocumented workers on the truck realize they are being used as scabs (strikebreakers) and move to the side of the strikers (both documented and undocumented).

8. Upon reviewing interviews with Owens as well as the Blexit website, we see that the movement focuses explicitly on getting African Americans to question democratic beliefs and values, in order to encourage movement toward conservatism. However, in our research on #Blexit, we did see other People of Color seeming to support the campaign. The Pew Research Center reports that in 2018, 90% of African Americans voted for a Democratic candidate, versus just 9% who voted for a Republican. See Pew Research Center (2018).

9. Nelson (2019) notes that the "plantation" association with the Democratic Party was first used by Richard Nixon in his 1968 presidential campaign and was used even earlier in history by Black conservatives. Nelson comments that the discourse used by Blexit is no different. "Blexit is the flashier, millennial, made-for-social-media edition." However, we would argue that the history of racist tropes as political strategy goes back further in U.S. history. Even conservative Kevin Phillips's (1969) analysis of the evolving Republican Party from the late 19th century suggests that race has been a defining factor in U.S. political behavior since at least Lincoln's election in 1860.

10. On June 15, 2012, the U.S. Department of Homeland Security (DHS), under executive action of President Barack Obama, announced the DACA program. The program allowed certain undocumented people who meet specific requirements for eligibility to receive a temporary 2-year work authorization and it deferred deportation removal. Some requirements set by U.S. Customs and Immigration Services (USCIS) for those seeking consideration of DACA were that they arrived in the United States before they were 16 years of age, they had continuously resided in the United States since June 15, 2007, and they were under the age of 31 as of June 15, 2012 (see www.uscis.gov/archive/consideration-deferred-action-childhood-arrivals-daca#guidelines). To be eligible, an applicant must also have been enrolled in school, graduated high school (or earned a GED), or have been an honorably discharged veteran of the U.S. military. Furthermore, applicants could not have been convicted of a felony or any significant misdemeanors. The DACA program was in effect for 5 years until it was rescinded on September 5, 2017, under the direction of President Donald Trump. The Supreme Court agreed to hear the case challenging Trump's rescinding of the policy. SCOTUS heard the case on November 12, 2019, and a decision was handed down in July 2020 in support of DACA.

11. The original podcast is from the series *The Joe Rogan Experience*, hosted by Joe Rogan. Rogan's interview with Owens is episode #1125 and aired May 31, 2018.

12. In 2019, the Trump administration moved to change asylum procedures, requiring applicants to pay a fee and judges to adjudicate requests sooner. These changes were made in an attempt to discourage Latina/o migrants, mostly from Central American, from applying for asylum.

13. Faces of the women in the photo have been blurred by authors to protect their identities. The photo was found on TooPics, a website that features popular/trending Instagram posts and hashtags. This particular photo was found in a "#Blexit" search at www.toopics.com/tag/blexit. The site continually refreshes new posts that use this hashtag.

14. See Khan-Cullors & bandele's (2018) memoir, "When They Call You a Terrorist" on the development of the Black Lives Matter movement.

15. This quote from Carol Anderson is cited in Nelson's interview with Candace Owens in 2019. See Nelson (2019).

16. In much of Derrick Bell's work, including his work on racial realism, he speaks specifically to the experiences of Black communities. However, we believe that many of the concepts that Bell has theorized, including racial realism, are relevant to the experiences of other People of Color.

17. Many Native American and other indigenous cultures tell stories of shape-shifting, where one creature can change form into a new manifestation.

18. Race traitors can be People of Color, from any group, who have internalized racism and white supremacist ideologies to the detriment of Communities of Color. Indeed, Owens is not the only example.

19. The term "race traitor" was introduced in Derrick Bell's *Faces at the Bottom of the Well* (1992b). In this book, Bell also applies the term to whites who engage in strategies to challenge and dismantle white dominance. This definition of a white race traitor was taken up by Noel Ignatiev and John Garvey shortly after, producing the edited book *Race Traitor* in 1996. This book focuses on the deconstruction of whiteness, what the authors (problematically) describe as "the struggle to abolish the white race from within" (Ignatiev & Garvey, 1996, p. 2). Ignatiev and Garvey's (1996) discussion of race traitors centers whites and whiteness and (problematically) claims that the strategies for anti-whiteness of Communities of Color fall outside the scope of their work.

Chapter 5

1. As you'll notice with our research on racial microaggressions, racial microaffirmations, and Critical Race Theory, these ideas have long gestation periods and earlier points of origin.

2. I (Danny) first read the Gates letter to his daughters in 1994. It was something that I knew was important and filed for later use. Twenty years later (January 2014) I presented the concept of racial microaffirmations at an invited lecture to the Principal Leadership Institute at UCLA's Graduate School of Education & Information Studies. I then presented a paper on the concept of racial microaffirmations titled "Toward Collective Action to Reclaim Public Narratives for Justice: Ameliorating an Impoverished Cultural Discourse on Affirmative Action in Higher Education," at the Annual Meeting of the American Education Research Association, Chicago, IL, April 18, 2015.

3. The excerpt here is taken from several pages throughout the preface of this memoir, including from pages xi to xvi.

4. For other articles that articulate racial justice strategies for the disruption of "white space" see Anderson (2015), Montoya (1994), Baszile (2004).

5. We explain Bell's (1992a) concept of racial realism in further detail in Chapter 4. Racial realism holds that racism has and always will be a permanent fixture in U.S. society.

6. Steele's research on self-affirmation theory led to a closer examination of race-based threats and the impact they have on People of Color. Later in his career, Steele developed the theory of stereotype threat to explain how perceived negative expectations of Students of Color can negatively impact self-esteem and academic

outcomes. See Steele and Aronson (1995). See also Cohen and Garcia (2005) for a study that explains a concept called "collective threat"—how the self-esteem of People of Color can be negatively impacted by those within one's own racial group who may be perceived as reinforcing negative racial group stereotypes. It should be noted that these studies do not consider individual and/or group agency or the structural conditions that shape racist viewpoints of People of Color.

7. Jones (2017) also found that "not nodding" could be interpreted as a signal of disrespect, and/or a signal that some African Americans did not want to be associated with others in this setting.

8. Dolores Delgado Bernal (1998) explains the concept of cultural intuition as culturally specific ways of knowing Chicana/o scholars bring to the research process that inform methodological decisions and strategies as well as the broader research design.

9. In 2018, on a trip to the National Museum of African American History and Culture, we found a permanent exhibit on Gestures of Acknowledgment. In this exhibit panel they mention "the Nod."

10. Stories, advice, and conversations.

11. We would also argue that Montoya's later work on name narratives as pedagogy could be a powerful form of racial microaffirmation used in classrooms, for marginalized students in particular. See Montoya, Vasquez, and Martínez (2014).

12. Norma Cantú (2008) highlights the significance of place (and land) in traditional Mexican dance styles performed in the United States.

13. Music in Latina/o communities, as in other Communities of Color, has historically served as a form of resistance to oppression and as an affirmation of cultural pride. *Corridos*, for example, is a Mexican music genre that has been used in these ways since the 19th century (Paredes, 1958). The documentary *Rumble: The Indians Who Rocked the World*, tells the story of the Native American influence on the development of rock 'n' roll in the United States and how it was erased from music history (Salas, Johnson, & Bainbridge, 2018). Similarly, in African American communities, jazz, blues, hip-hop and other important genres have their roots in resistance, while also being appropriated by white listeners (see Chang & Herc, 2005; Floyd, 1996; Jones, 1999). The history of appropriation, profit, and historical erasure of music created by Communities of Color is a result of institutional racism and white supremacy.

14. Anzaldúa (1999) uses the term *linguistic terrorism* to name the ways that the Spanish language is stigmatized, and its use among Chicana/o communities punished in the United States (p. 80). Linguistic terrorism describes how language suppression is discursively utilized as an exercise of power and strategy of domination over Chicana/o communities in the United States, often beginning in schools and extending to other social institutions where linguistic norms are established to marginalize and exclude Chicanas/os and Latinas/os. Anzaldúa (1999) also describes how "language is a male discourse" and these processes of subordination are not only racist, but also patriarchal (p. 76).

15. Under the leadership of Jim Enote, the director of the Zuni A:shiwi A:wan Museum & Heritage Center, 50 artists from the Zuni nation have embarked on a project called the Zuni Map Art Project. Enote states that he "wanted to make maps that were both elegant, evacuative, and profoundly important to the Zuni People." He goes on to state that "these maps become a thing that helps a family or group

to start speaking about places. To start learning from each other and talking about places in a way that is uniquely Zuni." He speaks of maps as affirming, and states that "when people have a map that is part of affirming their identity, it tells them that they are of this place" (see Enote & McLerran, 2011, and the online *Emergence Magazine*, at (emergencemagazine.org/story/counter-mapping/) for a video description of the Zuni Map Art Project. Like the Zuni Map Art Project, we also recognize that the field of Ethnic Studies has been a source of racial microaffirmation throughout our careers—seeing, affirming, and validating ourselves in space, history, and text. We also argue that not seeing oneself in space, history, and text is a racial microaggression.

16. In Chapter 2, we explain visual microaggression as a type of racial microaggression. We believe that visual microaffirmation is a type of racial microaffirmation, and that the model we present in Figure 2.1 could be adapted and used to explore the types, contexts, effects of, and responses to racial microaffirmations.

17. Some examples of racial microaffirmations in the history of African American communities in the United States can be found in early photojournalism. The National Museum of African American History and Culture in Washington, DC, recently opened the exhibit "African Americans in Full Color," which displays early 20th-century African American photojournalism (see nmaahc.si.edu/blog-post/african-americans-full-color). Among these publications were *Ebony* and *Jet,* magazines that offered affirmative Black imagery and featured achievements of African Americans. The entire *Ebony* and *Jet* photo archive went up for auction in 2019 after its publishing company filed for bankruptcy. Some photos from the collection were featured in a *New York Times* article about the archive collection and auction in July 2019 (see www.nytimes.com/2019/07/16/us/ebony-magazine-photographs-auction.html). Since then, the National Museum of African American History and Culture announced that it had acquired a significant portion of the collection (see www.washingtonpost.com/entertainment/museums/foundations-donate-historic-jetebony-archive-to-african-american-museum/2019/07/25/caaee662-af11-11e9-bc5c-e73b603e7f38_story.html).

Chapter 6

1. Valencia (2010) theorized cultural deficit theory to describe the phenomenon of blaming the cultures, families, and communities of Latinas/os and African Americans to explain the social inequities, including lower educational outcomes, that exist in the United States.

2. Parks was commissioned by *Life* magazine in 1956 to document the lives of three Black families living in Alabama during the Jim Crow segregation era. This "Department Store" photo captured one of the family members, Joanne Thorton Wilson, and her young niece. The sign was actually at the entrance to a movie theater, near a department store. In the *New York Times* (2013) Wilson tells the story of the photo, explaining that her niece smelled the popcorn wafting from the theater entrance, but that Wilson did not want to take her through the back entrance to buy it for her. So she stood on the sidewalk under the sign thinking "where I could go to get her popcorn" (see lens.blogs.nytimes.com/2013/06/06/the-woman-in-the-picture/)

3. See Maya Angelou's website at www.mayaangelou.com/blog/.

4. The University of California, Santa Barbara (UCSB) library currently houses *The Teatro Campesino Archives*, a collection of over 20 years of work created by the theater group that includes interviews, films, audio recordings, photographs, and other materials. For the finding aid to this collection see pdf.oac.cdlib.org/pdf/ucsb/spcoll/cusb-cema5.pdf

5. A possible example we should mention here is a package of bills introduced to the California legislature by Assemblywoman Sydney Kamlager-Dove (D-Los Angeles). These bills would require state-licensed doctors, physician assistants, and nurses to undergo 8 hours of implicit bias training and testing every 2 years. See www.latimes.com/politics/la-pol-ca-implicit-bias-legislation-california-20190422-story.html

6. Coates (2017) explains that the rise of support for Donald Trump was a direct response to the progressive politics of former President Barack Obama and the policies that sought to improve the lives of Communities of Color. Coates provides a historically insightful account of these waves of progress and retrenchment of the rights of People of Color dating back to the early 19th century.

References

Abel, E. (2010). *Signs of the times: The visual politics of Jim Crow*. Berkeley, CA: University of California Press.

Acuña, R. (1972). *Occupied America: The Chicano's struggle toward liberation*. San Francisco, CA: Canfield Press.

Adelman, L. (2008). Unnatural causes: Is inequality making us sick? [Television series]. San Francisco, CA: Public Broadcasting Service (PBS).

Ahuja, G. (2009). What a doll tells us about race. *ABC News*. Retrieved from abcnews.go.com/GMA/story?id=7213714&page=1

Alexander, M. (2010). *The new Jim Crow: Mass incarceration in the age of color-blindness*. New York, NY: The New Press.

Allen, W. R., & Solórzano, D. (2001). Affirmative action, educational equity and campus racial climate: A case study of the University of Michigan Law School. *UC Berkeley La Raza Law Journal*, *12*, 237–363.

Alvarez, M. (2018, June 26). Where are the children? Not in Trump's priorities [Blog post]. National Immigration Law Center. Retrieved from www.nilc.org /2018/06/26/children-not-in-trumps-priorities/

Anderson, E. (2015) The white space. *Sociology of Race & Ethnicity*, *1*(1), 10–21.

Anderson, E. (2018, June 9). This is what it feels like to be black in white spaces. *The Guardian*. Retrieved from www.theguardian.com/commentisfree/2018/jun/09 /everyday-racism-america-black-white-spaces

Ansell, D. A. (2017). *The death gap: How inequality kills*. Chicago, IL: The University of Chicago Press.

Anzaldúa, G. (1999). *Borderlands/La Frontera: The new mestiza* (2nd ed.). San Francisco, CA: Aunt Lute Books.

Anzaldúa, G. (2002). La Prieta. In C. Moraga & G. Anzaldúa (Eds.), *This bridge called my back* (pp. 220–233). Durham, NC: Duke University Press.

Bagwell, O. (1994). Malcolm X: Make it plain [Documentary]. USA: Blackside.

Baker, P. (2019, February 15). Trump declares a national emergency, and provokes a constitutional clash. *The New York Times*. Retrieved from www.nytimes. com/2019/02/15/us/politics/national-emergency-trump.html

Baldwin, J., Capouya, E., Hansberry, L., Hentoff, N., Hughes, L., & Kazin, A. (1961, Summer). The Negro in American culture. *CrossCurrents*, *11*(3), 205–224.

Baszile, D. T. (2004) Who does she think she is? Growing up nationalist and ending up teaching in white space. In D. Cleveland (Ed.), *A long way to go: Conversations about race by African American faculty and graduate students* (pp. 158–70). New York, NY: Peter Lang.

Battle-Baptiste, W., & Rusert, B. (Eds.). (2018). W. E. B. Du Bois's data portraits: Visualizing Black America. New York, NY: Princeton Architectural Press.

Beatty Moody, D. L., Leibel, D. K., Darden, T. M., Ashe, J. J., Waldstein, S. R., Katzel, L. I., . . . Zonderman, A. B. (2019). Interpersonal-level discrimination indices, sociodemographic factors, and telomere length in African-Americans and Whites. Biological Psychology, 141, 1–9. doi.org/10.1016/j.biopsycho.2018.12.004

Bell, D. (1992a). Racial realism. Connecticut Law Review, 24(2), 363–379.

Bell, D. (1992b). Faces at the bottom of the well: The permanence of racism. New York, NY: Basic Books.

Bell, D. (1999). The power of narrative. Legal Studies Forum, 23(3), 315–348.

Bermudez, E. (2018, June 16). I am raising my daughter to speak three languages. A stranger demanded I 'speak English' to her. Los Angeles Times. Retrieved from www.latimes.com/local/california/la-me-speak-english-20180616-story.html

Bernhard, M., & Delwiche, T. (2014). "I, too, Am Harvard" draws national attention, promotes discussion. The Harvard Crimson. Retrieved from www.thecrimson.com/article/2014/3/5/i-too-am-harvard/

Berry, C. D., & Duke, B. (Producers and Directors). (2011). Dark girls [Documentary]. USA: Urban Winter Entertainment.

Blow, C. (2019, July 28). The rot you smell is a racist POTUS: Trump and his views are the real infestations in America. New York Times. Retrieved from www.nytimes.com/2019/07/28/opinion/trump-racist-baltimore.html

Boal, A. (2000). Theatre of the oppressed. London, England: Pluto Press.

Bonilla-Silva, E. (2001). White supremacy and racism in the post-civil rights era. Boulder, CO: Lynne Rienner Publishers.

Brown v. Board of Education, 347 U.S. 483 (1954).

Broyles-González, Y. (1994). El teatro campesino: Theater in the Chicano movement. Austin: University of Texas Press.

Cantú, N. (2008). The semiotics of land and place: Matachines dancing in Laredo, Texas. In O. Najera-Ramirez, N. Cantu, & B. Romero (Eds.), Dancing across borders: Danzas y bailes Mexicanos (pp. 97–115). Urbana: University of Illinois Press.

Carcamo, C. (2014, June 21). Q&A: Explaining the crisis on the Southwest border as children seek refuge. The Los Angeles Times. Retrieved from www.latimes.com/nation/la-na-ff-immigration-answers-20140621-story.html

Carcamo, C., & Repard, P. (2018, April 29). People "associated with" Central American caravan have entered U.S. illegally, federal officials say. The Los Angeles Times. Retrieved from www.latimes.com/local/lanow/la-me-ln-sd-caravan-20180428-story.html

Carroll, G. (1998). Environmental stress and African Americans: The other side of the moon. Westport, CT: Praeger.

Carter, R. (1988). The NAACP's legal strategy against segregated education, 1925-1950. Michigan Law Review, 86(6), 1083–1095.

Center for Constitutional Rights. (2012). Stop and frisk, the human impact: The stories behind the numbers, the impact on our communities. Retrieved from http://stopandfrisk.org/the-human-impact-report/

Chae, D. H., Epel, E. S., Nuru-Jeter, A. M., Lincoln, K. D., Taylor, R. J., Lin, J., Blackburn, E.H., & Thomas, S. B. (2016). Discrimination, mental health, and leukocyte telomere length among African American men. *Psychoneuroendocrinology, 63*, 10–16.

Chae, D. H., Nuru-Jeter, A. M., Lincoln, K. D., & Jacob Arriola, K. R. (2012). Racial discrimination, mood disorders, and cardiovascular disease among Black Americans. *Annals of Epidemiology, 22*(2), 104–111.

Chae, D. H., Lincoln, K. D., Adler, N. E., & Syme, S. L. (2010). Do experiences of racial discrimination predict cardiovascular disease among African American men? The moderating role of internalized negative racial group attitudes. *Social Science & Medicine, 71*(6), 1182–1188. doi.org/10.1016/j.socscimed.2010.05.045

Chang, C., & Poston, B. (2019, January 24). "Stop-and-frisk in a car": Elite LAPD unit disproportionately stopped black drivers, data show. *Los Angeles Times.* Retrieved from www.latimes.com/local/lanow/la-me-lapd-traffic-stops-20190124-story.html

Chang, J., & Herc, D. J. K. (2005). *Can't stop won't stop: A history of the hip-hop generation.* New York, NY: Picador.

Chávez, L. R. (2008). *The Latino threat: Constructing immigrants, citizens, and the nation.* Stanford, CA: Stanford University Press.

Chomsky, A. (2014). *Undocumented: How immigration became illegal.* Boston, MA: Beacon Press.

Clark, K. B., & Clark, M. P. (1947). Racial identification and preference in Negro children. In T. M. Newcomb & E. L. Hartley (Eds.), *Readings in social psychology* (pp. 169–178). New York, NY: Holt, Reinhart & Winston.

Clark, K. B., & Clark, M. P. (1950). Emotional factors in racial identification and preference in Negro children. *Journal of Negro Education, 19*(3), 341–350. doi.org/10.2307/2966491

Clark, K. B., Chein, I., & Cook, S. W. (2004). The effects of segregation and the consequences of desegregation: A (September 1952) social science statement in the *Brown v. Board of Education of Topeka* Supreme Court case. *American Psychologist, 59*(6), 495–501. doi.org/10.1037/0003-066X.59.6.495

Clark, R., Anderson, N., Clark, V., & Williams, D. (1999). Racism as a stressor for African Americans: A biopsychosocial model. *American Psychologist, 54*(10): 805–816.

CNN (2010). Black or white: Kids on race. Special coverage on CNN.com. Retrieved from www.cnn.com/SPECIALS/2010/kids.on.race/

Coates, T. (2017). *We were eight years in power: An American tragedy.* New York, NY: One World.

Cohen, G. L., & Garcia, J. (2005) "I am us": Negative stereotypes as collective threats. *Journal of Personality and Social Psychology, 89*, 566–582.

Cohen, G. L., Garcia, J., Purdie-Vaughns, V., Apfel, N., & Brzustoski, P. (2009) Recursive processes in self-affirmation: Intervening to close the minority achievement gap. *Science, 324*(5925), 400–403.

Collins, P. (1986). Learning from the outsider within: The sociological significance of Black feminist thought. *Social Problems, 33*(6), S14–S32.

Constantine, M. G. (2007). Racial microaggressions against African American clients in cross-racial counseling relationships. *Journal of Counseling Psychology, 54*(1), 1–16.

Constantine, M. G., & Sue, D. W. (2007). Perceptions of racial microaggressions among black supervisees in cross-racial dyads. *Journal of Counseling Psychology, 54*(2), 142–153.

Cox, P. R. (2004). Don't tell lies, Lucy!: A cautionary tale. London, England: Usborne Publishing.

Crenshaw, K., Gotanda, N., Peller, G., & Thomas, K. (Eds.). (1995). *Critical race theory: The key writings that formed the movement.* New York, NY: The New Press.

Culp, J. (1996). Telling a Black legal story: Privilege, authenticity, "blunders," and transformation in outsider narrative. *Virginia Law Review, 82,* 60–93.

Davis, J. H. (2018, May 16). Trump calls some unauthorized immigrants 'animals' in rant. *The New York Times.* Retrieved from www.nytimes.com/2018/05/16/us/politics/trump-undocumented-immigrants-animals.html

Davis, P. (1989). Law as microaggression. *Yale Law Journal, 98,* 1559–1577.

Delgado, R. (1982). Words that wound: A tort action for racial insults, epithets, and name-calling. *Harvard Civil Rights-Civil Liberties Law Review, 17,* 133–182.

Delgado, R. (1989). Storytelling for oppositionists and others: A plea for narrative. *Michigan Law Review, 87*(8), 2411–2441.

Delgado, R. (Ed.). (1995). *Critical race theory: The cutting edge.* Philadelphia, PA: Temple University Press.

Delgado Bernal, D. (1998). Using a Chicana feminist epistemology in educational research. *Harvard Educational Review, 68*(4), 555–579.

Delgado Bernal, D., Pérez Huber, L., & Malagon, M. (2019). Bridging theories to name and claim a critical race feminista methodology. In T. Chapman, J. DeCuir-Gunby, & P. Schutz (Eds.), *Critical race research methods and methodologies in education* (pp. 109–121). New York, NY: Routledge.

de Onís, C. (2017). What's in an "x"?: An exchange about the politics of "Latinx." *Chiricú Journal: Latina/o Literatures, Arts, and Cultures, 1*(2), 78–91.

Dinan, S. (2018, November 28). Judge blocks Trump asylum changes: Caravan can demand protections even after illegal entry. *The Washington Times.* Retrieved from www.washingtontimes.com/news/2018/nov/20/judge-blocks-trump-asylum-changes-rulings-means-ca/

Domenech Rodríguez, M. (2014). *No way but through* [Video file]. Retrieved from rgs.usu.edu/tedxusu/portfolio-items/melanie-m-domenech-rodriguez/

Du Bois, W. E. B. (1897). Strivings of the Negro people. *Atlantic Monthly, 80,* 194–198.

Du Bois, W. E. B. (1899). *The Philadelphia Negro: A social study.* Philadelphia: University of Pennsylvania.

Du Bois, W. E. B. (1903). *The souls of Black folk.* Chicago, IL: A. C. McClurg & Co.

Du Bois, W. E. B. (1910, November). Strivings of the Negro people. *The Crisis: Record of the Darker Races, 1*(1), 3–6.

Du Bois, W. E. B. (1920/2004). *Darkwater: Voices from within the veil.* New York, NY: Washington Square Press.

Du Bois, W. E. B. (1940/1984). *Dawn of dusk: An essay toward an autobiography of a race concept.* Piscataway, NJ: Transaction Publishers.

Dunbar-Ortiz, R. (2014). *An indigenous peoples' history of the United States.* Boston, MA: Beacon Press.

Dyson, M. E. (2001, March) Brother, can you spare a nod? *Savoy,* 93–94.

Enote, J., & McLerran, J. (Eds.). (2011). *A:shiwi A:wan Ulohnanne—The Zuni world*. Flagstaff, AZ: A:shiwi A:wan Museum and Heritage Center and the Museum of Northern Arizona.

Essed, P. (1991). *Understanding everyday racism: An interdisciplinary theory*. Newbury Park, CA: Sage.

Fagan, J. (2010). Second supplementary report in *Floyd et al., v. City of New York et al*. New York, NY: United States District Court, Southern District of New York. Retrieved from ccrjustice.org/files/FaganSecondSupplementalReport.pdf

Fagan, J. (2012). Executive summary, stop and frisk: Updated data confirms earlier findings of rights violations. *Center for Constitutional Rights*. New York, NY: Retrieved from www.ccrjustice.org/files/Fagan-2012-summary-FINAL.pdf.

Fegley, S. G., Spencer, M. B., Goss, T. N., Harpalani, V., & Charles, N. (2008). Colorism embodied: Skin tone and psychosocial well-being in adolescence. In W. F. Overton, U. Müller, & J. L. Newman (Eds.), *Jean Piaget symposium series. Developmental perspectives on embodiment and consciousness* (pp. 281–311). New York, NY: Taylor & Francis Group/Lawrence Erlbaum Associates.

Flores Niemann, Y. (2012). The making of a token: A case study of stereotype threat, stigma, racism, and tokenism in academe. In G. Gutiérrez y Muhs, Y. F. Niemann, C. G. González, & A. P. Harris (Eds.), *Presumed incompetent: The intersections of race and class for women in academia* (pp. 337–355). Boulder, CO: Utah State University Press.

Floyd v. City of New York, No. 08 Civ. 01034 (SAS) 2013 U.S. Dist. LEXIS 132881 (S.D.N.Y Aug. 12, 2013).

Floyd, Jr., S. A. (1996). *The power of Black music: Interpreting its history from Africa to the United States*. New York, NY: Oxford University Press.

Franklin, J. D., Smith, W. A., & Hung, M. (2014). Racial battle fatigue for Latina/o students: A quantitative perspective. *Journal of Hispanic Higher Education*, 13(4), 303–322. doi.org/10.1177/1538192714540530

Freedman, L. (Producer/Filmmaker). (2018). *Unaccompanied: Alone in America*. Immigration Counseling Service & Thumbs Up Video Productions. Retrieved from www.unaccompaniedchildren.org

Freire, P. (2000). *Pedagogy of the oppressed* (4th ed.). New York, NY: Continuum.

Friedland, R. (1992). Space, place, and modernity: The geographical moment. *Contemporary Sociology*, 21(1), 11–15.

Garcia, G. A., Johnston, M. P., Garibay, J. C., Herrera, F. A., & Giraldo, L. G. (2011). When parties become racialized: Deconstructing racially themed parties. *Journal of Student Affairs Research and Practice*, 48(1). doi.org/10.2202/1949-6605.6194

García Bedolla, L. (2005). *Fluid borders: Latino power, identity, and politics in Los Angeles*. Berkeley: University of California Press.

Gates, H. L., Jr. (1994). *Colored people: A memoir*. New York, NY: Vintage Press.

Gates, H. L., Jr. (2019). *Stony the road: Reconstruction, white supremacy, and the rise of Jim Crow*. New York, NY: Penguin Press.

Gaxiola Serrano, T., & Solórzano, D. (2018). The role of interest convergence in California's education: Community colleges, Latinas/os and the state's future. In A. De Los Santos, G. Keller, R. Tannenbaum, & A. Acereda (Eds.), *Hispanic students move forward: Assessment, development, and achievement* (pp. 117–140). Albany: State University of New York Press.

Gee, G., Ro, A., Shariff-Marco, S., & Chae, D. (2009). Racial discrimination and health among Asian Americans: Evidence, assessment, and directions for future research. *Epidemiologic Reviews, 31*(1), 130–151.

Geronimus, A., Hicken, M., Keene, D., & Bound, J. (2006). "Weathering" and age patterns of allostatic load scores among Blacks and Whites in the United States. *American Journal of Public Health, 96*(5), 826–833.

Gildersleeve, R., Croom, N., & Vasquez, P. (2011). "Am I going crazy?!": A critical race analysis of doctoral education. *Equity & Excellence in Education, 44*(1), 93–114.

Gillborn, D. (2006). Rethinking white supremacy: Who counts in 'WhiteWorld.' *Ethnicities, 6*(3), 318–340.

Gillborn, D. (2008). *Racism and education: Coincidence or conspiracy?* London, England: Routledge.

Gitlin, T. (2015). You are here to be disturbed. *The Chronicle of Higher Education*. Retrieved from www.chronicle.com/article/A-Plague-of-Hypersensitivity/229963

Glaser, B., & Strauss, A. (1967). *The discovery of grounded theory.* Chicago, IL: Aldine.

Gómez, L. E. (2018). *Manifest Destinies, Second Edition: The Making of the Mexican American Race* (2nd ed.). New York, NY: NYU Press.

Gomez, V., & Pérez Huber, L. (2019). Examining racist nativist microaggressions on DACAmented college students in the Trump era. *California Journal of Politics and Policy, 11*(2), 1–16. doi.org/10.5070/P2CJPP11243089

Gonzalez, J, (2000). *Harvest of empire: A history of Latinos in America.* New York, NY: Penguin.

Goyer, J. P., Garcia, J., Purdie-Vaughns, V., Binning, K. R., Cook, J. E., Reeves, S. L., & Cohen, G. L. (2017). Self-affirmation facilitates minority middle schoolers' progress along college trajectories. *Proceedings of the National Academy of Sciences, 114*(29), 7594–7599.

Gravlee, C. C., Dressler, W. W., & Bernard, H. R. (2005). Skin color, social classification, and blood pressure in southeastern Puerto Rico. *American Journal of Public Health, 95*(12), 2191–2197.

Greenwald, A. G., & Krieger, L. H. (2006). Implicit bias: Scientific foundations. *California Law Review, 94*(4), 945–967.

Grier-Reed, T. (2010). The African American student network: Creating sanctuaries and counterspaces for coping with racial microaggressions in higher education settings. *Journal of Humanistic Counseling, Education, and Development, 49*(2), 181–188.

Griffith, E. E. H. (1998). *Race and excellence: My dialogue with Chester Pierce* (1st ed.). Iowa City: University of Iowa Press.

Grutter v. Bollinger, 123 S. Ct. 2325 (2003).

Guinier, L. (2004). From racial liberalism to racial literacy: *Brown v. Board of Education* and the interest-divergence dilemma. *Journal of American History, 91*(1), 92–118.

Guinier, L. (2015). *The tyranny of the meritocracy: Democratizing higher education in America.* New York, NY: Beacon Press.

Gutiérrez y Muhs, G. y, Niemann, Y. F., González, C. G., & Harris, A. P. (Eds.). (2012). *Presumed incompetent: The intersections of race and class for women in academia.* Boulder, CO: Utah State University Press.

Guzmán, B. (2012) Cultivating a guerrera spirit in Latinas: The praxis of mothering. *Journal of the Association of Mexican American Educators, 6*(1), 45–51.

Haney López, I. (2006). *White by law: The legal construction of race.* New York, NY: NYU Press.

Harper, S. (2017). Racially responsive leadership: Addressing the longstanding problem of racism in higher education. In J. S. Antony, A. M. Cauce, & D. E. Shalala (Eds.), *Challenges in higher education leadership: Practical and scholarly solutions* (pp. 117–129). New York, NY: Routledge Press.

Harrell, S. P. (2000). A multidimensional conceptualization of racism-related stress: Implications for the well-being of people of color. *American Journal of Orthopsychiatry, 70*(1), 42–57.

Harris, A. P. (2008). From color line to color chart: Racism and colorism in the new century. *Berkeley Journal of African-American Law & Policy, 10*(1), 52–69.

Harris, C. (1993). Whiteness as property. *Harvard Law Review, 106*(8), 1707–1791.

Hayes-Bautista, D., & Chapa, J. (1987). Latino terminology: Conceptual bases for standardized terminology. *American Journal of Public Health, 77*(1), 61–68.

Hill, L. B. K., Kobayashi, I., & Hughes, J. W. (2007). Perceived racism and ambulatory blood pressure in African American college students. *Journal of Black Psychology, 33*(4), 404–421.hooks, b. (1990). *Yearnings: race, gender, and cultural politics.* Boston, MA: South End Press.

Huang, F. L., & Cornell, D. G. (2019). School teasing and bullying after the presidential election. *Educational Researcher, 48*(2), 69–83.

Hurtado, S., Alvarado, A. R., & Guillermo-Wann, C. (2015). Thinking about race: The salience of racial identity at two- and four-year colleges and the climate for diversity. *The Journal of Higher Education, 86*(1), 127–155.

Hurtado, S., Milem, J., Clayton-Pedersen, A., & Allen, W. (1999). *Enacting diverse learning environments: Improving the climate for racial/ethnic diversity in higher education* [Monograph]. ASHE-ERIC Higher Education Report, 26(8). Washington, DC: The George Washington University Graduate School of Education and Human Development.

Ignatiev, N., & Garvey, J. (Eds.). (1996). *Race Traitor.* New York, NY: Routledge.

Jerald, M. C., Ward, L. M., Moss, L., Thomas, K., & Fletcher, K. D. (2017). Subordinates, sex objects, or sapphires? Investigating contributions of media use to Black students' femininity ideologies and stereotypes about Black women. *Journal of Black Psychology, 43*(6), 608–635.

Johnson, K. R. (2012). Immigration and civil rights: Is the new Birmingham the same as the old Birmingham? *William & Mary Bill of Rights Journal, 21*(2), 367–397.

Jones, C. (2000). Levels of racism: A theoretic framework and a gardener's tale. *American Journal of Public Health, 90*(8), 1212–1215.

Jones, J. M., & Rolón-Dow, R. (2018). Multidimensional models of microaggressions and microaffirmations. In G. C. Torino, D. P. Rivera, C. M. Capodilupo, K. L. Nadal, & D. W. Sue (Eds.), *Microaggression theory: Influence and implications* (pp. 32–47). Hoboken, N.J: Wiley.

Jones, J. R. (2017) Racing through the halls of congress: The "Black nod" as an adaptive strategy for surviving in a raced institution. *DuBois Review: Social Science Review on Race, 14*(1), 165–187.

Jones, L. (1999). *Blues people: Negro music in white America*. New York, NY: Harper Perennial.

Jordan, M. (2018, July 31). A migrant boy rejoins his mother, but he's not the same. *The Los Angeles Times*. Retrieved from www.nytimes.com/2018/07/31/us/migrant-children-separation-anxiety.html

Kaiser Family Foundation (2018, June 27). *Key health implications of separation of families at the border*. Retrieved from www.kff.org/disparities-policy/fact-sheet/key-health-implications-of-separation-of-families-at-the-border/.

Kang, J., Bennett, M., Carbado, D., Casey, P., Dasgupta, N., Faigman, D., . . . Mnookin, J. (2012). Implicit bias in the courtroom. *UCLA Law Review, 59*, 1124–1186.

Kendi, I. X. (2016). *Stamped from the beginning: The definitive history of racist ideas in America*. New York, NY: Nation Books.

Khan-Cullors, P., & bandele, a. (2018). *When they call you a terrorist: A Black Lives Matter memoir*. New York, NY: St. Martin's Press.

Kohli, R. (2017). *Internalized racism: The consequences and impact of racism on people of color*. UCLA Center for Critical Race Studies in Education (CCRSE). Retrieved from issuu.com/almaiflores/docs/rk_internalized_racism/1

Kohli, R., & Solórzano, D. G. (2012). Teachers, please learn our names!: Racial microaggressions and the K–12 classroom. *Race Ethnicity and Education, 15*(4), 441–462.

Kopan, T. (2018, November 16). More than 14,000 immigrant children are in U.S. custody, an all-time high. *San Francisco Chronicle*. Retrieved from www.sfchronicle.com/nation/article/More-than-14-000-immigrant-children-are-in-U-S-13399510.php

Laclau, E., & Mouffe, C. (2014). *Hegemony and socialist strategy: Towards a radical democratic politics*. (2nd ed.). New York, NY: Verso.

Lacy, K. (2007). *Blue-chip Black: Race, class, and status in the new Black middle class*. Berkeley, CA: University of California Press.

Ladson-Billings, G. (1998) Just what is critical race theory and what's it doing in a nice field like education? *International Journal of Qualitative Studies in Education, 11*, 7–24.

Lakoff, G. (2006). *Thinking points: Communicating our American values and vision*. New York, NY: Farrar, Straus and Giroux.

Larsen, N. (1928). *Quicksand and Passing*. New York, NY: Alfred Knopf.

Lawrence, C., III. (1993). If he hollers, let him go: Regulating racist speech on campus. In M. Matsuda, C. Lawrence III, R. Delgado, & K. W. Crenshaw (Eds.), *Words that wound: Critical race theory, assaultive speech, and the first amendment* (pp. 53–88). Boulder, CO: Westview Press.

Layous, K., Davis, E. M., Garcia, J., Purdie-Vaughns, V., Cook, J. E. & Cohen, G. L. (2017). Feeling left out, but affirmed: Protecting against the negative effects of low belonging in college. *Journal of Experimental Social Psychology, 69*, 227–231.

Ledesma, M., & Solórzano, D. (2013). Naming their pain: How everyday microaggressions impact students and teachers. In D. Carter Andrews & F. Tuitt (Eds.), *Contesting the myth of a "post racial" era: The continued significance of race in U.S. education* (pp. 112–127). New York, NY: Peter Lang.

Levchak, C. C. (2018). *Microaggressions and modern racism: Endurance and evolution*. New York, NY: Springer Berlin Heidelberg.

Lin, G. (2016, March). *The windows and mirrors of your child's bookshelf: Grace Lin TEDxNatick* [Video file]. Retrieved from www.youtube.com /watch?v=_wQ8wiV3FVo

Littlefield, A., & Vasquez, T. (2018, June 27). Bethany Christian Services is fostering migrant kids. It also has a history of coercive adoptions. *Rewire.News*. Retrieved from rewire.news/article/2018/06/27/christian-group-fostering-migrant -kids-history-coercive-adoptions/

Lopez, D. (2017). *Sixth grade Latina/o youth: Voicing their experiences and responses to racial Microaggressions* (Master's thesis). California State University, Long Beach, CA. Proquest Dissertation and Theses Database (Publication No. 10605045).

Lorde, A. (1992). Age, race, class, and sex: Women redefining difference. In M. Andersen & C. P. Hill (Eds.), *Race, class, and gender: An anthology* (pp. 177–184).

Lukianoff, G., & Haidt, J. (2015). How trigger warnings are hurting mental health on college campuses. *The Atlantic*. Retrieved from www.theatlantic.com /magazine/archive/2015/09/the-coddling-of-the-american-mind/399356/

Lukianoff, G., & Haidt, J. (2018). *The coddling of the American mind: How good intentions and bad ideas are setting up a generation for failure*. New York, NY: Penguin Books.

Marable, M. (2002). *The great wells of democracy: The meaning of race in American life*. New York, NY: Basic Books.

Masta, S. (2018). "I am exhausted:" Everyday occurrences of being Native American. *International Journal of Qualitative Studies in Education, 31*(9), 821–835.

Matsuda, M. J., Lawrence, C., III, Delgado, R., & Crenshaw, K. W. (1993). *Words that wound: Critical race theory, assaultive speech, and the first amendment*. Boulder, CO: Westview Press.

Memmi, A. (1968). *Dominated man: Notes towards a portrait*. New York, NY: Orion Press.

Memmi, A. (1974). *The colonizer and the colonized*. New York, NY: Earthscan Press.

Mendoza-Denton, N. (2017). Bad hombres: Images of masculinity and the historical consciousness of US-Mexico relations in the age of Trump. *HAU: Journal of Ethnographic Theory, 7*(1), 423–432.

Miller, C., & Werner-Winslow, A. (2016, November 29). *Ten days after: Harassment and intimidation in the aftermath of the election*. Southern Poverty Law Center (SPLC): Montgomery, AL. Retrieved from www.splcenter.org/20161129/ ten-days-after-harassment-and-intimidation-aftermath-election

Miroff, N. (2018, November 8). Trump administration tightens immigration asylum rules as caravans continue to push for U.S. border. *The Washington Post*. Retrieved from www.washingtonpost.com/world/national-security/trump-administration -to-tighten-asylum-rules-as-caravans-approach/2018/11/08/69a06a08-e2a7 -11e8-a1c9-6afe99dddd92_story.html?utm_term=.3c5f00cb1869.

Monaghan, P. (1993, July 23). 'Critical race theory' questions role of legal doctrine in racial inequality: Lani Guinier, ill-fated Justice Dept. nominee, is one of its traditional adherents. *Chronicle of Higher Education*, A7, A9.

Montoya, M. E. (1994). Máscaras, trenzas, y greñas: Un/masking the self while un/ braiding Latina stories and legal discourse. *Chicano-Latino Law Review, 15*(1), 1–37.

Montoya, M. E., & Valdes, F. (2008). Latinas/os and the politics of knowledge production: LatCrit scholarship and academic activism as social justice action. *Indiana Law Journal, 83*, 1197–1233.

Montoya, M. E., Vasquez, I. M., & Martínez, D. V. (2014) Name narratives: A tool for examining and cultivating identity. *Chicana/o Latina/o Law Review 32*(2), 113–152. Retrieved from escholarship.org/uc/item/4k526207.pdf

Morales, S. (2017, June). *Re-defining counterspaces: New directions and implications for research and praxis* (Issue No. 8). Research Brief Series, UCLA Center for Critical Race Studies in Education.

Moreno, C., Jackson-Triche, M., Nash, G., Rice, C., & Suzuki, B. (2013, October). *Independent investigative report on acts of bias and discrimination involving faculty at the University of California, Los Angeles.* Los Angeles, CA: UCLA Office of the Chancellor.

Morris, A. (2015). *The scholar denied: W. E. B. Du Bois and the birth of modern sociology.* Oakland: University of California Press.

Morrissey, K. (2018, April 29). Migrants from Central American caravan face a long road to asylum in U.S. *Los Angeles Times.* Retrieved from www.latimes.com/local/lanow/la-me-caravanqa-20180429-story.html

Muñoz, S. M., & Vigil, D. (2018). Interrogating racist nativist microaggressions and campus climate: How undocumented and DACA college students experience institutional legal violence in Colorado. *Journal of Diversity in Higher Education, 11*(4), 451–466. doi.org/10.1037/dhe0000078.

Nadal, K. L. (2013). *That's so gay!: Microaggressions and the lesbian, gay, bisexual and transgender community.* Washington, DC: American Psychological Association.

Najera-Ramirez, O. (2009). Staging authenticity: Theorizing the development of Mexican folklórico dance. In O. Najera-Ramirez, N. Cantu, & B. Romero (Eds.), *Dancing across borders: Danzas y bailes Mexicanos.* (pp. 277–292) Urbana: University of Illinois Press.

National Advisory Commission on Civil Disorders. (1968). *The Report of the National Advisory Commission on Civil Disorders.* Washington, DC: U.S. Government Printing Office.

Nelson, R. (2019). Candace Owens is the new face of black conservatism. *The Washington Post Magazine.* Retrieved from www.washingtonpost.com/news/magazine/wp/2019/03/06/feature/candace-owens-is-the-new-face-of-black-conservatism-but-what-does-that-really-mean/?utm_term=.3ce14d5ea896

New York Times Editorial Board. (2013, March 22). Walking while Black in New York. *New York Times*, p. A16.

Ngai, M. (2004). *Impossible subjects: Illegal aliens and the making of modern America.* Princeton, NJ: Princeton University Press.

Okwonga, M. (2014, October 16). The nod: A subtle lowering of the head you give to another Black person in an overwhelmingly white place. *Matter Magazine.* Retrieved from medium.com/matter/the-nod-a-subtle-lowering-of-the-head-to-another-black-person-in-an-overwhelmingly-white-place-e12bfa0f833f

Omi, M., & Winant, H. (1994). *Racial formation in the United States: From the 1960s to the 1990s.* New York, NY: Routledge.

Omi, M., & Winant, H. (2013). Resistance is futile?: A response to Feagin and Elias. *Ethnic and Racial Studies, 36*(6), 961–973.

O'Toole, M. (2020, May 20). Young, alone, and a target for deportation. Under Trump policy, migrant children are being cut off from family and counsel. *Los Angeles Times*. Retrieved from https://enewspaper.latimes.com/infinity/article _share.aspx?guid=c622b4ed-3859-4618-a3df-0fc2fcd6ae7c

Owens, C. [RealCandaceO]. (2018, January 16). Regarding #DACA: Send them ALL home! –Unlimited illegal immigration has harmed the black community for decades. Put Americans first, not law-breaking illegal immigrants. In conclusion: WALL! [Tweet]. Retrieved from twitter.com/realcandaceo /status/953419170258890752?lang=en

Pantoja, A. D., Menjívar, C., & Magaña, L. (2008). The spring marches of 2006: Latinos, immigration, and political mobilization in the 21st century. *American Behavioral Scientist, 52*(4), 499–506.

Paredes, A. (1958). *With a pistol in his hand: A border ballad and its hero*. Austin: University of Texas Press.

Park, I. J. K., Du, H., Wang, L., Williams, D. R., & Alegría, M. (2018). Racial/ ethnic discrimination and mental health in Mexican-origin youths and their parents: Testing the "linked lives" hypothesis. *Journal of Adolescent Health, 62*(4), 480–487.

Park, R. (1928). Human migration and the marginal man. *American Journal of Sociology, 33*(6), 881–893.

Parks, G. (1956). *Department store, Mobile, Alabama, 1956* [Photograph]. Gordon Parks Foundation, Pleasantville, NY.

Partlow, J., & Miroff, N. (2018, November 24). Deal with Mexico paves way for asylum overhaul at U.S. border. *The Washington Post*. Retrieved from www .washingtonpost.com/world/national-security/deal-with-mexico-paves-way -for-asylum-overhaul-at-us-border/2018/11/24/87b9570a-ef74-11e8-9236 -bb94154151d2_story.html?utm_term=.9b35bcccb1f0

Pérez, E. (1999). *The decolonial imaginary: Writing Chicanas into history*. Bloomington: Indiana University Press.

Pérez Huber, L. (2008). Building critical race methodologies in educational research: A research note on critical race *testimonio* as method. *Florida International University Law Review, 4*(1), 159–173.

Pérez Huber, L. (2009a). Challenging racist nativist framing: Acknowledging the community cultural wealth of undocumented Chicana college students to re-frame the immigration debate. *Harvard Educational Review, 79*(4), 704–729.

Pérez Huber, L. (2009b). Disrupting apartheid of knowledge: *Testimonio* as methodology in Latina/o critical race research in education. *International Journal of Qualitative Studies in Education, 22*(6), 639–654.

Pérez Huber, L. (2010). Using Latina/o critical race theory (LatCrit) and racist nativism to explore intersectionality in the educational experiences of undocumented Chicana college students. *Educational Foundations, 24*(1–2), 77–96.

Pérez Huber, L. (2011). Discourses of racist nativism in California public education: English dominance as racist nativist microaggressions. *Educational Studies, 47*(4), 379–401.

Pérez Huber, L. (2015). Constructing "deservingness": DREAMers and Central American unaccompanied children in the national immigration debate. *Association of Mexican American Educators (AMAE) Journal, 9*(3), 22–34.

Pérez Huber, L. (2016). "Make America great again!": Donald Trump, racist nativism and the virulent adherence to white supremacy amid U.S. demographic change. *Charleston Law Review, 10,* 215–248.

Pérez Huber, L. (2018, June). *Racial microaffirmations as a response to microaggressions.* (Research Brief No. 15). Los Angeles, CA: Center for Critical Race Studies at UCLA.

Pérez Huber, L., Camargo Gonzalez, L., & Solórzano, D. (2018). Considerations for using critical race theory and critical content analysis: A research note. *Understanding and Dismantling Privilege, 8*(2), 8–26.

Pérez Huber, L., Camargo Gonzalez, L., & Solórzano, D. *Theorizing a critical race content analysis for children's literature about people of color.* Submitted for publication.

Pérez Huber, L., & Cueva, B. M. (2012). Chicana/Latina *testimonios* on effects and responses to microaggressions. *Equity & Excellence in Education, 45*(3), 392–410. doi.org/10.1080/10665684.2012.698193

Pérez Huber, L., & Huber-Verjan, L. (2015, February). *'But I'm Latino, so they're saying I'm a bandit!': Critical race theory, visual microaggressions and the historical image of Mexican banditry.* Paper presented to the California State University, Los Angeles, Department of Chicana/o Studies, Los Angeles, CA.

Pérez Huber, L., Huidor, O., Malagón, M., Sánchez, G., & Solórzano, D. (2006). *Falling through the cracks: Critical transitions in the Latina/o educational pipeline* (Report No. 7). Los Angeles, CA: UCLA Chicano Studies Research Center.

Pérez Huber, L., Johnson, R. N., & Kohli, R. (2006). Naming racism: A conceptual look at internalized racism in U.S. schools. *Chicana/o-Latina/o Law Review, 26,* 183–206.

Pérez Huber, L., Lopez, C. B., Malagon, M. C., Velez, V., & Solórzano, D. G. (2008). Getting beyond the 'symptom,' acknowledging the 'disease': Theorizing racist nativism. *Contemporary Justice Review, 11*(1), 39–51.

Pérez Huber, L., & Malagon, M. C. (2007). Silenced struggles: The experiences of Latina and Latino undocumented college students in California. *Nevada Law Journal, 7,* 841–861.

Pérez Huber, L., & Solórzano, D. G. (2015a). Visualizing everyday racism: Critical race theory, visual microaggressions, and the historical image of Mexican banditry. *Qualitative Inquiry, 21*(3), 223–238.

Pérez Huber, L., & Solórzano, D. G. (2015b). Racial microaggressions as a tool for critical race research. *Race, Ethnicity, and Education, 18*(3), 297–320.

Pérez Huber, L., & Solórzano, D. G. (2015c). *Racial microaggressions: What they are, what they are not, and why they matter* (Latino Policy & Issues Brief No. 30). Los Angeles, CA: UCLA Chicano Studies Research Center.

Pérez Huber, L., & Solórzano, D. G. (2018). Teaching racial microaggressions: Implications of critical race hypos for social work. *Journal of Ethnic & Cultural Diversity in Social Work, 27,* 54–71.

Pérez Huber, L., Vélez, V. N., & Solórzano, D. (2018). More than 'papelitos:' A QuantCrit counterstory to critique Latina/o degree value and occupational prestige. *Race Ethnicity and Education*, 21(2), 208–230. doi.org/10.1080/136 13324.2017.1377416

Pew Research Center (2018, November 8). *The 2018 midterm vote: Divisions by race, gender, education*. Retrieved from www.pewresearch.org/fact-tank/2018/11/08 /the-2018-midterm-vote-divisions-by-race-gender-education/

Phillips, K. P. (1969). *The Emerging Republican Majority: Updated Edition*. Princeton, NJ: Princeton University Press.

Pierce, C. (1969). Is bigotry the basis of the medical problem of the ghetto? In J. Norman (Ed.), *Medicine in the ghetto* (pp. 301–314). New York, NY: Meredith Corporation.

Pierce, C. (1970). Offensive mechanisms. In F. Barbour (Ed.), *The Black seventies* (pp. 265–282). Boston, MA: Porter Sargent.

Pierce, C. (1974). Psychiatric problems of the Black minority. In S. Arieti (Ed.), *American handbook of psychiatry* (pp. 512–523). New York, NY: Basic Books.

Pierce, C. (1975a). The mundane extreme environment and its effects on learning. In S. Brainard (Ed.), *Learning disabilities: Issues and recommendations for research* (pp. 1–23). Washington, DC: National Institute of Education, U.S. Department of Health, Education and Welfare.

Pierce, C. (1975b). Poverty and racism as they affect children. In I. Berlin (Ed.), *Advocacy for child mental health* (pp. 92–109). New York, NY: Brunner/Mazel Publishers.

Pierce, C. (1980). Social trace contaminants: Subtle indicators of racism in TV. In S. Withey & R. Abeles (Eds.), *Television and social behavior: Beyond violence and children* (pp. 249–257). Hillsdale, NJ: Lawrence Erlbaum.

Pierce, C. (1988). Stress in the workplace. In A. Coner-Edwards & J. Spurlock (Eds.), *Black families in crisis: The middle class* (pp. 27–34). New York, NY: Brunner/Mazel.

Pierce, C. (1989). Unity in diversity: Thirty-three years of stress. In G. Berry & J. Asamen (Eds.), *Black students: Psychological issues and academic achievement* (pp. 296–312). Newbury Park, CA: Sage.

Pierce, C. (1995). Stress analogs of racism and sexism: Terrorism, torture, and disaster. In C. Willie, P. Rieker, B. Kramer, & B. Brown (Eds.), *Mental health, racism, and sexism* (pp. 277–293). Pittsburgh, PA: University of Pittsburgh Press.

Pierce, C., Carew, J., Pierce-Gonzalez, D., & Wills, D. (1978). An experiment in racism: TV commercials. In C. Pierce (Ed.), *Television and education* (pp. 62–88). Beverly Hills, CA: Sage.

Pierce, C., Earls, F., & Kleinman, A. (1999). Race and culture in psychiatry. In A. Nicholi (Ed.), *Harvard handbook of psychiatry* (3rd ed.) (pp. 735–743). Cambridge, MA: Harvard University Press.

Pierce, C., & Profit, W. (1991). Homoracial and heteroracial behavior in the United States. In S. Okpaku (Ed.), *Mental health in Africa and the Americas today* (pp. 257–64). Nashville, TN: Chrisolith.

Pitzer, A. (2018, June 21). Trump's tent city for children is a concentration camp. *San Francisco Chronicle*. Retrieved from www.sfchronicle.com/opinion/article /Trump-s-tent-city-for-children-is-a-13016150.php

Pressley, A. [@AyannaPressley]. (2019, July 14). THIS is what racism looks like. WE are what democracy looks like. And we're not going anywhere. Except back to

DC to fight for families you marginalize and vilify everyday. [Tweet]. Retrieved from twitter.com/ayannapressley/status/1150460489199173632

Profit W., Mino, I., & Pierce, C. (2000). Blacks, stress in. In G. Fink (Ed.), *Encyclopedia of stress*, Volume 1 (A–D) (pp. 324–330). San Diego, CA: Academic Press.

Rankine, C. (2014). *Citizen: An American lyric*. Minneapolis, MN: Graywolf Press.

Roediger, D. R. (1999). *The wages of whiteness: Race and the making of the American working class*. London, England: Verso.

Rogan, J. (Host). (2018, May 5). *JRE #1125 - Candace Owens* [Audio podcast.]. Retrieved from /podcasts.joerogan.net/podcasts/candace-owens

Rogers, J., Franke, M., Yun, J. E., Ishimoto, M., Diera, C., Geller, R., . . . Brenes, T. (2017). *Teaching and learning in the age of Trump: Increasing stress and hostility in America's high schools*. Los Angeles, CA: UCLA's Institute for Democracy, Education, and Access. Retrieved from idea.gseis.ucla.edu/publications /teaching-and-learning-in-age-of-trump

Rogers, J., Ishimoto, M., Kwako, A., Berryman, A., & Diera, C. (2019). *School and society in the age of Trump*. Los Angeles, CA: UCLA's Institute for Democracy, Education, and Access. Retrieved from idea.gseis .ucla.edu/publications/school-and-society-in-age-of-trump/publications/files /school-and-society-in-the-age-of-trump-report

Rowe, M. (2008). Micro-affirmations and micro-inequities. *Journal of the International Ombudsman Association, 1*(1), 45–48.

Ryan, P. M. (2002). *Esperanza rising*. New York, NY: Scholastic Press.

Saito, N. T. (1997). Alien and non-alien alike: Citizenship, "foreignness," and racial hierarchy in American law. *Oregon Law Review, 76*, 261–346.

Salas, S., Johnson, T. (Producers), & Bainbridge, C. (Director) (2018). *Rumble: The Indians who rocked the world*. United States: Les Films Rezolution Pictures.

Sánchez, G. (1997). Face the nation: Race, immigration and the rise of nativism in late twentieth century America. *International Migration Review, 31*(4), 1009–1030.

Schuette v. Coalition to Defend Affirmative Action, Integration and Immigration Rights and Fight for Equality (BAMN), 572 U.S. 291. (2014). *Supreme Court Slip Opinion*. Retrieved from www.supremecourt.gov/opinions/13pdf/12-682_8759.pdf

Shapiro, T. M. (2017). *Toxic inequality: How America's wealth gap destroys mobility, deepens the racial divide, and threatens our future*. New York, NY: Basic Books.

Sherman, D. K., & Cohen, G. L. (2006) The psychology of self-defense: Self-affirmation theory. *Advances in Experimental Social Psychology, 38*, 183–242.

Smith, S. (2004). *Photography on the color line: W. E. B. Du Bois, race, and visual culture*. Durham, NC: Duke University Press.

Smith, W. A. (2004). Black faculty coping with racial battle fatigue: The campus racial climate in a post-civil rights era. In D. Cleveland (Ed.), *A long way to go: Conversations about race by African American faculty and graduate students* (pp. 171–190). New York, NY: Peter Lang.

Smith, W. A., Allen, W. R., & Danley, L. L. (2007). "Assume the position . . . you fit the description." Psychosocial experiences and racial battle fatigue among African American male college students. *American Behavioral Scientist, 51*(4), 551–578.

Smith, W. A, Yosso, T. J., & Solórzano, D. G. (2006). Challenging racial battle fatigue on historically white campuses: A critical race examination of race-related stress. In C. Stanley (Ed.), *Faculty of color teaching in predominantly white colleges and universities* (pp. 299–327). Bolton, MA: Anker Publishing.

Smith, W. A., Yosso, T. J., & Solórzano, D. G. (2007). Racial primes and Black misandry on historically white campuses: Toward critical race accountability in educational administration. *Educational Administration Quarterly, 43*(5), 559–585.

Solórzano, D. G. (1989). Teaching and social change: Reflections on a Freirean approach in a college classroom. *Teaching Sociology, 17,* 218–225.

Solórzano, D. G. (1993). *The road to the doctorate for California's Chicanas and Chicanos: A study of Ford Foundation minority fellows.* Berkeley, CA: California Policy Seminar.

Solórzano, D. (1997). Images and words that wound: Critical race theory, racial stereotyping, and teacher education. *Teacher Education Quarterly, 24*(3), 5–19.

Solórzano, D. (1998a). Critical race theory, race and gender microaggressions, and the experience of Chicana and Chicano scholars. *International Journal of Qualitative Studies in Education, 11*(1), 121–136.

Solórzano, D. (1998b). Role models, mentors, and the experiences of Chicana and Chicano Ph.D. scientists. In H. Frierson, (Ed.), *Mentoring and* diversity *in higher education, Volume 2* (pp. 91–103). Greenwich, CT: JAI Press.

Solórzano, D. G. (2013). Critical race theory's intellectual roots: My email epistolary with Derrick Bell. In M. Lynn & A. Dixson, (Eds.), *Critical race theory in education handbook* (pp. 48–68). New York, NY: Routledge.

Solórzano, D. G. (2014, January). *Using the tools of critical race theory to examine racial microaggressions in academic and social spaces.* Invited lecture to the Principal Leadership Institute at the UCLA Graduate School of Education & Information Studies, Los Angeles, CA.

Solórzano, D. G. (2015, April) *Toward collective action to reclaim public narratives for justice: Ameliorating an impoverished cultural discourse on affirmative action in higher education.* Paper presented at the annual meeting of the American Education Research Association, Chicago, IL.

Solórzano, D. G. (2016). A critical race examination of *McLaurin v. Oklahoma*: How Derrick Bell helped me understand George McLaurin's seat. In G. Ladson Billings & W. Tate (Eds.), *"Covenant keeper": Derrick Bell's enduring educational legacy* (pp. 39–55). New York, NY: Peter Lang.

Solórzano, D. G. (2019). Toward a critical race theory for teacher education. In P. Jenlick (Ed.), *Teacher preparation at the intersection of race and poverty in today's schools* (pp. 107–112). Lanham, MD: Rowman & Littlefield.

Solórzano, D., & Allen, W. (2000). *A case study of racial microaggressions and campus racial climate at the University of California, Berkeley.* Expert report commissioned by the plaintiffs in *Castaneda, et al. v. UC Regents, et al.,* United States Federal Court, Northern District of California.

Solórzano, D., Allen, W., & Carroll, G. (2002). Keeping race in place: A case study of racial microaggressions and campus racial climate at the University of California, Berkeley. *UCLA Chicano/Latino Law Review, 23,* 15–111.

Solórzano, D., Ceja, M., & Yosso, T. (2000). Critical race theory, racial microaggressions and campus racial climate: The experiences of African American college students. *Journal of Negro Education, 69,* 60–73.

Solórzano, D. G., & Delgado Bernal, D. (2001). Examining transformational re-sistance through a critical race and LatCrit theory framework: Chicana and Chicano students in an urban context. *Urban Education, 36*(3), 308–342.

Solórzano, D., & Pérez Huber, L. (2012). Microaggressions, racial. In J. Banks (Ed.), *Encyclopedia of diversity in education* (pp. 1489–1492). Thousand Oaks, CA: Sage Publications.

Solórzano, D., Peréz Huber, L., & Huber-Verjan, L. (2020). Theorizing racial mi-croaffirmations as a response to racial microaggressions: Counterstories across three generations of critical race scholars. *Seattle Journal for Social Justice, 18*(2), 185–215.

Solórzano, D., & Solórzano, R. W. (1995). The Chicano educational experience: A framework for effective schools in Chicano communities. *Educational Policy, 9*(3), 293–314.

Solórzano, D., & Vélez, V. (2016). Using critical race spatial analysis to examine the Du Boisian color-line along the Alameda corridor in Southern California. *Whittier Law Review, 37*, 423–437.

Solórzano, D., & Vélez, V. (2017). Using critical race spatial analysis to examine redlining in Southern California communities of color—Circa 1939. In D. Mor-rison, S. Annamma, & D. Jackson (Eds.), *Critical race spatial analysis: Map-ping to understand and address educational inequity* (pp. 91–108). Sterling, VA: Stylus.

Solórzano, D. & Villalpando, O. (1998). Critical race theory, marginality, and the experience of minority students in higher education. In C. Torres & T. Mitchell, (Eds.), *Emerging issues in the sociology of education: Comparative perspectives* (pp. 211–224). Albany, NY: SUNY Press.

Solórzano, D. G., & Yosso, T. J. (2001). Maintaining social justice hopes within ac-ademic realities: A Freirean approach to critical race/LatCrit pedagogy. *Denver Law Review, 78*, 595–621.

Solórzano, D. G., & Yosso, T. (2002). Critical race methodology: Counter-storytell-ing as an analytical framework for education research. *Qualitative Inquiry, 8*, 23–44.

Spencer, M. B. (1984). Black children's race awareness, racial attitudes, and self-concept. A reinterpretation. *Journal of Child Psychology and Psychiatry, 25*(3), 433–441.

Spencer, M. B. (2008). Lessons learned and opportunities ignored since *Brown v. Board of Education*: Youth development and the myth of a color-blind society. *Educational Researcher, 37*(5), 253–266.

Steele. C. M. (1988) The psychology of self-affirmation: Sustaining the integrity of the self. *Advances in Experimental Social Psychology, 21*, 261–302.

Steele, C. M., & Aronson, J. (1995) Stereotype threat and the intellectual test per-formance of African Americans. *Journal of Personality and Social Psychology, 69*(5), 797–811.

Sternthal, M. J., Slopen, N., & Williams, D. R. (2011). Racial disparities in health: How much does stress really matter? *Du Bois Review, 8*(1), 95–113.

Strauss, A., & Corbin, J. (1990). *Basics of qualitative research: Grounded theory procedures and techniques.* Newbury Park, CA: Sage.

Sue, D. W. (2010). *Microaggressions in everyday life: Race, gender, and sexual ori-entation.* Hoboken, NJ: John Wiley & Sons.

Sue, D. W., Bucceri, J., Lin, A. I., Nadal, K. L., & Torino, G. C. (2007). Racial microaggressions and the Asian American experience. *Cultural Diversity and Ethnic Minority Psychology, 13*(1), 72–81.

Sue, D. W., Capodilupo, C. M., Torino, G. C., Bucceri, J. M., Holder, A. M. B., Nadal, K. L., & Esquilin, M. (2007). Racial microaggressions in everyday life: Implications for clinical practice. *American Psychologist, 62*(4), 271–286.

Sue, D. W., & Constantine, M. G. (2007). Racial microaggressions as instigators of difficult dialogues on race: Implications for student affairs educators and students. *College Student Affairs Journal, 26*(2), 136–143.

Takaki, R. (2008). *A different mirror: A history of multicultural America* (Revised edition). New York, NY: Back Bay Books.

Takenaga, L., & Gardiner, A. (2019, July 19). 16,000 readers shared their experiences of being told to 'go back.' Here are some of their stories. *The New York Times.* Retrieved from www.nytimes.com/2019/07/19/reader-center/trump-go-back-stories.html

Tatum, B. D. (1997). *"Why are all the black kids sitting together in the cafeteria?": And other conversations about race.* New York, NY: Basic Books.

Teatro Campesino. (1976). *University of California Santa Barbara Library, Teatro Campesino Archives.* Retrieved from www.library.ucsb.edu/special-collections/cema/etc.

Title IX of the Education Amendments of 1972, Pub. L. No. 92-318, S. 659, 92nd Cong., § 901a (1972).

Trask, H. (1999). *From a native daughter: colonialism and sovereignty in Hawaii.* Honolulu, HI: Latitude 20 Books.

Tronya, B., & Hatcher, R. (1992). *Racism in children's lives: A study of mainly white primary schools.* New York, NY: Routledge.

Truong, K. A., & Museus, S. D. (2012). Responding to racism and racial trauma in doctoral study: An inventory for coping and mediating relationships. *Harvard Educational Review, 82*(2), 226–254.

Truong, K. A., Museus, S. D., & McGuire, K. M. (2016). Vicarious racism: A qualitative analysis of experiences with secondhand racism in graduate education. *International Journal of Qualitative Studies in Education, 29*(2), 224–247.

U.S. Census Bureau. (2019, August 20). *Hispanic heritage month 2019.* Profile America facts for features: CB19-07. Retrieved from www.census.gov/content/dam/Census/newsroom/facts-for-features/2019/hispanic-heritage-month.pdf

U.S. Department of Health and Human Services. (2020, March). *Unaccompanied alien children information. Reports to Congress on separated children.* Retrieved from https://www.hhs.gov/programs/social-services/unaccompanied-alien-children/index.html

University of California Senate-Administration Work Group on the Moreno Report. (2013, December). *Report to the President, Academic Council, and Chancellors.* Oakland, CA: University of California Office of the President. Retrieved from www.ucop.edu/moreno-report/moreno-senate-admin-work-group-12-23-13.pdf

Vachon, J. (1938). *A drinking fountain on the county courthouse lawn, 1938* [Photograph]. Washington, DC: Library of Congress. Retrieved from www.loc.gov/rr/print/list/085_disc.html

Valencia, R. R. (2010). *Dismantling contemporary deficit thinking: Educational thought and practice.* New York, NY: Routledge.

Valencia, R. R., & Solórzano, D. G. (1997). Contemporary deficit thinking. In R. R. Valencia (Ed.), *The evolution of deficit thinking: Educational thought and practice* (pp. 160–210). Oxford, England: RoutledgeFalmer.

Van Ausdale, D., & Feagin, J. R. (2001). *The first R: How children learn race and racism.* Lanham, MD: Rowman & Littlefield.

Vega Rodriguez, S. (2018). Praxis of resilience & resistance: "We can STOP Donald Trump" and other messages from immigrant children. *Association of Mexican American Educators Journal, 12*(3), 122–147. doi.org/10.24974/amae.12.3.403

Vega Rodriguez, S. (2019). Teatro vs. Trump: Children in South Central Los Angeles fight back. *Aztlán: A Journal of Chicano Studies, 44*(1), 189–198.

Vega, C. (2019). *Strolling and straddling academic boundaries: Chicana, Latina, and Indigenous motherscholars in the academy* (Doctoral dissertation). ProQuest ID: Vega_ucla_0031D_18171. Merritt ID: ark:/13030/m5fn68qz. Retrieved from escholarship.org/uc/item/3zp8k23k

Vélez, V., Pérez Huber, L., Benavides Lopez, C., de la Luz, A., & Solórzano, D. G. (2008). Battling for human rights and social justice: A Latina/o critical race media analysis of Latina/o student youth activism in the wake of 2006 anti-immigrant sentiment. *Social Justice, 35*(1), 7–27.

Vélez, V., & Solórzano, D. (2017). Critical race spatial analysis: Conceptualizing GIS as a tool for critical race research in education. In D. Morrison, S. Annamma, & D. Jackson (Eds.), *Critical race spatial analysis: Mapping to understand and address educational inequity* (pp. 8–31). Sterling, VA: Stylus.

Volokh, E. (2015a, June 23). The UC's PC police. *Los Angeles Times.* Retrieved from www.latimes.com/nation/la-oe-0623-volokh-uc-microaggressions-20150623-story.html

Volokh, E. (2015b, June 16). UC teaching faculty members not to criticize race-based affirmative action, call America 'melting pot,' and more. *The Washington Post.* Retrieved from www.washingtonpost.com/news/volokh-conspiracy/wp/2015/06/16/uc-teaching-faculty-members-not-to-criticize-race-based-affirmative-action-call-america-melting-pot-and-more/

Walton, G. M., & Cohen, G. L. (2011) A brief social-belonging intervention improves academic and health outcomes of minority students. *Science, 331*(6023), 1447–1451.

Ward, J. V. (1996) Raising resisters: The role of truth-telling in the psychological development of African American Girls. In B. J. Leadbeater & N. Way (Eds.), *Urban girls: Resisting stereotypes, creating identities* (pp. 85–99). New York, NY: New York University Press.

Watson, K. (2019). *Revealing and uprooting cellular violence: Black men and the biopsychosocial impact of racial microaggressions* (Unpublished dissertation). University of California, Los Angeles.

Weyeneth, R. R. (2005). The architecture of racial segregation: The challenges of preserving the problematical past. *The Public Historian, 27*(4), 11–44.

Williams, D. R. (2016, June). *Measuring discrimination resource* (Online report). Scholars at Harvard. Retrieved from scholar.harvard.edu/files/davidrwilliams/files/measuring_discrimination_resource_june_2016.pdf

Williams, D. R. (2018). Stress and the mental health of populations of color: Advancing our understanding of race-related stressors. *Journal of Health and Social Behavior, 59*(4), 466–485.

Williams, D. R., Gonzalez, H. M., Williams, S., Mohammed, S. A., Moomal, H., & Stein, D. J. (2008). Perceived discrimination, race and health in South Africa. *Social Science & Medicine, 67*(3), 441–452. doi.org/10.1016/j.socscimed.2008.03.021

Williams, D. R., John, D. A., Oyserman, D., Sonnega, J., Mohammed, S. A., & Jackson, J. S. (2012). Research on discrimination and health: An exploratory study of unresolved conceptual and measurement issues. *American Journal of Public Health, 102*(5), 975–978.

Williams D. R., Priest, N., & Anderson, N. (2016). Understanding associations between race, socioeconomic status and health: Patterns and prospects. *Health Psychology, 35,* 407–411.

Williams, D. R., & Purdie-Vaughns, V. (2016). Needed interventions to reduce racial/ethnic disparities in health. *Journal of Health Politics, Policy and Law, 41*(4), 627–651.

Williams, D. R., Yan Yu, Jackson, J. S., & Anderson, N. B. (1997). Racial differences in physical and mental health: Socio-economic status, stress and discrimination. *Journal of Health Psychology, 2*(3), 335–351. doi.org/10.1177/135910539700200305

Wong, G., Derthick, A., David, E., Saw, A., & Okazaki, S. (2014). The what, the why, and the how: A review of racial microaggressions research in psychology. *Race and Social Problems, 6,* 181–200.

Woodson, Sr., R. L. (1996). Personal responsibility. In G. Curry (Ed.), *The affirmative action debate* (pp. 111–120). Reading, MA: Basic Books.

Yosso, T. (2000). *A critical race and LatCrit approach to media literacy: Chicana/o resistance to visual microaggression* (Unpublished doctoral dissertation). University of California, Los Angeles.

Yosso, T. (2005). Whose culture has capital? A critical race theory discussion of community cultural wealth. *Race, Ethnicity and Education, 8,* 69–91.

Yosso, T., Smith, W., Ceja, M., & Solórzano, D. 2009. Critical race theory, racial microaggressions, and campus racial climate for Latina/o undergraduates. *Harvard Educational Review, 79*(4), 659–690.

Yosso, T., & Solórzano, D. (2005). Conceptualizing a critical race theory in sociology. In M. Romero & E. Margolis (Eds.), *Blackwell companion to social inequalities* (pp. 117–146). London, England: Blackwell.

Zeiders, K. H., Doane, L. D., & Roosa, M. W. (2012). Perceived discrimination and diurnal cortisol: Examining relations among Mexican American adolescents. *Hormones and Behavior, 61*(4), 541–548.

Index

The letter *f* after a page number indicates a figure.

About the Authors

Daniel G. Solórzano is professor of social science and comparative education and director of the Center for Critical Race Studies in Education in the Graduate School of Education and Information Studies at the University of California, Los Angeles (UCLA). His teaching, research, and publishing interests include Critical Race Theory in education, racial microaggressions, critical race pedagogy, and critical race spatial analysis. Dr. Solórzano has authored over 100 research articles and book chapters on issues related to educational access and equity for underrepresented student populations in the United States, Critical Race Theory, and racial microaggressions. Over his 48-year career, Dr. Solórzano has taught at the Los Angeles County Juvenile Hall, the California Community College, the California State University, and the University of California Systems. Among his awards, he has received the UCLA Distinguished Teacher Award, the American Education Research Association Social Justice in Education Award, the Critical Race Studies in Education Association Derrick A. Bell Legacy Award, and the Association for Studies in Higher Education (ASHE) Mildred Garcia Exemplary Scholarship Award. In 2014 Solórzano was selected as a Fellow of the American Education Research Association. In 2017, he received the inaugural Revolutionary Mentor Award from the AERA Critical Educators for Social Justice (CESJ). In 2019, he delivered the AERA Distinguished Lecture on Racial Microaggressions. Solórzano received the Distinguished Alumni Award from the Claremont Graduate University and the 50th Anniversary Alumni Award from the Chicano Latino Student Affairs Center at the Claremont Colleges in 2020. Also in 2020, Solórzano was elected to the National Academy of Education.

Lindsay Pérez Huber is an associate professor in the Social and Cultural Analysis of Education (SCAE) master's program in the College of Education at California State University, Long Beach. Dr. Pérez Huber's research agenda is concerned with using interdisciplinary perspectives to analyze racial inequities in education, the structural causes of those inequities, and how they mediate educational trajectories and outcomes of Students of Color. She has conducted studies in K–12 schools, community colleges, and 4-year universities. Her research specializations include race, immigration, and higher education; racial microaggressions; and critical-race gendered methodologies and epistemologies. Her work is known for further developing theoretical and conceptual frameworks in Critical Race Theory (CRT), bridging CRT and Chicana feminist perspectives in education, and for contributing to a greater understanding of Latina/o undocumented student experiences. Dr. Pérez Huber has served as vice president for the Critical Race Studies in Education Association (CRSEA), and as a visiting scholar at the UCLA Chicano Studies Research Center (CSRC) and the UCLA Center for Critical Race Studies in Education (CCRSE). She is a National Academies Ford Foundation Fellow, an American Association of Hispanics in Higher Education (AAHHE) Faculty Fellow, and the 2019 Derrick Bell Legacy Award winner for the Critical Race Studies in Education Association (CRSEA).